ARGUING WITH THE PAST

How do writers create dialogues with past writing? How do readers of the present day engage with the difference of past literature? What part does forgetting play in the understanding of narrative? How do we make contact with the desires and debates of past readers? And in what ways do they enter our present?

Arguing with the Past engages with these issues through discussion of fiction and long narrative, drawing on a broad range of writing of earlier periods and on recent narrative theory. Gillian Beer looks at the work of writers as diverse as Thomas Carlyle and Philip Sidney, Samuel Richardson and George Eliot. Three chapters on Virginia Woolf demonstrate how Woolf's reading of past literature, philosophy, and science gave her an intellectual and emotional purchase on problems of feminism and modernism.

Reading takes place always in the present moment and is informed by current needs, dreads, preoccupations, pleasures. But the encounter with earlier writing allows us also to challenge our communal assumptions and to shake up our categories. To do this, Gillian Beer argues, we must avoid the 'evolutionist' model of literary development in which texts are praised for their 'almost modern awareness' and for being 'ahead of their time'. We cannot become past readers. But we can learn to hear the voices of earlier debates within the text and so invigorate the responsiveness with which we read now.

Gillian Beer is Reader in Literature and Narrative at the University of Cambridge and a Fellow of Girton College, Cambridge.

ARGUING WITH THE PAST

Essays in narrative from Woolf to Sidney

GILLIAN BEER

ROUTLEDGE
London and New York

First published 1989
by Routledge
11 New Fetter Lane, London EC4P 4EE
29 West 35th Street, New York, NY 10001

Printed in Great Britain
by Butler & Tanner Ltd, Frome, Somerset

British Library Cataloguing in Publication Data

Beer, Gillian
Arguing with the past: essays in narrative
from Woolf to Sidney.
1. Fiction in English, to 1983 – critical studies
I. Title
823.′009

Library of Congress Cataloging in Publication Data

Beer, Gillian.
Arguing with the past: essays in narrative
from Woolf to Sidney/Gillian Beer
p.   cm.
Includes index.
ISBN 0 415 02607 5. – ISBN 0 415 02608 3 (pbk.)
1. English literature – History and criticism.
2. Narration (Rhetoric)   I. Title.
PR408.N37B44   1989
820′.9 – dc19

To Allon White

Since the days of man's life do not endure for ever, our ancestors invented letters and signs ... so, by an ingenious means, the dead might engage in conversation with the living, and might reveal the secrets of their wishes, actions and plans, to those who were to follow, even though they were manifestly separated by great distances of time and space.

(Preamble to a charter issued by Drogo, Bishop of Thérouanne, in 1075, abbreviated and translated)

Understanding begins when something addresses us. This is the primary hermeneutical condition.

(Hans Georg Gadamer, *Truth and Method*)

But the instrument played upon by the Writer, namely, the mind of the Reader, has not been arranged for the purpose of thus being played upon, and its strings do not wait to vibrate in obedience to the Writer's touch, but are always on the point of sounding and jangling uninvited.

(Vernon Lee [Violet Paget] 'On Style')

CONTENTS

PREFACE

In this volume I have selected from my work solely essays on fiction and long narrative and have focused on the question of how writers and readers respond to, internalize, and resist past writing. We carry on an argument with the past; we also use the past as evidence with which to pursue argument. Here, from time to time, I find myself arguing with my own past. I have not revised earlier essays except to clarify the relations between those on Virginia Woolf. These particular essays develop out of each other, brooding further on ideas and quotations at first cursorily noted.

Most of the essays in this volume were written for particular occasions and published in the following places. I am grateful for permission to gather them here: 'Origins and oblivion in Victorian narrative', in R. B. Yeazell (ed.), *Sex, Politics, and Science in the Nineteenth Century Novel: Selected Papers from the English Institute* (Baltimore and London: Johns Hopkins University Press, 1986); a rather different version of '*Pamela* and *Arcadia*: reading class, genre, gender', in M. A. Doody and Peter Sabor (eds), *Samuel Richardson: Tercentenary Essays* (Cambridge: Cambridge University Press, 1989); 'Richardson, Milton, and the status of evil', in *The Review of English Studies*, new series, 19 (1968); 'Circulatory systems: money, gossip, and blood in *Middlemarch*', in *Cahiers Victoriens et Edouardiens: Studies in George Eliot*, ed. M. Amalric, no. 26 (1987); 'Beyond determinism: George Eliot and Virginia Woolf', in Mary Jacobus (ed.), *Women Writing and Writing about Women* (London: Croom Helm in association with Oxford University Women's Studies Committee, 1979); 'The Victorians in Virginia Woolf: 1832–1941', in Joanne Shattock (ed.), *Dickens and Other Victorians: Essays in Honour of Philip Collins* (London: Macmillan, 1988); 'Virginia Woolf and prehistory', in Eric Warner (ed.), *Virginia*

Woolf: A Centenary Perspective (London: Macmillan, 1984); 'Hume Stephen, and elegy in *To the Lighthouse*', *Essays in Criticism*, 34 (1984). 'Carlylean transports' was written at the invitation of Jonathan Rée for a conference on 'Literary History and History of Philosophy' organized by the British Society for the History of Philosophy, April 1988. Flu prevented me at the last moment from being there and joining the discussions.

I am particularly grateful to Sarah Nichols of the English Faculty Office for her prompt and willing help in typing sections of this book. As always, I have been fortunate to have the resources of the Cambridge University Library, the English Faculty Library, and Girton College Library.

Written arguments are part of that larger conversational network which is one of the great pleasures of life. Many of the ideas here have developed in discussions with students in the English Faculty and Girton College. Colleagues and friends, particularly Jill Mann and John Stevens, have voiced tonic scepticism, urged me on, and never allowed me to forget the sophistication that medieval literature demands of, and develops in, readers. Allon White was a source of conversation, friendship, repartee, and insight throughout the years that most of these essays were written, and I dedicate the book to him – as he knew.

Cambridge

ACKNOWLEDGEMENTS

Author and publisher gratefully acknowledge permission given by Harcourt Brace Jovanovich, Inc., to reproduce excerpts from the following works:

Virginia Woolf, *A Common Reader*, copyright 1925 by Harcourt Brace Jovanovich, Inc., and renewed 1953 by Leonard Woolf, reprinted by permission of the publisher.

'A sketch of the past' from Virginia Woolf, *Moments of Being*, copyright 1976 by Quentin Bell and Angelica Garnett, reprinted by permission of Harcourt Brace Jovanovich, Inc.

The Letters of Virginia Woolf, copyright 1976 by Quentin Bell and Angelica Garnett, reprinted by permission of Harcourt Brace Jovanovich, Inc.

Virginia Woolf, *A Writer's Diary*, copyright 1954 by Leonard Woolf and renewed 1982 by Quentin Bell and Angelica Garnett, reprinted by permission of Harcourt Brace Jovanovich, Inc.

'Elizabeth Barrett Browning' from Virginia Woolf, *Collected Essays*, copyright 1950 and renewed 1978 by Harcourt Brace Jovanovich, Inc., reprinted by permission of the publisher.

'Geraldine and Jane' from Virginia Woolf, *Collected Essays*, copyright 1932 by Harcourt Brace Jovanovich, Inc., and renewed 1960 by Leonard Woolf, reprinted by permission of the publisher.

'I am Christina Rossetti' from Virginia Woolf, *Collected Essays*, copyright 1932 by Harcourt Brace Jovanovich, Inc., and renewed 1960 by Leonard Woolf, reprinted by permission of the publisher.

1

INTRODUCTORY

Reading will always be informed by current needs, dreads, pre-occupations, pleasures. The cultural conditions within which we receive the texts will shape the attention we bring to them. Literary history, like all history, starts now. We shall read as 1989 or, with luck, 1999 readers, but we need not do so hauling without noticing our cultural baggage. The encounter with the otherness of earlier literature can allow us to recognize and challenge our own assumptions, and those of the society in which we live. In order to do so we must take care not to fall into the habit of assuming the evolutionist model of literary development, so often taken for granted. In this, texts are praised for their 'almost modern awareness' or for 'being ahead of their time'. This presentist mode of argument takes *now* as the source of authority, the only real place.

Engaging with the *difference* of the past in our present makes us aware of the trajectory of our arrival and of the insouciance of the past – their neglectfulness of our prized positions and our assumptions. To do this, we need to learn the terms of past preoccupations. We may then experience the pressure within words, now slack, of anxieties and desires. To focus such enquiry we can observe how writers interpret the past of their personal and communal culture. We can use this awareness, if we will, to gratify our sense of our own correctness, 'an almost modern understanding' – but that leaves out too much text. Rather, the study of past writing and past reading can disturb any autocratic emphasis on the self and the present, as if they were stable entities. It can make us aware too of how far that view continues despite postmodernism.[1]

We never read only 'in our own person'. The writing is there before us; its words, its syntax, its narrative sequences organize our entry

1

into the text and order our roles within it. We may understand ourselves to be free agents as we read, but the range of our freedom is extended by the written work – and limited by it too. The writing characterizes our performance: Jane Austen makes us witty as we read. The effect may not persist. The passionate compunction we discover as we read George Eliot will ebb as we close the book. The readerly wariness that Beckett induces may not much inhibit our attachments. The ungainsayable commitment that Coetzee makes us know is hard to sustain beyond the time of the text. Humanist criticism was mistaken in assuming a straight translation possible from reading-self to socialized self. Reading is a sequestered activity; it is hard work to render its effects communal, and that work demands a series of vigorous displacements, not straight enactment.

Whereas in the theatre we take part in an openly communal experience, the process of reading is nowadays solitary. However, the intermitted reading of long narrative means that it broods within all our other current life-activities. These other activities – and landscapes also – may come to form part of our repertoire of memory when we look back on the text. Particularly is this so when the work has made a profound impression: the plains of Yugoslavia and the bleak clangour of Tottenham Court Road slide past my eyes again when I think of *Anna Karenina*. Each reader introjects landscapes, rooms, and faces into the text to form an entirely personal residuum of reference, not available to others. But, as readers, we share also a communal 'I', which is that unspoken second person of the text. As Georges Poulet puts it, 'Whenever I read, I mentally pronounce an *I*, and yet the I which I pronounce is not myself.'[2] This I/other is a figure scattered among, as much as composed from, the many discursive positions offered by the writing, athwart the positions the reader occupies in current history.

Our encounter with the work is sprung upon the linguistic resources it offers, and our resistance to it as well as our immersion in it cannot refuse its terms. But these terms are not invariant; words on the page do not have fixed limits. They reach us doubly freighted with debate: the arguments, engagements, and estrangements within which they were embedded at the time of the work's production, the arguments, estrangements, and engagements within which we read now. All the essays in this collection, written over several years (and one long ago), read, in present terms, prose writers engaging with past writing and past reading. The writers respond not only in debate but in affection, riding the rhythms of past prose, as Richardson does with Sidney even as he redisposes the class questions Sidney did not see as questions. The last three essays concern Virginia Woolf, whose internalization of past writing and past persons gets under the guard of the parody she deploys. Her work fictionalizes the modernist claim to a new start, undermines it even as it proposes it.

The concept of the dialogue with the past, developed particularly by Habermas and Gadamer, but there from antiquity, emphasizes the expanding and corrective interaction of present reading with past writing. 'Understanding begins', writes Gadamer, 'when something addresses us. This is the primary hermeneutical condition.'

> The hermeneutically trained mind will also include historical consciousness. It will make conscious the prejudices governing our own understanding, so that the text, as another's meaning, can be isolated and valued on its own. . . .
>
> For so long as our mind is influenced by a prejudice, we do not know, and consider it as a judgment. How then are we to isolate it? It is impossible to make ourselves aware of it while it is constantly operating unnoticed, but only when it is, so to speak, stimulated. The encounter with a text from the past can provide this stimulus. For what leads to understanding must be something that has already asserted itself in its own separate validity.[3]

The 'stimulating' of our prejudices or, to put it more neutrally, of our formative conditions is achieved not by drawing the work into a concept of 'relevance' but by accepting its initiating distinctness from ourselves, though the writing will be activated for each person only by the process of reading.

Reading the past

Discourse does not take place outside history. However, no historical period consists only of its present. Evidence of this is provided not only by architecture and legal systems but also – with particular intensity – by past writing when read within and read into the present. History is in this sense less linear than constellatory. The parameters of reading periods are unstable and difficult to descry. Whereas we skein out literary *production* into controllable periods – the Romantics, the Victorian age, modernism – *reading periods* are quite otherwise organized, trawling a variety of pasts and varying from person to person, though circumscribed by what is available within the community. Reading communities, moreover, differ greatly from one another even within the same place and time. And in much recent discussion of the 'canon' and its powers the changing composition of the canon itself has been overlooked: the interlocked accepted works of the late eighteenth century were very different from those of the late nineteenth century, for example, and different again from our own institutionalized grouping of texts.

Reading takes place always in the present. The heat of writing has already been cooled in published work by the mortification of cold print. What Todorov calls the 'perpetual present' of narrative enacts the difference between writing and reading.[4] The distance between *time* of writing and time of reading varies immensely, of course, and will lead to the need for different forms of explanation. But the *space* between writing and reading is always and absolutely there. That is the space of enactment and recoil: the argument with the past.

Sometimes writers inscribe it within the text, making the absence the ironic control on which the work is sprung. In this volume I argue that George Eliot does that with the unwritten time of her own adult life, which falls between the setting of her novel *Middlemarch* and the period of its writing and first reading. Later readings trouble the poise of that ironic relationship by extending temporal distance, so slackening the detailed reference to change, and challenging the normative position ascribed to the first readers.

The present is both an absolute and an endlessly drifting position. In Iser's account of interaction between text and reader the language he uses renders the text prior to the reader but surpassed by reading; what is written is not shown as having the capacity to re-enter argument: 'the linguistic signs and structure of the text exhaust their function in triggering developing acts of comprehension.' The active reader extends the bounds or fills the gaps left by the tutelary writing which 'offers guidance as to what is to be produced, and therefore cannot itself be the product'.[5] But reading does more.

Much otherwise invaluable reception theory has emphasized the present of reading without taking account of the historical conditions of the work's production. This omission obliterates the hermeneutic circle of novel and first readers, the complexity of whose relations is written into the work. The presence of those voices (arguing, repeating, refusing, diversifying the range of the book's linguistic community), once heard, makes for a fuller, more specific, and often more disturbing resonance to our reading now. Readers are not all cleverer since Henry James, only cleverer at reading Henry James. Past writing can teach us lost reading and experiential skills, and with those skills we can begin to learn the *difference* of the past.

One merit of the notion of arguing with the past is that it sustains the possibility of the writing persistently re-entering dialogue. As Dominick LaCapra puts it in *Rethinking Intellectual History*:

> The past has its own 'voices' that must be respected, especially when they resist or qualify the interpretations we would like to place on them. A text is a network of resistances, and a dialogue is a two-way affair; a good reader is also an attentive and patient listener. Questions are necessary to focus interest in an investigation, but a fact may be pertinent to a frame of reference by contesting or even contradicting it.[6]

Such a position seems to me to be preferable to Harold Bloom's antithetical imagination, which conceives past and present, writing and reading, as embattled contraries, and survival as being possible only by the evasion or stupefying of what precedes:

> 'Influence' to Nietzsche meant vitalization. But influence, and more precisely poetic influence, has been more a blight than a blessing, from the Enlightenment until this moment. Where it has vitalized, it has operated as misprision, as deliberate, even perverse revisionism.[7]

'To imagine is to misinterpret' has proved to be one of those remarks which level more than they liberate.

For example, unless we believe in fixed entities – man and woman – we need to be alert to the processes of gender formation and gender change. We cannot construe this in isolation from other elements within a culture, and, moreover, we shall better discover our own fixing assumptions if we value the *unlikeness* of the past. The formation of gender, and its condensation in the literature of the time, is not cut loose from economics, or architecture, or class, or, come to that, animal care. No one of these is the single source of authority either: there is no sole source of oppression, though there are dominant forms of it in class, race, and gender power-structures. Self-understanding internalizes the shapes for experience proffered by earlier literature (as I have elsewhere argued concerning Ovid and the language of women's sensibility).[8] In the literature of the past we are presented with immensely detailed interconnecting systems: power and pleasure caught into representations so particular as to be irreplaceable. So the informing of the text with our learnt awareness of historical conditions is not a matter simply of providing 'context' or 'background'. Instead it is, more exactly, in-forming, instantiation.

Yet we can never become past readers: learnt awareness dramatizes what could then be assumed, and so changes it from an inert to an active element in the text. But reading only along the grain of our pressing cultural and personal needs, even what Bloom calls 'misreading', may too easily become a matter of subjugating the text and evading the awkward questions it poses. The reader claims sovereignty. The text becomes the subject, and subjected. It falls silent or speaks only what the sovereign wishes to hear. This is no way to uncover other experience or to tap into difficult questions. The subjectivist hierarchy, when it is interpreted as empowering the reader absolutely, reduces writing to single signification. Sometimes, it is true, a particular single signification is so gripping, so necessary within a historical moment, that it suffices for that reader, that group. Such hermeneutic retrenchment may have a sound political function, especially if it brings sharply into focus a pattern of debate within the work hitherto little observed, or marks discursive elements unfulfilled at the historical moment of the text's production. But there will always be more to the text than the single sharply posed question reveals or than the reader's particular experience necessitates.

The privileging of complexity in literary works, objected to by some interpreters, is a privileging of contestation. Complexity challenges the reader by refusing single resolution, by offering questions we had not thought of, and suggestions not on our terms. It persuades the reader into experience not chosen. The reader cannot foresee the fullness of the written text. Nor can interpretation encompass it.

Ceasing to read

Any reader may choose to cease reading – and this is a power too little addressed in narrative theory. The reader, having ceased to read – flung the book across the room or put it down one morning thinking to pick it up again and then not wished (or wished not) to do so – is left with a problem: the book remains, half read. If the book has bored the reader it may peel flat away from the memory. More often, though, it continues to be read in the mind, brooded over, repudiated. Truncated reading can monumentalize the work, fixing it in the memory. The reader's only sharp revenge is the refusal to finish reading. The unfinished reading may revenge itself by returning. In such suspended reading the element of debate, of struggle with the text, is intensified.

There are many half-read works in most readers' minds; but incomplete reading is not a respectable activity. Indeed, rereading is the only thoroughly respectable mode in some circles: 'I haven't reread it recently' may often mean 'I never got round to reading it'. In studying the books read by past writers we emphasize – and properly so – those that the writer is known to have loved, and perhaps often returned to. However, this seems to me to be only one path to interpretation, and a misleading one if it expunges unsatisfactory experiences or incomplete reading. Hermeneutically, spasmodic reading may be more troubling, unfinished texts more haunting, repudiated reading more provoking, than the thoroughly assimilated book we study. I am not recommending sloppy reading, nor encouraging readers to let the book drop from their hands. I do suggest, though, that we need to take account of truncated or baffled readings as part of the creative process. Intense but unsuccessful reading may be a goad to thought, not its numbing.

In work elsewhere on Darwin's reading I was able to draw on Darwin's own exact descriptions of the diverse intensity of reading he gave to different works ('skimmed', 'read thoroughly', 'failed in reading').[9] It would be rash to assume a steady relation between the thoroughness of reading and the stimulus provided. Darwin from time to time scrupulously records that he has failed in reading something: 15 April 1840, 'Failed in reading Dryden's Poems except Absalom and Ach. wh. I rather liked'; 20 September, 'Failed in reading Niebuhr's Rome'.

It would be an ingenious and confident commentator who could tell precisely what, if anything, Darwin retained from his failed reading of Dryden – though clearly something teased him and drew him back, since already on 15 March, a month earlier, he had recorded, 'Skimmed Pope and Dryden Poems – need not try them again.' Yet three years later, on 1 October 1843, he records 'Scotts Life of Dryden'. The recurrence of Dryden's name in the reading lists is intriguing, but the kinds of pleasure and recalcitrance he possessed for Darwin remain obscure. Niebuhr, however, has been claimed as an influence on Darwin, and Darwin's comment that he 'failed in reading' him by no means necessarily rules out that claim. Indeed, difficulty, distaste, and even boredom, particularly when stimulus and pleasure have been anticipated by repute, create a powerful difficulty that may lead to a more sustained brooding on the problems raised by an author than does an enthusiastic, complete, and therefore resolved reading. Whereas Darwin simply sweeps aside some works with the comment 'poor', it is to be noted that in both the examples cited above he feels *himself* to have failed: 'failed in reading'. The dialectic is interrupted but not set aside with the book. It is extended in the reader's own thoughts and may therefore move on at a tangent from the initiating problem. So, specifically, in this volume, I suggest that Carlyle's reading of Kant continued to form obstructions and tunnels in his thought for years just because he was uncertain that he had grasped Kant's argument or its value.

Continuing to read

Writers are readers too – and not only of other people's works. The writer reads as she or he composes, reads as she reviews her half-composed text, reads again as she revises. Each of these readings has a different relation to the text. Revision, which looks back upon the whole temporal process of the achieved work (still and always incomplete), is very different from the instantaneity of reading and writing within the composition of the text. At that time the horizon is local and a much greater speculative space remains. The writer does not yet know what is to be written, though the whole may be projected, and in that phase the writer still to some degree shares the fan of future possibilities that the reader will riffle through moment by moment, page by page. The multiple possible futures of the work give much of our driven freedom as we read: we weigh, discount, hope, revive alternative outcomes. The cluster of hypothesized futures gives much of the pleasure and anxiety to reading. The reading writer, in the process of writing, has further and pressing anxieties: above all, is completion possible? Can the work ever be finished? Most conclusions are disappointing, not only because we have come to the end, but because of the inadequacy of any one chosen pathway from among the many mapped out. In an essay in this volume I suggest that Richardson's reading of a seventeenth-century continuation of Sidney may have triggered his desire to prolong, and to dispute with, Sidney's almost endless narrative.

A primary mystery for the child within a family group – a mystery which few outgrow though they may set it aside or control it intellectually – is that the others were there before you, and before you *were*. The entry into an already formed group is a recurrent experience throughout an individual's life. It is also, in great intensity, the reader's experience. Within the novel, plot creates a further, paranoid, intensification of this predicament by suggesting a prior ordering at work. The text was already there – and so were other readers. The hermeneutic network in which the reader participates when reading works of the past is one that both promises novelty and yet is already formed. The paradox precedes our reading. None the less the experience of reading offers to make all things new. Moreover, the 'perpetual present' of narrative allows fresh participation on each occasion of reading. It is true that the reader may shift narrative positions more freely on a second than on a first reading, particularly in plots of intrigue: for example, we evade the narrative traps set for Emma on a second reading of Jane Austen's novel; but we do not escape undergoing again Emma's mortification. Our helpless knowingness the second time round proves not to absolve us any more than our helpless bungling alongside her on the first occasion. In each case the novel's writing describes the conditions of our knowledge; its terms, its grammar and syntax, write us into the epistemological sequences of the work. That is, though we *know* in advance the work's outcome, we *discover* sentence by sentence the roles and responses ordered for us within the work. We may refuse to comply. We may ab-rupt the complicity demanded, read against the grain. But even so we shall, if we continue reading, do so within conditions which have closed upon us by means of generic exclusions, discursive variety, plot repertoires. When we rebel we shall do so as readers on the book's terms.

Reading does not stop when we close the book. The ruminative process of selection, imagistic repetition, and recoil continues to inform our thought. The work may also now freely enter memory. Books once read do not stay inside their covers. Once in the head they mingle, forming networks of allusion with other reading and other experiences of the time. Though reading is an initially isolative experience, no narrative, once read, is recalled either in its entirety or in absolute isolation. Woolf explored this network of intertexts, and the passion of reminiscence they sustain, particularly in *To the Lighthouse* and *Between the Acts*. Books once read enter also the process of forgetting. Nietzsche insisted on the need to forget, to dwell within a local horizon; that was his quarrel with history, and also with science.[10]

Both, in his terms, set the mind adrift on too large an ocean. Reading is bound up with forgetting, not only of incidents, but of the language of each page. In the first essay in this collection I examine a cultural moment when the process of forgetting took on the aspect of crisis.

The strength of repeated reading is that it allows us to re-member, to read again – and to discover that the work is now other again than we recollect, its points of resistance and expansion shifted. And yet it holds its ground. The encounter across time, in the reader's changing present, can begin anew.

The work of the past was first read and written within quite other conditions, conditions which imply a different argumentative tension between reading and writing. That other implied argument poses questions that we do not automatically start from now. No community can ever be sufficiently described in the terms available to it. Nor can it ask all the salient questions concerning itself. The outsider's eye, across space or time, makes observations which do not simply supplement but may transform the questions to be asked. We are those outsiders; but then so also are the books we study.

NOTES

1 Some of the ideas here adumbrated are developed further, in relation to the representation of women, in my forthcoming essay 'Representing women: re-presenting the past', in Catherine Belsey and Jane Moore (eds), *A Feminist Reader* (London, 1989).

2 Georges Poulet, 'Phenomenology of reading', *New Literary History*, I (Baltimore, 1969), p. 56.

3 Hans Georg Gadamer, *Truth and Method* (London, 1975), p. 266. See also Jürgen Habermas, *Knowledge and Human Interests* (London, 1978), p. 315: 'the unity of knowledge and interest proves itself in a dialectic that takes the historical traces of suppressed dialogue and reconstructs what has been suppressed.' Martin Heidegger had argued in *Identity and Difference* (New York, 1969), in 'The onto-theo-logical constitution of metaphysics', pp. 49–50, that 'the character of the conversation with the history of thinking is no longer *Aufhebung*, but the step back. . . . . The step back goes from what is unthought, from the difference as such, into what gives us thought.'

4 Tzvetan Todorov, 'The quest of narrative', in his *The Poetics of Prose* (Oxford, 1977), p. 132: 'Narrative logic implies, ideally, a temporality we might call the "perpetual present". Time here is constituted by the concatenation of countless instances of discourse; it is these latter which define the very idea of the present.'

5 Wolfgang Iser, *The Act of Reading: A Theory of Aesthetic Response* (Baltimore and London, 1978), pp. 107–8.

6 Dominick LaCapra, *Rethinking Intellectual History: Texts, Contexts, Language* (Ithaca and London, 1983), p. 64.

7 Harold Bloom, *The Anxiety of Influence: A Theory of Poetry* (Oxford, 1973), p. 50. Bloom's emphasis on his work as a theory of *poetry* has not prevented later critics from applying it to fiction, nor does there seem any reason why it should not 'hold across genres.

8 Gillian Beer, ' "Our unnatural no-voice": Heroic Epistle, Pope, and women's gothic', in Claude Rawson (ed.), *The Heroic and its Transformations, The Yearbook of English Studies*, 12 (1982); forthcoming in Leo Damrosch (ed.), *Modern Essays on Eighteenth Century Literature* (Oxford, 1989).

9 Gillian Beer, 'Darwin's reading and the fictions of development', in David Kohn (ed.), *The Darwinian Heritage* (Princeton, 1985), esp. pp. 546–9.

10 Friedrich Nietzsche, 'The use and abuse of history', *Thoughts out of Season*, part 2 (Edinburgh and London, 1909), p. 95: 'Excess of history has attacked the plastic power of life'; 'Science . . . tries to remove all limitation of horizon and cast men into an infinite boundless sea.'

2

ORIGINS AND OBLIVION IN VICTORIAN NARRATIVE

Forgetfulness is categorized as a malfunction of memory, and yet forgetting is our commonest experience. We do not remember great tracts of life, great tracts of narrative. Of its nature, what has been forgotten is not available to be discussed. Remembering is achievement – and memory is prized as we prize all human achievement, with a sense of the exceptional. A summary example of how acceptable is memory, how unacceptable forgetting, is that in working on this project I found it impossible to gain access to material in catalogues except by looking under memory: *forgetting* (except in the clinical intensification of amnesia) and even *oblivion* were not available as subsections.[1] Forgetting is the habitual activity of each human being; oblivion covers all that has been forgotten. We all ride, largely unperturbed, what Shakespeare in *Richard III* called 'the swallowing Gulfe of dark Forgetfulnesse, and deepe Oblivion' (III. vii). But there are times when the act of forgetting becomes crisis and the recognition of oblivion becomes threatening to a community. One such time was the end of the sixteenth century in England; another was the Victorian period.

In this essay I suggest connections between the ordinary act of ceasing to remember and deep anxieties about the extent of oblivion, the remoteness and unreclaimableness of origins, in Victorian creativity. I want to consider how and why some Victorian narratives resist or dwell upon the dissolution of record, and so to study an intersection between general reading process and a particular historical period.

It is not surprising that forgetting and oblivion are frequently seen as antagonists within literature: a common great theme has been the heroic task of the poet who makes things last by writing them. However, it may be an unobserved professional deformation that as critics we tend to identify forgetting with inefficient reading and fail to notice how important in our experience of a fiction is the dissolution in memory of the specificity of the text. We remember (or pretend to remember) the totality of a narrative and so misread its passing. We dwell on particular passages with intense semantic attention, and we triumphantly recall the names of minor characters. But long narrative must either accept or combat the reader's constant forgetting. Many early novelists had few qualms about dissolution.

The multi-plot form of many of the greatest Victorian fictions, particularly those of Dickens, Thackeray, and George Eliot, makes it difficult for the reader to remember all that passes by.[2] In Hardy that difficulty becomes the mainspring of narrative meaning. I do not propose in this short paper (nor am I qualified) to enter the controversy among experimental psychologists as to whether all memory is stored (even though some is unusable) or whether most experiences pass through us and are irretrievably lost. In any case, the loss of individual memory was not the only form of the problem that beset Victorian writers. They were enforcedly made aware that life had been going on for millions of years before human memory existed: no memory of that state was possible; life and story did not require the human race. In such a situation, human beings' imaginative zeal in 'decipherment', what Richard Owen and others called 'the writing on the rocks', gave an entry into the pre-human past for human consciousness.[3] Another point of entry was what W.B. Carpenter, Eneas Sweetland Dallas, and, later, Freud thought of as the possibility that 'involuntary, unconscious thought' harboured traces of existence prior to the individual's history and continuous with the extreme and infinitely remote emergence of humankind.[4]

Eneas Sweetland Dallas, in the 1860s, conceives imagination as a 'function' rather than a faculty, a function of what he calls 'the Hidden Soul' or 'unconscious' with its 'perpetual magic of reminiscence hidden from our conscious life'. And, in Derridean style, he writes that 'imagination ... is only a name for the free, unconscious play of thought. But the mind in free play works more as a whole than in conscious and voluntary effort.'[5] Dallas's emphasis on imagination as an expression of the 'involuntary and unconscious' mind accords with Walter Benjamin's description of Proust's acts of memory:

Is not the involuntary recollection, Proust's *mémoire involontaire*, much closer to forgetting than what is usually called memory? ...

When we awake each morning, we hold in our hands, usually weakly and loosely, but a few fringes of the tapestry of lived life, as loomed for us by forgetting. However, with our purposeful activity and, even more, our purposive remembering each day unravels the web and ornaments of forgetting.

Benjamin's praise of forgetting, like his praise of boredom in 'The Storyteller', has in it a grave and conscious reversal of our expectations. In 'The Storyteller' he remarks, 'There is nothing that commends a story to memory more effectively than that chaste compactness which precludes psychological analysis.'[6] Victorian fiction, with its emphasis on multiplicity and arboreal form combined with psychological analysis, might seem at the opposite pole from such storytelling: copiousness and hyperproductivity invite selection, not complete recall.

My project does not use the metaphor of 'background', with literature as the foreground and all other writing as a system of clues that will give access to literary experience. Rather, I want to examine creative narratives such as those of the geologist Sir Charles Lyell, Darwin, or the philologist Max Müller, and Winwood Reade, *alongside* Victorian works of fiction. I have argued elsewhere that the process of interchange of metaphors and concepts between fields is at its most active 'in areas of unresolved conflict or problem' and that 'the function of transposition may be as much to disguise as to lay bare.'[7] It is in the spirit of that observation that I analyse the means writers used to control a newly intensified sense of evanescence associated with concepts of geological time, of extinction, and of irreversible and random genetic mutation. Each of these diminished the claims of memory. Oblivion is prospective as well as past, universal as well as individual. Both fear of the sun's cooling and the new study of pre-history play a part in the hazards of Victorian experience and in the encoding of that experience in fiction. It is to modernist and postmodernist narrative that we turn for the topic of forgetting, the emphasis on fissure, palimpsest, and faulture. But it is within Victorian written culture that we find the incentives – intellectual and emotional – towards that interrupted organization.

In some recent postmodernist fiction, forgetting has emerged both as topic and as remarked process in the reader's activity. In *One Hundred Years of Solitude* Gabriel García Márquez describes the insomnia plague and the forgotten massacre, and at the same time confuses throughout the book the reader's notation of events and time by reusing names repeatedly for different individuals. Milan Kundera in *The Book of Laughter and Forgetting* signals the topic in his title and illustrates it in the episodes (and the episodic structure) of the book. Malcolm Bradbury in *The History Man* sets up a moralized tension between the post-causal immediacy of present-tense narrative, which figures the hero's irresponsible revolutionism, and the counterweight of forgotten history. At the end of the book we as readers are made to discover our own collusion with Howard. Like him, and encouraged by the book's organization, we have forgotten his wife, Barbara, who plays no part in the work's latter phases but re-emerges in the final scene to cut her wrist: an act of suicide that admonishes the reader of the connection between guilt, failure, and forgetting. Forgetting has become associated in our narratives with guilt and trauma. Freud's moral struggle was to restore memories and by such recuperation to make them part of accountable consciousness. Since Freud, individuals' acts of forgetting are interpreted as purposeful, rather than as part of a general process of evanescence.

Though a recognition of strained memory has become topical, readers habitually allow narrative language and sometimes narrative sequence to dissolve, unhampered by any insistence on retention, unless the text persistently prompts them to recall and store. For example, one of the pleasures of picaresque fiction is the reader's licence to discard narrative, just as the hero sloughs off experience. Many Victorian novelists set up a creative problem for themselves and their readers by combining the amplitude and arboreal form of their large narratives with an increasing insistence on the moral duty to recall and connect. Elizabeth Ermarth wittily condenses the question: 'In all realistic novels one of the chief moral problems characters face is that of making proper connections, literally by marriage, and figuratively by sustained increase of conscious grasp. The power to accomplish that is often associated with memory.'[8] In Victorian multi-plot novels the reader, even more than the characters, is required to recognize his or her own activity of remembering and to value it. We are made to feel responsible for sustaining memory and are put on our guard against natural forgetting. Such insistence on remembering, as Wolfgang Iser points out in *The Act of Reading*, may produce satiety. The 'consensual' novel (Ermarth's term) seeks to offer a full and single understanding of the whole and in particular to encompass its own beginning and ending. That naturalization of beginning and ending draws on the ontogenetic model of the life cycle.

Consider, then, the disturbances implicit in scientific findings that suggested that the model of the single life cycle could not be extended to describe the natural order and its history, and that narrative acts had no necessary coherence with the time patterns of the material world.

Human memory, even at its most extended, is not coincident with the past. The living world existed previous to the human race, outside language: it can be brought within language and narrative only by the deciphering of traces and fragments, the assemblage of record. Prehistory was a new study and a new imagination, in the mid-nineteenth century. 'Real events' were the business of the Victorian novelist as well as of the natural historian, and it may be that we should see the Victorian insistence on the 'real' as in some measure a response to the loss of a close-knit beginning and ending in the natural world. No longer held in by the Mosaic time order, that history became a mosaic of another sort, a piecing together of subsets into an interpretable picture. Words like *traces* and *decipherment* become central to geology, evolutionary theory, and fictional narrative at this time. Interpretation was the only assurance. So Lyell alludes to Barthold Georg Niebuhr's achievements in historiography to illuminate the importance of geological researches: 'As we explore this magnificent field of enquiry, the sentiment of a great historian of our times may continually be present to our minds, that "he who calls what has vanished back again into being, enjoys a bliss like that of creating."'
Near the outset of *Principles of Geology*, Lyell quotes the geologist James Hutton, whose work in *A System of the Earth* (1785) had undermined the testimony of 'granitic writing' and decipherment:

No small sensation was excited when Hutton seemed, with unhallowed hand, desirous to erase characters already regarded by many as sacred. 'In the economy of the world', said the Scotch geologist, 'I can find no traces of a beginning, no prospect of an end'; a declaration the more startling when coupled with the doctrine, that all past ages on the globe had been brought about by the slow agency of existing causes. The imagination was first fatigued and overpowered by endeavouring to conceive the immensity of time required for the annihilation of whole continents by so insensible a process; and when the thoughts had wandered through these interminable periods, no resting-place was assigned in the remotest distance.[9]

16

Hutton asserted that geology had nothing to do 'with the origin of things'. An unspoken and unwritten – because humanly unobserved – world precedes us, of which Huxley said 'the question of the moral government of such a world could no more be asked than we could reasonably seek for moral purpose in a kaleidoscope.'[10] Macherey, in *Towards a Theory of Literary Production*, has reminded us that the idea of an origin is an appeal to bounds, a means of staying the slide into oblivion, and – in his analysis – a way of giving authority to bourgeois hegemony. The questioning of historical origins and of a nameable originator may give some of the anxious zest to the Victorian insistence on causality. Certainly, Hutton's definition of a world in which there are 'no traces of a beginning, no prospect of an end' is a highly inconvenient shape for fiction – particularly for fiction that wishes to lay claim to coherence with a representable order of society and a 'real' material world.

The Victorians were made preternaturally sensitive to the processes of forgetting and to the extent of what has been forgotten. They were made aware also of the vigorous life that long preceded human memory. Their fascination with history is one response to that awareness – as well as an intensifying symptom. But history was preoccupied with power, and what evolutionary theory brought out in contrast was the thronging powerlessness of the individual organisms who were the medium of change. At the end of *Middlemarch* George Eliot celebrates the 'incalculably diffusive' outcome of Dorothea's life and of other unrecounted lives and ends her 'domestic epic' with a bare gradualism that just admits the possibility of improvement: 'For the growing good of the world is partly dependent on unhistoric acts; and that things are not so ill with you and me as they might have been, is half owing to the forgotten numbers who lived faithfully a hidden life, and rest in unvisited tombs.'[11] The 'forgotten numbers' are the permitting medium of our present experience.

The insistence on displacing the experience of the individual life cycle into that of the society or species is so familiar to us that we rarely, too rarely perhaps, examine it. The vacillation between ontogeny and phylogeny has been the most powerful new metaphor of the past hundred years, affecting areas as diverse as race history and musicology. The growth of the single organism was an ancient metaphor; the growth of species and the paralleling of the two were new. One means by which the Victorians imaginatively healed their sense of the enormity of oblivion was by the concepts of 'recapitulation' and 'survivals': the embryo 'recapitulates' the phases of evolutionary development, while remote tribes are 'survivals' from the 'childhood of man'. Freud openly used the vacillation between individual organism and species history in the case of Dr Schreber (1911) and *Totem and Taboo* (1913), and he continued to hold this view through the 1930s, as demonstrated in *Moses and Monotheism*. The past precedes human memory and is irrecoverable, except by conjoining ontogeny and phylogeny. Freud uses this essentially Victorian conjunction in the postscript to 'Notes on a case of paranoia':

> The mythopoeic forces of mankind are not extinct, but ... to this very day they give rise in the neuroses to the same psychical products as in the remotest past ages. ... I am of opinion that the time will soon be ripe for us to make an extension of a thesis which has long been asserted by psychoanalysts, and to complete what has hitherto had only an individual and ontogenetic application by the addition of its anthropological counterpart, which is to be conceived phylogenetically. 'In dreams and in neuroses', our thesis has run, 'we come once more upon the child and the peculiarities which characterize his modes of thought and his emotional life.' 'And we come upon the savage too,' we may now add, 'upon the primitive man, as he stands revealed to us in the light of the researches of archaeology and ethnology.'[12]

Sir Charles Lyell, whose *Principles of Geology* stretched time backwards an unknown and irrecoverable extent, emphasized the differing narrative properties of his account of the world and the accounts of previous geologists.

> We often behold, at one glance, the effects of causes which have acted at times incalculably remote, and yet there may be no striking circumstances to mark the occurrence of a great chasm in the chronological series of Nature's archives. In the vast interval of time which may really have elapsed between the results of operations thus compared, the physical condition of the earth may, by slow and insensible modifications, have become entirely altered; one or more races of organic beings may have passed away, and yet have left behind, in the particular region under contemplation, no trace of their existence.[13]

The short span of time previously allowed to events has implied, said Lyell, a narrative of catastrophe and revolution, of upheaval and reversal, a magical or nightmare romance:

> How fatal every error as to the quantity of time must prove to the introduction of rational views concerning the state of things in former ages, may be conceived by supposing the annals of the civil and military transactions of a great nation to be perused under the impression that they occurred in a period of one hundred instead of two thousand years. Such a portion of history would immediately assume the air of a romance; the events would seem devoid of credibility, and inconsistent with the present course of human affairs. A crowd of incidents would follow each other in quick succession. Armies and fleets would appear to be assembled only to be destroyed, and cities built merely to fall in ruins. There would be the most violent transitions from foreign or intestine war to periods of profound peace, and the works effected during the years of disorder or tranquility would appear alike superhuman in magnitude. He who should study the monuments of the natural world under the influence of a similar infatuation, must draw a no less exaggerated picture of the energy and violence of causes.[14]

Previous geologists were like the seven sleepers who awoke to a transformed world, unaware of their immense slumbers. The reach of time in Lyell's narrative is turned into a means of comfort by suggesting continuity and slight change as the agencies of transformation.

But that quiet world of slippage, erosion, and dead forms is disturbed again by Robert Chambers in *Vestiges of the Natural History of Creation* (1844) and Charles Darwin in *On the Origin of Species by Means of Natural Selection, or the Preservation of Favoured Races in the Struggle for Life* (1859). The full title of Darwin's work brings out the ideological contrast between his arguments and those of Chambers. For Chambers, what is left in the world is 'vestiges' – fragmentary records of a primordial creation – and 'natural history' is the storying of creation, arranging it in a narrative sequence that will not question the initiating act. Darwin, on the other hand, substitutes process for initiation, place, or person. 'Of the origin ... by means of': originating is no longer to be identified with an originator, or with a place of origin. It would be going too far to describe Darwin's project as 'free play without origins' as Derrida describes the nature of poetry, but it is a significant move away from the idea of history and of natural history as a tracking back to a recoverable origin. Darwin develops Lyell's metaphor of the material world as language, or as a Borgesian, language-ridden history of language, itself written in an alien tongue.

> For my part, following out Lyell's metaphor, I look at the natural geological record, as a history of the world imperfectly kept, and written in a changing dialect; of this history we possess the last volume alone, relating only to two or three countries. Of this volume, only here and there a short chapter has been preserved; and of each page, only here and there a few lines. Each word of the slowly-changing language, in which the history is supposed to be written, being more or less different in the interrupted succession of chapters, may represent the apparently abruptly changed forms of life, entombed in our consecutive, but widely separated for-mations.[15]

The account of forgotten worlds that Lyell and Darwin provided relied not upon catastrophe but upon an immense elongation of time and on a recognition of how recent – and how frail – was the hold of the human within the natural order. Lyell thought it quite probable that the human race would die out again and the world revert to earlier states. Darwin emphasized that few if any current species-forms would carry forward into the prolonged future. Not only individuals but whole species take part in the immense and irrecoverable process of forgetting and of being forgotten. Lyell's and Darwin's work raised the problem of how to sustain a narrative form that would satisfy the demand for coherence while acknowledging evanescence.

Hayden White in 'The narrativization of real events' writes:

> I assume we agree that narrativization is what Fredric Jameson calls 'the central function or instance of the human mind' or a form of human comprehension that is productive of meaning by its imposition of a certain formal coherence on a virtual chaos of 'events' which in themselves (or as given to perception) cannot be said to possess any particular form at all, much less the kind that we associate with 'stories'. The question is with what *kind of meaning* does storying endow these events which are the products of human agency in the past and which we call 'historical events'.

Making an important distinction, White goes on to remark that there is no sense in speaking of 'events per se', only 'events under description'.[16] White writes of the 'storying' of events that are the products of human agency. The Victorians were faced also with the problem of 'storying' events prior to the human and regardless of the human – and of making sense of the human story in this enlarged field. Is the forgotten period simply a repetition of what is now enacted, or is it increasingly different, more alien, less retrievable? Is the present therefore less universal than it has seemed, more purely local and passing also? Was there a particular historical problem for the Victorians in relation to the project of realism? Could realism itself be said to emerge from a dismayed recognition of the extensiveness of oblivion, the manifold and unremitting activities of forgetting?

Darwinian theory brings into question the value of memory. It highlights the extent of our inevitable ignorance of the lived past, both our own past and that of the physical order of the world. It denies, in its earlier stages, the inscribing of experience as inherited characteristics. It emphasizes 'luck' as opposed to 'cunning', to use Samuel Butler's later pair of contraries. It refuses both chance and necessity and – with Lyell – emphasizes the inadequacy of our perspective as observers. It also prepares for a recovery of the human position through the idea of the unconscious. However, for Lyell, for Darwin, and for Huxley, the unconscious was not the guardian of prior memories but rather a separate domain, relating to the earth's movements, and to 'natural' instead of 'artificial' selection, genetic as opposed to reasoned continuity.[17]

In Hardy's small, profound poem, 'Heredity', we hear the menace and promise of impersonal genetic continuity:

> I am the family face;
> Flesh perishes, I live on,
> Projecting trait and trace
> Through times to times anon,
> And leaping from place to place
> Over oblivion.[18]

That poem, with its emphasis on haphazard and partial genetic survival (a survival that obliterates individual significance), was written towards the end of a period that had almost intolerably extended the awareness of 'oblivion'.

'History' becomes 'natural history', with the profoundly equivocal meaning that 'natural' bears at this period: 'natural history', 'natural theology', 'natural selection'. The ironic relationships between these terms pivot upon their common element 'natural'. Human beings are both newly and completely part of the natural order – in evolutionary theory they are not set apart from other species. Yet they must also become the chroniclers of tracts of time in which they had no place: 'before the lowest Silurian stratum was deposited, long periods elapsed ... during these vast, yet quite unknown, periods of time, *the world swarmed with living creatures*' (emphasis added). That perception Darwin saw as crucial to this theory, indisputable yet beyond memorial. He, like Lyell, commented on the difficulty of believing in the vastness of time and the tendency to close the gaps in the record. Darwin saw the narrative problem of recording such 'vast intervals': 'When we see the formations tabulated in written works, it is difficult to avoid believing that they are closely consecutive.' Tabulation erases intermittence. The record is paltry in the extreme.

> I have made these few remarks because it is highly important for us to gain some notion, however imperfect, of the lapse of years. During each of these years, over the whole world, the land and the water have been peopled by hosts of living forms. What an infinite number of generations, which the mind cannot grasp, must have succeeded each other in the long roll of years! Now turn to our richest geological museums, and what a paltry display we behold![19]

In *Science and the Hebrew Tradition* Huxley later comments on the importance of the imperfection of the geological record: 'This imperfection is a great fact, which must be taken into account in all our speculations, or we shall constantly be going wrong.'[20]

Here we have possible incentives within the culture for the rise of the detective story, with its emphasis on lost clues, determined reading, recuperable losses, the deciphering of traces: a way of controlling the hermeneutic plethora, 'the imposition of a certain formal coherence on a virtual chaos of "events"' (Hayden White). Detective fiction is a form that draws the reader's attention to his or her own processes of forgetting and of inattention. It establishes a nameable origin for its action. It restores coherence at the price of amplitude, though as Frank Kermode observes:

> Even in a detective story which has the maximum degree of specialised hermeneutic organisation, one can always find significant concentrations of interpretable material that has nothing to do with clues and solutions and that can, if we choose, be read rather than simply discarded, though propriety recommends the latter course.[21]

These 'significant concentrations of interpretable material' may be said to be the 'hosts of living forms' redundant to story, history, or even explanation.

For Victorian writers, the detective or mystery story emerges as the form in which it remains satisfyingly possible to go back and rediscover the true initiation of a history. In such an organization we are assured that 'the traces of the past [lie] deep – too deep to be effaced.' Wilkie Collins here connects the imagery of geology and decipherment with that of subconscious memory and trauma. He emphasizes the survival of traces, not their obliteration. In such a plot truth-telling and interpretation are close to paranoia. Nothing is contingent; everything can be retraced to a single initiating source. In paranoid plot the loss of authentic origin makes the acts of decipherment and interpretation both self-generating and self-consuming. In *The Woman in White*, Hartright's monomania is sane, but barely so:

> I began to doubt whether my own faculties were not in danger of losing their balance. It seemed almost like a monomania to be tracing back everything strange that happened, everything unexpected that was said, always to the same hidden source and the same sinister influence.[22]

Nothing may be forgotten by the reader or the first-person narrator, since all information is usable. Such fiction thrives on the guilt of misinterpretation and the satisfaction of the single solution, an austere reassembly of evidences.

In a world jostling with multiformity, fissured by incomplete meaning, the dogged and dedicated search for the single solution, the recovered origin, becomes one pressing narrative response. The reader is both chastened and heartened, chastened by his or her misclued memory, the tendency to retain what is not needed and discard the unnoticed that was crucial. The form of the detective story emphasizes the reader's attention to his or her own reading process and, at the conclusion, makes possible the satisfactory rereading of the past. For, in writing, death is never absolute. By turning back the pages we retrieve the earlier form. Obliteration is impossible: the traces never give way. This is indeed a technical problem for detective story writers, but also part of the synchronic pleasures that the form offers. The rise of the detective story may have to do, I suggest, with the Victorian anxiety about forgetting. Origins, within detective narratives, are still figured as recoverable by means of astute reading. But such reading is also transparently a fictive act, devoted to a form that declares its elucidations to be fictional.

In discussion of origins, the ontogenetic/phylogenetic/ontogenetic interchange may help also to account for the insistent search for parentage in Victorian fiction. Dianne F. Sadoff, in *Monsters of Affection*, has offered a fascinating Freudian reading of the role of the father in Victorian novels and in the novelists' imaginations.[23] The individual's psychohistory, however, is supplemented by shared perturbations, particularly communal perturbations such as the loss of congruity between human history and the history of the natural order. The insistence on the father, who is both an immediate and an uncertain origin, is a means of stabilizing the human record. The search for the mother, as in *Daniel Deronda*, shares the genetic recognition that W.R. Grove offered in his 1866 presidential address to the British Association for the Advancement of Science:

> From the long continued conventional habit of tracing pedigrees through the male ancestor, we forget in talking of progenitors that each individual has a mother as well as a father, and there is no reason to suppose that he has in him less of the blood of the one than of the other.[24]

Women are forgotten in the history of descent as they largely are in the historical record. In the new emphasis on genetic descent as the primary means of storying the past, it became necessary to recognize the generative power of the mother.

Without denying either the social or the psychosexual incentives for this topic, we may better understand the intensity of the theme if we measure it in relation to longer-spanning anxieties that preceded Darwin and were fed by Lyell and Chambers, among others. In Dickens's *Bleak House* the themes of lost parentage, of obliterated record or 'traces', and the consternation of a lawsuit preoccupied with 'pedigree' and with the descent of the great family are at last voided of content. Throughout this book it is the *effort* of memory that is the focus. Decipherment is the reader's task; writing is the scrivener's and the copyist's. The legal documents that are copied turn out to be burdened with Nothingness, just as the scrivener is Nobody – Nemo. Krook forgets nothing and can decipher nothing, only copy it. At the end of *Bleak House*, when the threatened apocalypse arrives, it takes the form of emptiness. The end of the lawsuit is the end of memory; there is no longer substance in the lawsuit, of either cash or meaning.

The lawsuit 'lapsed and melted away'; Richard can only 'begin the world' in another world. The immense clutter of Dickens's creativity allows us to forget much as we read, while, increasingly, in his later work, Dickens introduces means of making us aware of our forgetfulness. In *Bleak House* he uses the multiple cluing of Tulkinghorn and Bucket and Guppy, with their different detective-story insistences, to revive and limit meaning. All these interlocking themes should be seen within the framework of Dickens's alerting the reader by means of abrupt cross-setting of systems in the introductory paragraph of the book, a paragraph that looks back to prehistory and forward to the death of the sun.

> London. Michaelmas Term lately over, and the Lord Chancellor sitting in Lincoln's Inn Hall. Implacable November weather. As much mud in the streets, as if the waters had but newly retired from the face of the earth, and it would not be wonderful to meet a Megalosaurus, forty feet long or so, waddling like an elephantine lizard up Holborn Hill. Smoke lowering down from chimney-pots, making a soft black drizzle, with flakes of soot in it as big as full-grown snow-flakes – gone into mourning, one might imagine, for the death of the sun.[25]

J. Hillis Miller has drawn attention to the irreconcilable gaps between the two narrators' accounts in this novel, gaps caused in part because the narrators live in different tenses – one opened out towards imminent apocalypse in the dangerous present tense, one reaching back to an understanding of the historical past.[26] But the cross-setting of systems goes further than that. The paragraph just cited sets side by side the new and old versions of origins and apocalypse and offers them in playful synchrony: 'waters . . . newly retired', 'Megalosaurus', 'the death of the sun'. Mosaic creation, evolutionary theory derived from Chambers, modern London with its street names, its particularity of local place, are all conjoined: a barely post-diluvian geology is set alongside soot like black snowflakes 'gone into mourning . . . for the death of the sun.' That allusion calls in still another Victorian anxiety: the new theory current since the physicist Hermann von Helmholtz's 1847 essay *Über die Erhaltung der Kraft*, which argued that the sun is gradually cooling and that the earth will become too cold for life.

Ten years after Dickens's novel, Max Müller offered his theory of myth in which metaphor figures as 'a disease of language' – a disease brought about by forgetfulness and resulting in mythology. The lost relation between substantive first meaning and later etymological shift results, Müller argues, in false personification. In Müller's system all signification leads back towards the sun and the phenomena of weather, and to the fear of non-recurrence. He claimed that primitive peoples feared that the sun would not rise again.[27] Frances Power Cobbe's *Darwinism in Morals* recounts a terrifying dream that goes deep into the current imagery of her culture: the loss of faith in *recurrence*, the loss of any assurance of 'eternal return', the recognition that oblivion is the matter not only of the past but of the future. We have already seen a slight reference to 'the death of the sun' in Dickens. By the 1870s it has begun to trouble dreams by night:

> I dreamed that I was standing on a certain broad grassy space in the park of my old home. It was totally dark, but I was sure that I was in the midst of an immense crowd. We were all gazing upward into the murky sky and a sense of some fearful calamity was over us, so that no one spoke aloud. Suddenly overhead appeared through a rift in the black heavens, a branch of stars which I recognised as the belt and sword of Orion. Then went forth a cry of despair from all our hearts! We knew, though no one said it, that these stars proved it was not a cloud or mist which, as we had somehow believed, was causing the darkness. No; the air was clear; it was high noon, and *the sun had not risen*! That was the tremendous reason why we beheld the skies. The sun would never rise again![28]

Max Müller's solar myth was so powerful because it gave expression to covert dreads then current: it cast itself as past enquiry, but expressed current fears. In Freud's 'Notes on a case of paranoia' Dr Schreber's 'delusional privilege' will be the power to look directly at the sun, which in Freud's analysis signifies the father. Solar myth becomes parental myth.

In *Vestiges* Chambers describes memory as 'that handmaid of intellect, without which there could be no accumulation of mental capital, but an universal and continual infancy'.[29] The mixture of economic and ontogenetic metaphors – capital and infancy – is striking here. In his most anti-capitalist novel, *Little Dorrit*, Dickens shows the appalling effects of memory that is clung to. Mrs Clennam, with her reading of the motto on her husband's watch, 'Do Not Forget', stultifies her own life and those of others. The vengeful repetitiveness of her memory means that no growth or change is possible. She is literally seized by the force of her resentment, which constantly replays the past. Her crazed clinging to the capital sum of memory (her husband's love affair) and her closed economic and emotional system feed everything back into the one originating event. ' "Do Not Forget". It spoke to me like a voice from an angry cloud. Do not forget the deadly sin, do not forget the appointed discovery, do not forget the appointed suffering. I did not forget.'[30] Mrs Clennam's is an extreme of mono-maniac memory that enforces the idea of the single origin. Through *Little Dorrit* Dickens suggests connections between the circulation or piling up of money and the circulation or piling up of memory. Forgetting and letting go prove to be the most difficult of achieve-ments, as we see in the history of Dorrit himself.

These combined dreads and 'delusional privileges' are taken into Hardy's imagination and powerfully share in his fictional process, particularly in *Tess of the D'Urbervilles*, with its solar myths of Stonehenge and the Druids and Tess's alliance to the sun. In Hardy people may long to be forgotten, not remembered. So Tess's lament opens, 'I would that folk forgot me quite', and ends:

> I cannot bear my fate as writ,
> I'd have my life unbe;
> Would turn my memory to a blot,
> Make every relic of me rot,
> My doings be as they were not,
> And gone all trace of me![31]

The combination of the discourses of writing ('blot' and 'trace') and of fossil evidence ('rot' and 'trace') lightly bears the weight of Victorian awareness of slight signs as the only surviving evidence of lives that can still never be reknown.

In Hardy we find a writer who was willing to encounter the activity of forgetting, to let go origins, and to encompass oblivion – with pain certainly, but without panic. He records that some times are 'silent beyond the possibility of echo'. He allows his reader the fullest experi-ence of discovering, of losing, and of forgetting, and parallels the profound insights of the evolutionary theorists. A great number of forms, argues Darwin, have been 'utterly lost'. Relations between current forms and 'their ancient and unknown progenitor' may be tracked, but the progenitor must remain unknown. 'Not one living species will transmit its unaltered likeness to a distant futurity. And of the species now living, very few will transmit progeny of any kind to a far distant futurity.'[32] Darwinian record, in *The Origin of Species*, is a record of descent and dispersal, not of learning or memory.

Storying in Hardy is *itself* tragic process; happiness lies only in the constellated moments of sense-experience. Much Victorian narrative, as opposed to modernist and postmodernist narrative, presents itself as a sufficient act of remembering, and of forgetting. Writing parallels record and memory, reading participates in the meta-memory immediately created; but reading participates, too, in the desuetude of memory, the ebbing of the experienced instant. Hardy allows the reader to have, to lose, and then to forget the loss – sometimes through the trauma of a plot's extremity, sometimes though the gentler hazard of narrative extension. As readers we glimpse in Hardy's writing lives unrecorded, this year's instalment of ephemeral being. Yet memory is also granted a heroic meaning, sustained past the end of the narrative, and not yet yielding to our oblivion. Marty South remembers Winterborne like the meaning of a knoll, a dip, a rise.

At the end of Hardy's *The Mayor of Casterbridge* Michael Henchard retreats into a countryside where nothing is forgotten, though only because nothing of human meaning has happened there between primeval times and now: 'that ancient country whose surface never had been stirred to a finger's depth, save by the scratching of rabbits, since brushed by the feet of the earliest tribes'. Characteristically, for Hardy, memory takes its furthest reach from touch and architecture. The tumuli are the only trace of former ancestral human lives. The last item of Henchard's will is 'that no man remember me' – a command that arrestingly negates itself.[33] His death is almost the sole event of that quiet country, but, as Hayden White reminds us, this is a question not of 'events in themselves' but of 'events under description'. Alongside Henchard's death we have the narrative description of the dwelling where his body lay. The architectural crumbling of materials is Hardy's characteristic enregisterment of the crumbling of narrative record. Forgotten lives, unrecorded beings, are hinted at in the description of natural materials built into dwellings and decaying back into nature:

> The walls, built of kneaded clay originally faced with a trowel, had been worn by years of rain-washings to a lumpy crumbling surface, channelled and sunken from its plane, its grey rents held together here and there by a leafy strap of ivy which could scarce find substance enough for the purpose.[34]

The clay is 'kneaded', 'faced with a trowel'. Origins, as in other such passages in Hardy, discreetly move in the vocabulary, here subdued and curtailed to a moment of workmanlike activity, 'originally faced with a trowel', which is succeeded by years of rain washing, and strapped by ivy. 'Strap' again suggests the workman, but the ivy is vagrantly active according only to its own needs. Purpose gives way.

In *Tess of the D'Urbervilles*, kind (both cattle and humans) survive only in totally metamorphosed forms – cattle as a glossy post. At the Dairy,

> long thatched sheds stretched round the enclosure, their slopes encrusted with vivid green moss, and their eaves supported by wooden posts rubbed to a glossy smoothness by the flanks of infinite cows and calves of bygone years, now passed to an oblivion almost inconceivable in its profundity.

Or, as Darwin put it, the 'hosts of living forms . . . an infinite number of generations, which the mind cannot grasp' have vanished in their turn into unrecorded oblivion. On the next page Tess is reminded 'that a family of some such names as yours in Blackmoor Vale came originally from these parts and that 'twere an old ancient race that had all but perished off the earth – though the new generations didn't know it.'[35] Again 'originally' sketches in a provisional beginning that serves to measure the distance into near-extinction.

Tess stands on the landscape, 'the hemmed expanse of verdant flatness, like a fly on a billiard-table of indefinite length, and of no more consequence to her surroundings than that fly.'[36] Hardy draws here upon the imagery of Winwood Reade's *The Martyrdom of Man*, published in the early 1870s and frequently reprinted until the Second World War. Reade's was the most eloquent and popular Victorian response to the tragic implications of Darwinian evolutionary theory:

> the earth resembles a picture, of which we, like insects which crawl upon its surface, can form but a faint and incoherent idea. . . . We belong to the minutiae of Nature, we are in her sight, as the raindrop of the sky; whether a man lives, or whether he dies, is . . . a matter of indifference to Nature. . . . Men . . . have no connection with Nature, except through the organism to which they belong.

The pain of the individual is both absolute and without major consequence. In response to the developmental 'progressive' reading of man's history, Reade writes bleakly:

> Pain is not less pain because it is useful; murder is not less murder because it is conducive to development. . . . Those who believe in a God of Love must close their eyes to the phenomena of life, or garble the universe to suit their theory.[37]

Reade, writing his strange history of the world, broods on the lost and irrecoverable nature of the past and on the constant stress between the individual's intense experience of life and the failure of this individual meaning to survive. Of all the non-fictional narratives of the time, Reade's comes closest to Hardy's creative contradictions.

Hardy's novels are haunted by Darwin's 'forgotten multitudes'; through 'unknown ages' the world has 'swarmed with living creatures', denizens of the natural order that include cows, plants, birds, men and women, hairy caterpillars. The sensuousness of our imagining of this unpurposed multitude is posed painfully against the individual purposiveness of trilobites or men: 'the creature had had a body to save, as he himself had now' – so thinks Knight, in Hardy's *A Pair of Blue Eyes*, in kinship with the fossil trilobite whose eyes stare at him from the cliff face as he expects to fall.[38] The arbitrariness of record puzzled Darwin and Huxley. They insisted on the need to preserve awareness of incompleteness and fissured history, the inadequacy of traces, as in itself important evidence: 'over the whole world, the land and the water have been peopled by hosts of living forms. . . . Now turn to our richest geological museums, and what a paltry display we behold.' Typically, with the word 'peopled', Darwin indicates the kinship of all those lived and lost lives, lives fully lived and fully forgotten. Evidence and record are both profoundly inadequate: 'What an infinite number of generations, which the mind cannot grasp, must have succeeded each other in the long roll of years!'[39]

'The mind cannot grasp' what has been forgotten. The world is always full. Memory fills up the extent of life available to it and makes us forget what lies beyond. Hardy keeps faith with oblivion, but disturbs our sense of completeness by the allusive system that anthropomorphically glimpses past and other states of being. Through geology, prehistory, the extension of the past, the insistence in evolutionary ideas on change and loss of nameable origins, the forgetting and deforming of meaning in language, the debilitating of memory as an agent of transformation and control in Darwinian theory – through all these factors, together with a common insistence on growth, the Victorians were made to be aware of how much was irretrievably forgotten, and to set great store by those signs and traces, those acts of decipherment that relieved oblivion and reconstituted themselves as origins.

NOTES

1 Compare Mircea Eliade, *Myth and Reality* (New York: Harper & Row, 1963), p. 136: 'It seems as if Western culture were making a prodigious effort of historiographic *anamnesis* . . . this *anamnesis* continues the religious evaluation of memory and forgetfulness.'

2 This leads Northrop Frye to write of Dickens's late novels as 'anti-narratives' (*The Secular Scripture* (Cambridge, Mass.: Harvard University Press, 1976), p. 40).

3 For example, Richard Owen, address to the British Association for the Advancement of Science, 1858: 'Yet, during all those æras that have passed since the Cambrian rocks were deposited which bear the impressed record of Creative power, as it was then manifested, we know, through the interpreters of these "writings on stone" that the earth was vivified by the sun's light and heat. . . . The earliest testimony of the living thing, whether shell, crust, or coral in the oldest fossiliferous rock, is at the same time proof that it died' (quoted in G. Basalla, W. Coleman, and R. Kargon (eds), *Victorian Science* (Garden City, NY: Doubleday, 1970), p. 313). Note the biblical suggestion of tablets, 'the impressed record of Creative power', and 'testimony'.

4 Eneas Sweetland Dallas, *The Gay Science* (London, 1866), vol. 2, p. 110: 'All pleasure has a tendency to forget itself, and there is no escape from the paradox that a large number of our joys, including some of the highest, scarcely, if ever, come into the range of consciousness.' Frances Power Cobbe, in *Darwinism in Morals* (London, 1872), p. 307, summarizes the then current terms as 'Latent Thought', 'Preconscious Activity of the Soul', and 'Unconscious Cerebration'. See also Samuel Butler, *Unconscious Memory* (London, 1880).

5 Dallas, op. cit., vol. 1, pp. 210, 305.

6 Walter Benjamin, 'The image of Proust', in *Illuminations* (London: Fontana/Collins, 1973), p. 204; 'The Storyteller', in ibid., p. 91.

7 Gillian Beer, 'Anxiety and interchange: *Daniel Deronda* and the implications of Darwin's writing', *Journal of the History of the Behavioral Sciences*, 19 (1983), p. 31.

8 Elizabeth Ermarth, *Realism and Consensus in the English Novel* (Princeton, NJ: Princeton University Press, 1983), p. 21.

9 Charles Lyell, *Principles of Geology; or, The Modern Changes of the Earth and its Inhabitants*, 10th rev. edn, 2 vols (London, 1867), vol. 1, pp. 89, 76; first published, 3 vols, 1830–3.

10 Thomas Henry Huxley, *Science and Christian Tradition* (London, 1894), p. 45.
11 George Eliot, *Middlemarch* (Harmondsworth: Penguin, 1965), p. 896.
12 Sigmund Freud, 'Notes on a case of paranoia', *The Pelican Freud Library* (Harmondsworth: Penguin, 1979), vol. 9, pp. 222–3.
13 Lyell, op. cit., vol. 1, p. 96.
14 ibid., p. 94.
15 Jacques Derrida, *Writing and Difference*, trans. Alan Bass (Chicago: University of Chicago Press, 1978), p. 292; Charles Darwin, *On the Origin of Species* (1859; repr. Cambridge, Mass.: Harvard University Press, 1964), p. 310.
16 Hayden White, 'The narrativization of real events', *Critical Inquiry*, 8 (1981), p. 795.
17 For a fuller discussion of these questions, see my *Darwin's Plots: Evolutionary Narrative in Darwin, George Eliot, and Nineteenth-Century Fiction* (London: Routledge & Kegan Paul, 1983).
18 'Heredity', in *The Complete Poems of Thomas Hardy*, New Wessex Edition (London: Macmillan, 1976), p. 434.
19 Darwin, op. cit., pp. 307, 287.
20 Thomas Henry Huxley, *Science and the Hebrew Tradition* (repr. New York: Greenwood Press, 1968), p. 85. Huxley follows these remarks by discussion and illustrations of the tracks of a species of enormous prehistoric creature and the unsolved mystery of their disappearance (pp. 87–9).
21 Frank Kermode, 'Secrets and narrative sequence', *Critical Inquiry*, 7 (1980), p. 87.
22 Wilkie Collins, *The Woman in White*, ed. Harvey Sucksmith, The World's Classics (Oxford: Oxford University Press, 1975), p. 69.
23 Dianne F. Sadoff, *Monsters of Affection: Dickens, Eliot, and Brontë on Fatherhood* (Baltimore: Johns Hopkins University Press, 1982).
24 Quoted in Basalla, Coleman, and Kargon (eds), op. cit., p. 346.
25 Charles Dickens, *Bleak House*, Authentic Edition (London, 1901), p. 1.
26 J. H. Miller, 'Introduction' to Charles Dickens, *Bleak House* (Harmondsworth: Penguin, 1971).
27 Max Müller, *Lectures on the Science of Language*, series 1 and 2 (London, 1861, 1862).
28 Francis Power Cobbe, 'Dreams as illustrations of unconscious cerebration', *Macmillan's Magazine*, 23 (April 1871), p. 515; repr. in Cobbe's *Darwinism in Morals*.
29 Robert Chambers, *Vestiges of the Natural History of Creation* (London, 1844; facsimile, New York: Humanities Press, 1969, with 'Introduction' by Gavin de Beer), p. 342.
30 Charles Dickens, *Little Dorrit*, Authentic Edition (London, 1901), p. 740. The reader is guarded from any embroilment in Mrs Clennam's memories. It is not until the end of the book that we hear her story. This work functions at the level of social and individual memory and forgetting, and I introduce it to delimit my argument, since I can read in it no trace of what I have called phylogenetic disturbance. Individualism is the work's scale as much as the value it sets against disorder. In this it differs from *Bleak House*.

31 *The Complete Poems of Thomas Hardy*, pp. 175, 177.
32 Darwin, op. cit., p. 344.
33 Thomas Hardy, *The Mayor of Casterbridge*, New Wessex Edition (London: Macmillan, 1975), p. 353.
34 ibid., p. 330.
35 Thomas Hardy, *Tess of the D'Urbervilles*, New Wessex Edition (London: Macmillan, 1975), p. 133; Darwin, op. cit., p. 287; Hardy, *Tess*, p. 134.
36 Hardy, *Tess*, p. 136.
37 Winwood Reade, *The Martyrdom of Man* (repr. London: Rationalist Press Association, 1924), pp. 428, 429, 435.
38 Thomas Hardy, *A Pair of Blue Eyes*, New Wessex Edition (London: Macmillan, 1976), p. 222.
39 Darwin, op. cit., p. 287.

3

PAMELA AND *ARCADIA:* READING CLASS, GENRE, GENDER

At the start of her essay on 'The Countess of Pembroke's *Arcadia*' Virginia Woolf muses on the succession of readers and readings that have entered Sidney's great volumes:

> We like to summon before us the ghosts of those old readers who have read their *Arcadia* from this very copy – Richard Porter, reading with the splendours of the Elizabethans in his eyes; Lucy Baxter, reading in the licentious days of the Restoration; Thos. Hake, still reading, though now the eighteenth century has dawned with a distinction that shows itself in the upright elegance of his signature. Each has read differently, with the insight and the blindness of his own generation. Our reading will be equally partial. In 1930 we shall miss a great deal that was obvious to 1655; we shall see some things that the eighteenth century ignored. But let us keep up the long succession of readers; let us in our turn bring the insight and the blindness of our own generation to bear upon the 'Countess of Pembroke's *Arcadia*', and so pass it on to our successors.

The 'insight and the blindness' of a late-twentieth-century reading will be (particularly after de Man's exploration of the terms) different again from that of 1930. Woolf comments at the end of her essay that 'in the *Arcadia*, as in some luminous globe, all the seeds of English fiction lie latent.' She opens out this image of silence, latency, and light into a consideration of the generic and the psychological implications harboured within Sidney's work.

> We can trace infinite possibilities: it may take any one of many different directions. Will it fix its gaze upon Greece and princes and princesses, and seek as it might so nobly, the statuesque, the

impersonal? Will it keep to simple lines and great masses and the vast landscapes of the epic? Or will it look closely and carefully at what is actually before it? Will it take for its heroes Dametas and Mopsa, ordinary people of low birth and rough natural speech, and deal with the normal course of daily human life? Or will it brush through those barriers and penetrate within to the anguish and complexity of some unhappy woman loving where she may not love; to the senile absurdity of some old man tortured by an incongruous passion? Will it make its dwelling in their psychology and the adventures of the soul? All these possibilities are present in the *Arcadia* – romance and realism, poetry and psychology.[1]

These questions of genre, of pastoral and epic, of natural speech and representation, of class position and psychological position, of stereotype and experiential drama, are all taken up into the work of one eighteenth-century writer and reader of *Arcadia*. That figure forms a blind spot in Woolf's own criticism, never coming into view: the figure of Samuel Richardson. Yet he was there in her creativity, as the first name of her sexually abstemious Mrs Dalloway indicates: she is Clarissa.

We know that Richardson had read Sidney's *Arcadia*, or read *in* it (since it is not a work that demands total word-by-word reading to declare its characteristic excellences). We need not assume that he read it for the first time when in 1724 his firm printed the fourteenth edition of Sidney's *Works*, but the activity would bring the work close to his eye and his thoughts. Moreover, that particular edition would have drawn to Richardson's attention the possibility of extending and rethinking Sidney's great work, of reading – and writing – it anew.[2]

The first two volumes of the edition that Richardson printed comprise Sidney's own five books of 'the Countess of Pembroke's *Arcadia*': the third volume opens with a supplement, 'A sixth book to the Countess of Pembroke's *Arcadia*, written by R.B. of Lincoln's Inn, Esq.'[3] This seventeenth-century addition takes up Sidney's hint in the last sentence of *Arcadia* that if you want any more you must sing it yourself or, as he more graciously puts it, the next generation of his characters 'may awake some other spirit to exercise his pen in that wherewith mine is already dulled'. R.B. takes up the invitation humbly and with a will, opening his book with the marriage of the Arcadian princess, Pamela. The third paragraph begins:

And now was the marriage-day come, when *Pamela*, attired in the stately ornament of beauteous majesty, led by the constant forwardness of a virtuous mind, waited on by the many thoughts of his fore-past crosses in her love, which now made up a perfect harmony in the pleasing discord of indeared affection, was brought to church.[4]

'The constant forwardness of a virtuous mind' provides a pithy characterization of what some readers have found hard to accept in Richardson's Pamela. The princess Pamela and the serving-maid Pamela share a grounded sense of their own worth and a willingness often wittily to voice their own claims. That is one of the radical congruities that Richardson asserts by means of the name he gives his heroine. If, like R.B., he was provoked into rethinking the afterworld of Sidney's *Arcadia*, his rethinking – unlike R.B.'s – was no slight continuation. Instead it was a new (if finally hedged) appraisal of the social order as manifested in relationships between men and women, masters and servants, town and country people.

By the time Richardson wrote *Pamela*, Sidney's heroic narrative had been famous for 150 years and had been succeeded by a host of French and English writers of romance. The work that Richardson knew was what we now call the *New Arcadia*, which incorporates Sidney's 1580s revisions, along with those of his sister the Countess of Pembroke in the 1593 folio, and a bridging passage by Sir William Alexander which appeared in the fifth edition of 1621.[5] Like *Pamela*, *Arcadia* is an accumulating text which incorporates the writer's and his readers' responses to the first version in the later revisions and continuations.

It is suggestive to find both that Richardson selected for his heroine a name which allied her with the world of romances rather than that of humdrum representation, and that he transgressed the social-class categories of romance in his naming. His choice of the name Pamela for his heroine was allusive, not naturalistic. Though to us it may seem an ordinary enough name, to his first readers it would have been highly surprising. Indeed, Fielding jokes about it in *Joseph Andrews*: 'She told me that they had a daughter of a very strange name, Pămela or Paméla; some pronounced it one way, and some another.' It was a literary name, apparently invented by Philip Sidney himself, and strongly associated with the romance tradition from then on. As an ordinary Christian name it had some vogue only *after* the appearance of Richardson's *Pamela*. We do not need to invent aspiring motives for Pamela's parents to explain its provenance: the name sets up disturbances in the hierarchies represented in the older text: hierarchies of class and of language, of social and material power.[6]

The hierarchies of naming had already been mocked in a comedy which Pamela discusses in *Pamela II* (IV, letter XII), Steele's *The Tender Husband*, where the heroine is called Biddy Tipkin. Under the influence of the romances, Steele's heroine repines at her name and renames herself Parthenissa, for, as she observes, there are strict class rules for names in romance: 'the Heroine has always something soft and engaging in Her Name'. ' 'Tis strange Rudeness those Familiar Names they give us, when there is *Aurelia, Sacharissa, Gloriana*, for People of Condition and *Celia, Chloris, Corinna, Mopsa*, for their Maids, and those of Lower Rank.' A little later Biddy is assured that she is not too young for love by direct allusion to *Arcadia*: 'Do you believe *Pamela* was One and Twenty before she knew *Musidorus*?'[7]

So Richardson's act of naming his servant-heroine Pamela *challenged* Arcadian doctrine as well. Richardson counter-proposed a working world, cluttered with a servant's duties. The naming proves, though, that within this world there is, as in Arcadia, time for speculation and desire, for anxious analysis of affairs of state – here expressed as affairs of the estate.

My argument does not propose Sidney as simple or single discursive progenitor of Richardson. The emphasis is on response, not influence, and, beyond that, on congruity and resistance. By the naming of his heroine Richardson implied *de facto* for his early readers – in a way that is now largely invisible, since *Arcadia* is no longer widespread pleasure reading – a riddling accord between the works.

In a brief but pithy article Jacob Leed has noted a number of correspondences between Richardson's Pamela and the princess Pamela in Sidney's *Arcadia*.[8] These correspondences he finds both in personality and in situation: Sidney's Pamela is 'vivacious, striking, and independent-minded ... in heavily emphasized contrast to her sister, Philoclea, who is an equally important heroine of the book'. Pamela in both *Arcadia* and *Pamela* is properly conscious of her own merits, Leed observes. He notes the parallels between their situations: both are imprisoned, both are threatened with forced marriages, both are 'involved in a problem of love between persons placed high and low in society'. Richardson, he argues, is less hostile to romance while writing *Pamela* than his later comments might lead us to believe. Leed's observations are sound – and the similarities could be multiplied; for example, the great meditations on suicide in each book, the figures of Cecropia and her low counterpart, Mrs Jukes – but on their own they do not take us far enough into the issues raised by Richardson's extension and revision of Sidney's text. A clue to differences between the works is given already in Leed's example of cross-class matching: as so often in pastoral (for example, in *The Winter's Tale*) one partner in a love match *appears to be* of a lower class; but Perdita proves to be the lost daughter of a king despite her shepherdess upbringing; similarly, Musidorus is a prince, only opportunistically disguised as a shepherd, Dorus, in order to gain access to Pamela. In Richardson, however, Pamela is – without reversal – of a lower class and has already risen by being a lady's maid. Leed concentrates on the apparent similarity between the situations in the two books. There is more to be discovered, however, by analysing also the *divergences* in Richardson's revisionary reading and rewriting of *Arcadia*.

In the figure of his Pamela, Richardson goes far beyond allusion to a single character, though that allusion is the reader's referential starting-point from which to observe difference as well as likeness. Richardson gathers within his single isolated figure, Pamela, aspects of both Sidney's princesses, Pamela and Philoclea. Sidney's Pamela displays 'the majesty of virtue', her sister Philoclea its playfulness and responsiveness. In Richardson, the two are mingled in his ordinary girl, seen by others as scared, 'pert', 'a baggage', 'a creature' – yet an adamant soul. Richardson goes further: he abrades the distinctions so hierarchically observed in the language and events of *Arcadia* between princess and serving-girl, Pamela and Mopsa. His writing raises questions of genre, moving away from romance and pastoral towards Protestant epic in *Pamela II* where Pamela is likened to the alternative possible state of an unfallen world imaged in 'old Du Bartas'.

Richardson responds to the immense discursive range of Sidney's work, endowing Pamela herself with a linguistic register which can move freely between the specificities of the servant's world she inhabits, the geographical region she comes from, and the high style of Bible and epic. Whereas in *Arcadia* the panoply of discourses emanates from a single conversational aristocratic voice, in *Pamela*, the letter form, though dialogic, attributes linguistic excellence specifically and predominatingly to the servant-heroine Pamela. Both Sidney and Richardson are composing their works for a precisely imagined readership of women. Questions of cross-dressing and of voyeurism are responded to, (very differently) by each of them. I shall here concentrate on the ways in which Richardson's allusion to *Arcadia* in the naming of his heroine works to unsteady assumed correspondences between social class, gender, and authoritative writing. Let us begin, though, from a point of congruity: the connection between writing, imprisonment and the self in the letter form.

The princess Pamela in Sidney's *Arcadia* finds herself, towards the end of the work's immense length, imprisoned with her sister Philoclea, unable to get news either of the outcome of the civil disturbances in the land or of the fate of their lovers, Musidorus and Pyrocles. Each of the women writes a letter to 'the general assembly of the *Arcadian* nobility' and these letters show their differing though equally perfect characters. The 'humble hearted Philoclea' passionately beseeches the life of her lover. Pamela, always majestically articulate, casts the desperation of her position in the terms of writing itself. The letter form requires that the writer have an identity and that the letter be addressed to knowable persons. However, for Sidney's Pamela here, it is a form of locked-up speech, a silenced voice. It demands reception and has none.

> In such a state, my Lord[s], you have placed me, as I can neither write nor be silent; for how can I be silent, since you have left me nothing but my solitary words to testify my misery? and how should I write, for as [for] speech I have none but my jailor that can hear me, who neither can resolve what to write, nor to whom to write? What to write is hard for me to say, as what I may not write, so little hope have I any of success, and so much hath no injury been left undone to me-wards. To whom to write, where may I learn, since yet I wot not how to entitle you? shall I call you my sovereigns? set down your laws that I may do you homage. Shall I fall lower, and name you my fellows? show me I beseech you the lord and master over us. But shall Basilius' heir name her self your princess? alas, I am your prisoner.[9]

Pamela's dilemma, like that of her later namesake, is such that she 'can neither write nor be silent'. She *cannot* write because she no longer knows who she is, in terms of the body politic. Is she any more a princess? She *must* write because her words alone can testify to her emotions, which endure beyond her civil state. The letter is the only evidence that she still exists. It is her bodying forth, the last expression of her power, and written in the expectation that they will 'prevent my power with slaughter'. Her lines 'signify', in repeating and extending utterance, her ineluctable sense of herself as a princess. She is beset, isolated. She grates the word 'princess' against the word 'prisoner' and strikes some frail sardonic sparks with them. But above all the activity of expression sustains her as a presence to whoever reads her, and to herself. Richardson seized that same connection between writing, imprisonment, and the self in his Pamela's continued writing when there seems no hope of delivery, for herself or her letters.

When Richardson's Pamela claims that her *soul* is of equal import-ance with the soul of a princess it turns out that she necessarily means that her body is so too. Soul and body, in the letter, take on the form of writing. Letters become the wafer of the body, the promise of the person. They become, during her trials, the one form for Richardson's Pamela of self-survival. By writing, and by reading her writing, she assures herself that she endures. Later she thickens and scrutinizes her self-understanding by re-reading. In *Pamela II* she comes to perceive that the lines she quotes from Dryden have even to some degree been true of herself also:

> And yet the soul, shut up in her dark room,
> Viewing so clear abroad, at home sees nothing:
> But like a mole in earth, busy and blind,
> Works all her folly up, and casts it outward
> To the world's open view[10]

Though placed within the greater range of narrative approaches, letters are important to *Arcadia*; they forward the plot, as challenges and chivalric exchanges; they herald upheaval in the state and in personal life, as in the tragic story of Parthenia and Argalus where the coming of the fatal challenge by letter is described with all the finicky desperation of anxiety:

And well she found there was some serious matter: for her husband's countenance figured some resolution betwęen lothness and neces-sity: and once his eye cast upon her, and finding hers upon him, he blushed; and she blushed because he blushed, and yet straight grew pale, because she knew not why he had blushed. But when he had read, and heard, and dispatched away the messenger (like a man in whom honour could not be rocked asleep by affection) with promise quickly to follow; he came to *Parthenia*, and as sorry as might be for parting, and yet more sorry for her sorrow, he gave her the letter to read. She with fearful slowness took it, and with fearful quickness read it; and having read it. Ah, my *Argalus*, said she, and have you made such haste to answer? (II, pp. 478–9)

The mutual love of this pair, so recently described as 'a happy couple, he joying in her, she joying in her self, but in herself, because she enjoyed him', is about to end in his death and, later, in her vengeance disguised as a knight.

At the opening of the third book, Dorus (Musidorus disguised as a shepherd) declares his desire for Pamela; he 'considered nothing but opportunity', and takes her in his arms 'offering to kiss her, and, as it were to establish a trophy of his victory'. (In the old *Arcadia* he almost raped her.) She repels him and he at length in despair writes her a letter. The description of the writing and the reception of the letter moves between intense feeling and comedy, as Dorus attempts to cram all his emotions into a verse letter: 'he thought best to counterfeit his hand ... and put it in verse, hoping that would draw her on to read the more, chusing the *Elegiac* as fittest for mourning.'

But never pen did more quakingly perform his office; never was paper more double-moistened with ink and tears; never words more slowly married together, and never muses more tired than now with changes and re-changes of his devices: fearing how to end, before he had resolved how to begin, mistrusting each word, condemning each sentence. This word was not significant, that word was too plain: this would not be conceived, the other would be illconceived: here sorrow was not enough expressed, there he seemed too much for his own sake to be sorry: this sentence rather showed art than passion, that sentence rather foolishly passionate, than forcibly moving. (II, p. 404)

(We may recall here Richardson's experience as a scribe composing a letter for the young women of his acquaintance to send to their lovers, and their trembling at the fear of being misconstrued.) Musid-orus leaves his letter in her 'standish' or inkstand, and to be doubly sure puts her inkstand on her bed-head 'to give her the more occasion to mark it.' The language then registers the eagerness and distaste of Pamela's receiving of it, overmastered by curiosity – her self-justifying delays surpassed by the automatic action of her eyes: 'Then she opened it, and threw it away, and took it up again, till (e'er she were aware) her eyes would read it.'

41

But when she saw the letter, her heart gave her from whence it came; and therefore clapping it to again she went away from it, as if it had been a contagious garment of an infected person: and yet was not long away, but that she wished she had read it, though she were loath to read it. Shall I, said she, second his boldness so far, as to read his presumptuous Letters? And yet (saith she) he sees me not now to grow the bolder thereby: and how can I tell whether they be presumptuous? The paper came from him, and therefore not worthy to be received; and yet the paper she thought was not guilty. At last, she concluded, it were not much amiss to look it over, that she might out of his words pick some farther quarrel against him. Then she opened it, and threw it away, and took it up again, till (e'er she were aware) her eyes would needs read it. (II, pp. 404–5)

Pamela in *Arcadia*, like Richardson's Pamela, has helplessly mixed feelings about her would-be seducer, here represented by the delicate comedy of her rationalization. In Richardson's *Pamela* the threat to the heroine is far more oppressive and the reader must construe without a guiding commentary the charged incongruities of Pamela's feelings. 'And I held down my face, all covered over with confusion.'[11]

The comedy and subtlety of Sidney's work comes not only from the controlled vacillation between discourses but also from the syntactical mimicking of the actions of mind and body, moment by moment as they occur. It is to this freedom and multiplicity of language 'to the moment' that Richardson so notably responds in the writing of *Pamela*. But at the same time Richardson breaks apart the assumed connection in Sidney's writing between social status and linguistic control. The language of *Arcadia*'s characters is stratified: poised, refined, and allusive for the aristocrats; punchy and verbose for the servants. Sensibility likewise is controlled by class. Nobility is the moral perquisite of princesses (though by no means all of *them*); racy pragmatism typifies the lower classes. Richardson's *Pamela* cuts right across these classifications. The sinuous discursive play of authorial narrative in Sidney is now represented by Pamela's own writing in her letters.

Ravelling and unravelling the discourses of *Arcadia* is the immense amorous conversation of the extended work, in which the writer at times playfully declares himself and his activities: 'But *Zelmane*, whom I left in the cave hardly bestead, having both great wits and stirring passions to deal with, makes me lend her my pen awhile to see with what dexterity she could put by her dangers' (II; 657). Zelmane, referred to thus always as female, is the disguised prince Pyrocles, who loves Philoclea and is beloved – vacillatingly, across gender – by Gynecia, Philoclea's mother. The gender and generation complications of *Arcadia* (and of the authorial relation to the grammar of description), are unsettled to a degree scarcely touched in *Pamela*.

The naming of Pamela was not an allusion only to a single character. It summoned up and made available for translation the achievement of *Arcadia*, as well as the symbolic repertoire of later romances. *Arcadia* offered, for re-appraisal, a mood of endless possibility chastened by peremptory trials; perspicuous analysis often realised as conceit; enquiry into the interest groups within a social order; and a pleasure-giving process in which page-by-page reading provokes and allays anxieties within each sentence that are more immediate than the anxieties of the plot. The invocation of *Arcadia* would set a narrative tempo, and would recall for the reader the reasoned leisure of the older work, a leisure which is employed at once erotically and ethically.

A further point: in calling his heroine Pamela, Richardson draws attention to a romance dimension of his tale. With the same stroke, I have suggested, he resists the romance tradition in which the scions of noble houses are inevitably the heroes and heroines of the work and servants have at best comic roles. The name therefore raises questions of descent and class. It also raises questions concerning the grammar of story. Will Pamela prove to be of high rank like her namesake? How can a serving-girl justify her aristocratic name? Is the name a secret promise of higher things proffered by author to reader? Does it mark her out as an exception to everyday possibilities? Questions of genre, gender, and social class are all raised by denominating his heroine as 'Pamela'.

Richardson was looking back to a work which was a great aristocratic classic and which, with all its comedy, combined religious and erotic dignity. The alliance with *Arcadia* enhanced his heroine's authority. He called on some of the same themes as Sidney. Both works, moreover, invoke an extraordinary variety of styles. Sidney shifts dextrously to and fro among discourses with a single sentence. His linguistic register is finely calibrated and yet capable of violent ricochets. For its full realisation, it demands the speaking voice – the voices, first, of himself and his sister; later, of the reader, as one can discover by reading aloud these apparently rambling sentences which then yield the precise swerves and emphases of intimate conversation.

In Richardson, the writing is largely occupied by Pamela's variable voice: and its silenced state as letter is the condition both of her predicament and of Richardson's concealment. Letters in Sidney's work are usually the result of long cogitation, but he excels at complex analysis of the psychological processes of composition and reception. In *Pamela*, the writing and receipt of letters are further refracted through their being themselves described in letters.

Like Richardson, Sidney was writing into a circle of female intimates, a circle preoccupied with moral complexities and fine-grained distinctions. Sidney writes to his sister of his book as a child 'done only for you': 'Your dear self can best witness the manner, being done in loose sheets of paper, most of it in your presence; the rest by sheets sent unto you, as fast as they were done' (I, pp. ii–iii). Richardson told Aaron Hill that his writing of *Pamela* was spurred on by the interest and encouragement of his wife and a young lady then living in his family.[12] The expected intimate female audience is, in each case, part of the composing of the book. Both are 'written to the moment' of those first loved women readers. The erotic movement of each work is controlled by a desire for the responsiveness of women. In this they are rare in post-medieval English literature and rarer still in their open acknowledgement of the ordering presence of a known female readership.

In both works the writers make strong identifications with women characters even while men characters blame the women characters for their beauty and the desire it arouses. In both works that beauty becomes a physical prison, within which the heroines are pinned by the violence and malice of others. They are then, insultingly, told that they produce the prison that contains them. So Amphialus 'by a hunger-starved affection was compelled to offer this injury to Philoclea'; he claims:

> What then shall I say? but that I, who am ready to lie under your feet, to venture, nay to lose my life at your last commandment: I am not the stay of your freedom, but love, love, which ties you in your own knots. It is you your self, that imprison yourself: it is your beauty which makes these castle walls embrace you: it is your own eyes, which reflect upon themselves this injury. (II, p. 420)

Mr B., having tricked Pamela and being about to imprison her on his Lincolnshire estate, writes to her thus:

The Passion I have for you, and your Obstinacy, have constrained me to act by you in a manner that I know will occasion you great Trouble and Fatigue, both of Mind and Body. Yet, forgive me, my dear Girl; for tho' I have taken this Step, I will by all that's good and holy, use you honourably. Suffer not your Fears to transport you to a Behaviour that will be disreputable to us both. For the Place where you'll receive this, is a Farm that belongs to me; and the People civil, honest and obliging. (p. 99)

Though nothing like so dextrous in argument as Amphialus, Mr B. succeeds in transferring the imprisonment from Pamela to himself: *he* is 'constrained' by passion and her obstinacy; he attaches the word 'disreputable' to her presumed future rather than his own actual behaviour. Both Philoclea and Richardson's Pamela retort ironically upon this emotional strategy, and its pre-empting of the languages of property and independence. Philoclea indignantly comments: 'You entitle your self my slave, but I am sure I am yours. If then violence, injury, terror, and depriving of that which is more dear than life it self, liberty, be fit orators for affection, you may expect that I will be easily perswaded.' (II, p. 418). Pamela demands: 'And pray ... how came I to be his Property? What Right has he in me, but such as a Thief may plead to stolen Goods?' (p. 116). Mrs Jewkes ripostes: 'Why was ever the like heard, says she – This is downright Rebellion, I protest!' The prison, and the falsehood of older women, men's agents, will later in the eighteenth century become a psychic necessity of the gothic, as they had been in medieval romance. The prison becomes a place of self-confirmation for the heroine.

In *Pamela II* there is, further, a recognition that the constriction of women requires a symbolic image which will call attention to the prolonged childhood demanded of women. Women's language is itself, Pamela argues, the counter product of containment:

But how I ramble – Yet, surely, Sir, you don't expect Method or Connexion from your Girl. The Education of our Sex will not permit that, where it is best. We are forced to struggle for Knowledge, like the poor feeble Infant in the Month, who ... is pinn'd and fetter'd down upon the Nurse's Lap; and who, if its little Arms happen, by Chance, to escape its Nurse's Observation, and offer but to expand themselves, are immediately taken into Custody, and pinn'd down to their passive Behaviour. So, when a poor Girl, in spite of her narrow Education, breaks out into Notice, her Genius is immediately tamed by trifling Imployments, lest, perhaps, she should become the Envy of one Sex, and the Equal of the other. (IV, p. 320)

The swaddling bands of the baby continue to constrict the free growth of the woman.

Pamela clings to reason and law; Mr B. asserts the cavalier virtues of honour, trust, and magnanimity: virtues in the possession of those with power. The battles that in Sidney range across the whole Arcadian landscape are here held within the house and garden. All the land within sight belongs to Mr B. The pond and the field with the cows in it are as far as Pamela can venture. So rooms become condensed body-images, and the body – in a rewriting of Renaissance imagery – becomes a landscape *moralisé*. The loft, the summer-house, the closet, the dressing-room: these are Pamela's body-spaces. We hear little about the public spaces of the house because, in her time as servant, she has little access to them. When, after marriage in *Pamela II*, she seeks an image for her new estate she lights on a counter-metaphor. She does not want to be a great estate like Chatsworth, where they levelled 'a mountain at a monstrous expense' and so produced a place where the destruction of all the natural contours of the landscape has left the house unconnected with its origins or wider setting (IV, 39).

Despite allusions to these aristocratic modes, Richardson is not writing pastoral, or romance.[13] He is claiming indeed to base his work on recent real events, and from time to time within the work he repudiates romance expectations, or allows the characters crossly to perceive the danger that they may be falling into the stale tropes of romance narrative. Mr B., in particular, feels uneasy at the thought that his story is a well-worn one: 'O my good Girl! said he, tauntingly, you are well read, I see; and we shall make out between us, before we have done, a pretty Story in Romance, I warrant ye!' (p. 42). He has expected to worst Pamela by his jaunty 'Who ever blamed *Lucretia*?' but she, who in the previous paragraph has been quoting *Hamlet* (the unnamed book she read 'a Night or two before'), remembers the outcome of Lucretia's story and claims it for herself: 'May I, said I, *Lucretia* like, justify myself with my death, if I am used barbarously?' Pamela, in her allusions, sees stories through to their end. The reader eyes Mr B.'s talk of their making 'a pretty story in Romance' with the hope of proleptic messages from the text which would undermine Mr B.'s knowingness. *Pamela* is, in this sense, a highly literary and intertextual composition. Richardson challenges pastoral, while recognizing the degree to which it includes always ideals of good government and raises questions of the state: 'Is the poor pipe disdained, which sometime out of Melibeous' mouth can show the misery of people under hard lords or ravening soldiers', Sidney wrote in the *Apology for Poetry*.[14]

Pamela's semantics glitter with double meanings, and this destabilizes the taken-for-granted values of Mr B.'s world in which she is always an outsider. The word 'plot' itself, as we shall see, becomes a mark of Pamela's sedition in the autocracy of Mr B.'s household as well as the well-ordered unrolling of story within a fiction. In the scene where Mr B., acting as accuser and judge, charges Pamela with 'treasonable papers' the lines between writing, amorous correspondence, the law, and the state are deliberately smudged (pp. 199–204). Pamela keeps her head, and her feet, in the midst of his devious appropriations and claims. He twice tells her that she must trust to his honour to come well out of her trial. His will is the only ordering principle of this social and verbal dictatorship. He has, earlier in the book, mocked the concept of honour as sound public reputation when Mrs Jervis speaks of 'the regard I have for your honour'. 'No more, no more, said he, of such antiquated topics.' Mrs Jervis, as good housekeeper, includes in her meaning of his 'honour' the right governance of his estate and household. He rejects such concerns as oldfashioned, and in the trial scene 'honour' seems to signify only a cavalier magnanimity outside the bounds of the law, whereas Pamela asserts: 'I thought myself right to endeavour to make my Escape from this Forced and illegal Restraint' (p. 200). Pamela has a little earlier been cutting about the aristocratic appropriation of words like 'honour', contenting herself instead with 'honesty': 'My Honesty (I am poor and lowly, and am not intitled to call it Honour) was in danger.'

The social and emotional combat between them takes the form of conceits and repartee. Words like 'plot', 'title', 'equal', 'liberties' and 'innocent exercises' in the following dialogue passage shift wittily across questions concerning social rank, social construction, civil order, literary construction, and the insurrectionary capacity of women. The repartee is expansive, allowing the reader time to savour the tussle of Mr B. (who speaks first) to take command of language. Pamela's intervening speech-tags, 'said I', 'said he', exercise a retrospective shaping control over the conversation. The letter form gives

Pamela control over the narrative past. Moreover, she puts sardonic pressure on Mr B.'s language by calling attention to its terms: 'those innocent Exercises, as you are pleased to call them'. She exposes and so withers the sexual predation such phrases conceal.

[Mr B. speaks:]I long to see the Particulars of your Plot, and your Disappointment, where your Papers leave off. For you have so beautiful a manner, that it is partly that, and partly my Love for you, that has made me desirous of reading all you write; tho' a great deal of it is against myself; for which you must expect to suffer a little. And as I have furnished you with the Subject, I have a Title to see the Fruits of your Pen. – Besides, said he, there is such a pretty Air of Romance, as you relate them, in your Plots, and my Plots, that I shall be better directed in what manner to wind up the Catastrophe of the pretty Novel.

If I was your equal, Sir, said I, I should say this is a very provoking way of jeering at the Misfortunes you have brought upon me.

O, said he, the Liberties you have taken with my Character, in your Letters, set us upon a Par, at least, in that respect. Sir, reply'd I, I could not have taken these Liberties, if you had not given me the Cause: And the *Cause*, Sir, you know, is before the *Effect*.

True, *Pamela*, said he; you chop Logick very prettily. What the Duce do we men go to School for? If our Wits were equal to Womens, we might spare much Time and Pains in our Education. For Nature learns your Sex, what, in a long Course of Labour and Study, ours can hardly attain to. – But indeed, every Lady is not a *Pamela*.

You delight to banter your poor Servant, said I.

Nay, continued he, I believe I must assume to myself half the Merit of your Wit, too; for the Innocent Exercises you have had for it from me, have certainly sharpen'd your Invention.

Sir, said I, could I have been without those *innocent* Exercises, as you are pleased to call them, I should have been glad to have been as dull as a Beetle. (pp. 201–2)

Pamela's dextrous chopping of logic ('the Cause, Sir, you know, is before the *Effect*') is laid beside her strong moral position. It gives the reader both a clandestine and an open pleasure. Pamela is 'naturally' intelligent. Mr B. indeed suggests this as an argument against the education of women: men's power needs women's ignorance: Pamela is the equal of Mr B. in wit, in work, in the play of discourse, in everything except wealth and power. But the lack of wealth and power makes her own range of linguistic command dangerous to her. Her proverbial phrase 'dull as a Beetle' sets Mr B. thinking along the lines of her possible marriage to 'some clouterly Plough-boy'. She ripostes: 'Sir, I should have been content and innocent; and that's better than being a Princess, and not so' (p. 202). Her ideal statement is both convincing and straight out of courtly pastoral. The idea of Pamela as 'the Ploughman's Wife' has a strong sexual charge for Mr B. It allows him fantasy identifications even as it exaggerates the social distance between them and demeans one who is demonstrating herself to be his verbal and moral superior.

Pamela is, moreover, threatening to take control of writing and to wrest 'the Catastrophe of the pretty Novel' from his control (p. 201). His plots and her plots conflict; it is she who devises the dramatic record of their conversation. 'Well' Pamela unguardedly remarks a little later, 'my Story, surely would furnish out a surprising kind of Novel, if it was to be well told' (pp. 212–13). She is presented as the teller of this tale; there is no open evidence of an organizing male author. The weakness in Pamela's position is that her writing, plotting, utterance, and body are all too closely contained: in a kind of physical conceit, she has sewn her letters into her garments and must undress to reach them. Her dress crackles with language: 'So I took off my Under-coat, and, with great Trouble of Mind, unsew'd them from it. And there is a vast Quantity of it' (p. 204).

Instead of *Arcadia*'s intimately confident all-seeing writer, Pamela and Mr B. struggle to wrest control of plot and language from each other. But again the points of congruity, as well as the differences, between the two works articulate Richardson's challenges to his readers' assumptions. Pamela's questioning of terms unsettles the social order implicit in Mr B.'s language. Moreover, she can reach assuredly across a linguistic register and series of discourses almost as inventive as those of *Arcadia*. In *Shamela* Fielding mocked the alternations of Pamela's language between italicized high apophthegm and low-minded commentary; he achieved his effect by excising the intervening range of discourses to which she has access. Fielding's social suggestion is that no maidservant could match aristocratic style. In the second half of *Pamela I* there is some loss of the tremor across senses in Pamela's language. She loses her alertness to shifty signification, which was necessitated by her mistrust of Mr B.: for example, the word 'gentleman' ceases to be bandied provocatively about and settles into plain description. When her fear of the sham marriage is withdrawn she can enjoy the word 'nuptials' unctuously and without reserve. But in *Pamela II* the dubiety reawakens, with the strengthened shadow of an obliterated author in the argument. The clash of wits and courtesy here, the teasing of the reader, is held in the endoubled first person of Pamela, who does the telling and purportedly controls the writing and who yet is written, both by the contrivances of Mr B. and by the connivance of Richardson's hand, plotting her.

The princesses in *Arcadia* are caught up in civil war, a war whose devastations undermine the pastoral state in which the book begins. Pamela, the rustic, is caught into a class and sexual power struggle which unsteadies Mr B.'s estate, though scarcely the country at large. In *Pamela I* man is the master, woman the servant. In *Pamela II*, within the less confrontational politics of the married state, the overweening claims of Mr B. are still pithily articulated by Pamela as going beyond constitutional powers: 'Could you ever have thought, Miss, that Husbands have a Dispensing Power over their Wives, which Kings are not allowed over the Laws? I have this day had a smart Debate with Mr. B., and I fear it will not be the only one upon this Subject' (III, p. 390).

The anger of the woman against the man, the servant against the master, the poor against the rich, the lowly against the aristocratic, are all condensed in Pamela. But so are the other aspects of that anger: the longing for alliance, for acceptance and equality, which declares itself as sycophancy more often than as love. Yet Pamela, even in the midst of some curdled exchanges of courtesy, insists on keeping her own name and not taking a title. She never turns out to be a princess in disguise, or a lost scion of a noble house. She is sharp-eyed about the claims of landed families and their assumptions that they will possess the land eternally. Her claim to gentility is a Christian one, as the inheritor of that other romance tradition of 'gentillesse' described in Chaucer's *Wife of Bath's Tale*:

> For, God it woot, men may wel often fynde
> A lordes sone do shame and vileynye;
> And he that wole han pris of his gentrye,
> For he was boren of a gentil hous,

50

And hadde his eldres noble and vertuous,
And nel hymselven do no gentil dedis,
Ne folwen his gentil auncestre that deed is,
He nys nat gentil, be he duc or erl;
For vileyns synful dedes make a cherl.
For gentillesse nys but renomee
Of thyne auncestres, for hire heigh bountee,
Which is a strange thyng to thy persone.
Thy gentillesse cometh fro God allone.
Thanne comth oure verray gentillesse of grace;
It was no thyng biquethe us with oure place.[15]

Hardy, much later, would ironize the tale of servant-girl and master by making that servant-girl, Tess of the D'Urbervilles, scion of a lost great family whose title Alec has bought out, and who herself would now be happier as Durbeyfield. Richardson's Pamela resists any attempt – or Richardson resists it for her – to make her part of an aristocratic family by descent. Her aristocracy is derived from her literary association only. Her consonance with Sidney's princess proves her title to high dignity at a literary level. Her bearing will be her entitlement to marriage into the landed gentry, and to our respect.

In Sidney's *Arcadia* the social equivalent of the servant Pamela is the servant Mopsa (a name for romance servants ratified by Biddy Tipkin's list). Mopsa (in *Arcadia*) has a certain earthy energy; she is a good but prolix storyteller (her version of Cupid and Psyche is cut short when she reaches the sentence: 'and so she went, and she went, and never rested the evening, where she went in the morning; till she came to a second aunt, and she gave her another nut' (I, p. 275). She is used as a catspaw by Dorus (Musidorus) in his pursuit of Pamela. Dressed as a shepherd he must woo the maid, and this he does only too effectively: 'With that he imprisoned his look for a while upon Mopsa, who thereupon fell into a very wide smiling' (I, p. 207). Mopsa is 'as glad as of sweetmeat' to go on an errand to fetch Dorus. She is a figure of fun, driven by her body and not fully in control of it. Dorus takes the chance of Mopsa being asleep to woo Pamela: 'He looked, and saw that Mopsa indeed sat swallowing of sleep with open mouth, making such a noise withal, as no body could lay the stealing of a nap to her charge' (I, p. 244). The humorous pressure on the word 'stealing' reminds us of assumptions about thieving servants –

and of the requirements that servants be constantly attentive – even while it counters the image of Mopsa's noisy sleeping.

The princess Pamela wakes Mopsa as a defence against Dorus:

He would have said farther, but *Pamela* calling aloud *Mopsa*, she suddenly started up, staggering, and rubbing her eyes, ran first out of the door, and then back to them, before she knew how she went out, or why she came in again: till at length, being fully come to her little self, she asked *Pamela*, why she had called her. For nothing said Pamela, but that ye might hear some tales of your servant's telling: and therefore now, said she, *Dorus*, go on. (I, p. 244)

The mechanistically exaggerated response is clownlike, as Mopsa, when her name is called, is galvanized out of sleep into hyperactivity, running out of the door and then back to them, 'before she knew how she went out, or why she came in again'. Dorus is Mopsa's 'servant' in courtly ritual because he is purportedly paying court to her but, of course, the aristocracy can truly woo only the aristocracy. She is Pamela's servant in a functional sense and so, in the hierarchy of *Arcadia*, has no full life of her own. If she is deluded in love, that is the matter of comedy.

Richardson's challenge to the social assumptions of older styles of romance involves the compression not only of Pamela and Philoclea, two princesses into one, but of Pamela and Mopsa, princess and serving-maid. Richardson takes entirely seriously the dynamics of the household. He places at the centre of attention, not princes and princesses in disguise, but the serving-girl undisguised who can combine homely imagery and high sentence in her utterance. Richardson's challenge proved so successful that in large measure the equivalences between the two Pamelas became obliterated by the fame of Richardson's figure. Pamela the serving maid became the 'original', as in *Pamela II* she declares that she wishes to become.

So I, Madam, think I had better endeavour to make the best of those natural Defects I cannot master, than by assuming Airs and Dignities in Appearance, to which I was not born, act neither Part tolerably. By this means, instead of being thought neither Gentlewoman nor Rustick, as Sir *Jacob* hinted, (*Linsey-wolsey*, I think, was his Term too) I may be look'd upon as an Original in my Way; and all Originals pass Muster well enough, you know, Madam, even with Judges. (IV, p. 39)

Hovering within the word 'original' is the eighteenth-century sense of 'eccentricity' as well as the recognition of her low birth, her 'original'. She is also claiming an originary status.

Pamela II, like the second part of *Don Quixote*, makes readers' responses to the first part of the work the action of the second. In it we have an episode which brings the question of Pamela's name into the open and ties it to the question of her equivocal class status as well as to the question of the book's own genre as domestic comedy, psychological drama, Christian epic, pagan romance. This is the very Cervantean episode of Sir Jacob Swynford's visit. Sir Jacob resolutely refuses to 'sit down at Table with Mr. B.'s girl; if she does, I won't' (III, p. 308). Sir Jacob is astonished by the hold that the unseen Pamela has established over her social superiors and over her husband: 'You talk in the Language of Romance', announces the forthright choleric Sir Jacob 'and from the House-keeper to the Head of the House, you're all stark-staring mad. ... I'm in an inchanted Castle, that's certain. What a Plague has this little Witch done to you all? – And how did she bring it about?' (III, p. 310).

Sir Jacob is gulled by the Countess of C., who presents Pamela as her youngest daughter, Jenny: the pregnant Pamela plays the role of the maiden Jenny. In this episode fun is more important than questions of propriety, but the fun brings out Pamela's disquieting power of flouting social categories. First there is the matter of her name. Sir Jacob sneers: 'But, *Pamela* – did you say? – A *queer* sort of Name! I have heard of it somewhere! – Is it a Christian or a Pagan name? – Linsey-wolsey – half one, half t'other – like thy Girl – Ha, ha, ha' (III, p. 315).

The hint that we should recollect where we have heard of the name before – even if Sir Jacob does not – is reinforced on the next page by his similarly vague recollection of a biblical allusion. Of course, when Pamela is presented as Lady Jenny, daughter of the countess, the old man immediately traces the lineaments of high descent in her face, and, in her manners, generations of high breeding. Her intelligence, likewise, he sees as exclusive to great families. Only the next day is it revealed to him that Lady Jenny is Pamela 'the Mistress of the House, and the Lady with the Pagan Name' (III, p. 319).

Pamela christianizes romance. She forgives the biter bit and welcomes him to her household: 'And the Tears, as he spoke, ran down his rough Cheeks; which moved me a good deal; for, to see a Man with so hard a Countenance weep, was a touching sight' (III,

p. 320). As Mr B. remarks: 'Now she has made this Conquest, she has completed all her Triumphs.' Pamela is simultaneously 'an Angel' and 'a Witch'. She rewrites the eclogues of romance into hymns. She wishes to resolve contradictions and to be at one with herself. She can do this however, only at the price of becoming extra-ordinary . She therefore cannot generate social change. She is a special case, an 'original', not evidence that cross-class marriages succeed and that serving-girls may be the true equals of their masters.

This problem of how to resolve what is various within herself may lie behind Pamela's harping on Sir Jacob's phrase 'Linsey-wolsey'. The example raises questions of class, of sexual feeling and of writing. Linsey-wolsey was a cloth woven from a mixture of wool and flax: such home-spun fabric might seem a virtuous product of cottage industry quite to Pamela's taste. But it is a mixed fabric, eking out wool with flax, a shilly-shally mixture neither rich nor poor, and so representing Pamela's awkward class position across the exalted and the rustic. More, linsey-wolsey was in some sixteenth- and seventeenth-century writers a metaphor for the mingled nature of sexual love, always edging over into lust – the *Oxford English Dictionary* cites Nashe, 'A man must not have his affection linsey-wolsey intermingled with lust', while Sylvester's translation of Du Bartas uses it in 'The Magnificence' as an image of the writer's failings who 'in my Works inchase/Lame, crawling lines':

And also mingle (Linsie-woolsie-wise)
This gold-ground Tissue with too-mean supplies. (II, p. 664, l. 2102)

So Pamela, in her desire for integrity and excellence, is made uneasy in several ways by Sir Jacob's incidental insight. It raises questions of sexual integrity, of genre, of social class, and of writing-process.

Pamela II is a more self-consciously literary work than *Pamela I*. Pamela is increasing the range of her reading, learning French and Italian, reading Telemachus, reading Cowley – becoming more experienced, that is to say, in the mingling of the Christian and the Pagan, the romance and religious writing. She began her training in literacy under the eye of Mr B.'s mother by transcribing Scripture. By the beginning of *Pamela II* she is assumed to be able to pick up the reference in Lady Davers's letter to Du Bartas, and is likened in her creativity to the paradisal fire of creative life which Du Bartas represents at the end of his description of Eden. The Du Bartas reference

also brings to mind Richardson's description of himself as a writer,
like a frugal widow nurturing fire from a few sticks.

Pamela's 'scribbling' has been often rebuked in the first volumes as
if it were a forbidden, masturbatory activity. But it is always thus
rebuked by those who want to contain her. In *Pamela II* it is represented as creative, salubrious (now with a strong procreative charge
in the imagery), self-stimulating, but productive of goodness, wisdom,
and wit in others. Lady Davers writes:

> But I'll tell you what has been a great Improvement to you: It is
> your own Writings. This Itch of Scribbling has been a charming
> Help to you. For here, having a natural Fund of good Sense, and
> a Prudence above your Years, you have, with the Observations
> these have enabled you to make, been Flint and Steel too, as I may
> say, to yourself: So that you have struck Fire when your pleas'd,
> wanting nothing but a few dry'd Leaves, like the First Pair in the
> old *Du Bartas*, to serve as Tinder to catch your animating Sparks.
> So that reading constantly, and thus using yourself to write, and
> enjoying besides the Benefit of a good Memory, every thing you
> heard or read became your own; and not only so, but was improved
> by passing thro' more salubrious Ducts and Vehicles; like some fine
> Fruits grafted upon a common Free-stock, whose more exuberant
> Juices serve to bring to quicker and greater Perfection the downy
> Peach, or the smooth Nectarine with its crimson Blush.
>
> Really, Pamela, I believe, I, too, shall improve by writing to
> you. – Why, you dear Saucy-face, at this Rate, you'll make every
> one that converses with you, better, and wiser, and wittier too, as
> far as I know, than they ever before thought there was Room for
> them to be. (III, pp. 54–5)

Lady Davers trills across several notes here, and her self-mocking style
combines with an appreciation of the way in which Pamela's self-
reading has accelerated her maturity. Pamela has been her own study,
allegorizing her virtue as a theme in a Christian epic, without quite
renouncing romance. Frugality and exuberance are both emphasized.

In the passage to which Lady Davers alludes, Du Bartas promises
eternal beauty of body and soul to 'innocence upright'. He concludes
his description of paradise thus:

> For as two bellowes, blowing turne by turne,
> By little and little make cold coales to burne,

55

And then their fire, inflames with growing heate
An yron bar, which on the anvil beate,
Seemes no more yron, but flies almost all
In hissing sparkes, and quicke bright cinders small:
So the world's soule should in our soule inspire
Th'eternall force of an eternall fire,
And then our soule (as forme) breath in our corse
Her counte-les numbers, and heav'n-tuned force,
Wherewith our bodies beawtie beawtified
Should (like our death-les soule) have never died.[17]

Pamela's quickening writing and blameless life represent the possibility of innocent development for mankind, Lady Davers's allusion
suggests. She is the new graft which improves the stock and produces
luscious nectarines; she is also the initiating fire-maker who breathes
life into the world. The Du Bartas passage, moreover, confirms Pamela's self-generating writing as the work of a Protestant epic muse: a
lineage that is tactfully, and highly, flattering to Richardson himself.
The reserved form of the allusion, which must be contextually placed
before the scale of its claims becomes clear, prevents any show of
hubris on Richardson's part.

Richardson, in *Pamela II*, creeps nearer to the surface of the text,
with its witty back-allusions and its discussion of issues embedded in
the first two volumes. One such issue is the question of Pamela's
'linsey-wolsey' status across classes. Pamela is 'an original', not a
generalizing possibility. Another issue is Pamela's knowingness. In
Pamela II her speed of riposte becomes openly a part of what is
admirable in her. A third issue that Richardson examines is disguise.
Let us first examine scenes in *Arcadia* and in *Pamela* where a man
pursues his courtship by disguising himself as a woman.

Vestiges of the Renaissance fascination with cross-dressing, and
questions of how to describe the disguised self, survive in *Pamela I*, but
there is none of the indulgence (or the stamina of redescription) that
is to be found in Sidney. Mr B. makes a fool of himself, and terrifies
Pamela, by disguising himself as Nan, her fellow maid. Sidney's
Zelmane (Prince Pyrocles dressed as a woman) is the more high-
minded equivalent of Mr B. dressed as Nan. Both watch their beloved
undress: '*Zelmane* would have put to her helping hand, but she was
taken with such a quivering that she thought it more wisdom to lean
herself to a tree, and look on.' Invited to join the other ladies in their

river-bathe, she excuses her/himself 'with having taken a late cold'; and, seeing Philoclea naked, '*Zelmane* could not chuse but run to touch, embrace and kiss her. But conscience made her come to her self' (I, pp. 246–7). The humour and eroticism of Sidney's description contrast sharply with Pamela's realization that she has been duped in believing Mr B. to be Nan. Mr B.'s reactions are represented entirely within her reading of them. The letter form here attempts to divest voyeurism of its glamour. 'But, I tremble to relate it, the pretended She came into Bed; but quiver'd like an Aspin-leaf; and I, poor Fool that I was! pitied her much. – But well might the barbarous Deceiver tremble at his vile Dissimulation, and base Designs' (p. 176). The titillation of the reader here is covert rather than wittily open as in Sidney. It lies in the conjunction of affective words ('quiver'd', 'tremble') with words expressing disgust ('vile Dissimulation', and 'base Designs').

Whereas to Sidney disguises and cross-dressing were means of bringing to light the complexity of human passion, and the power groupings at work in class and gender, to Richardson disguise is always demeaning. For that reason, though others fail to recognize her intent, Pamela early in the work insists that her change back into the homely fabrics which accorded with her station before she came to Lady B.'s is an apt expression of her intention to return to that station willingly. She insists that she means no disguise by it, though Mr B. is jolted into new paroxysms of desire. In *Pamela II* the masked ball is the trigger for Mr B.'s half-hearted unfaithfulness to her – and is also the scene of Richardson's most open references to *Arcadia*.[18]

The pleasures of the upper classes include that of disguise. Pamela is not shown as compromising herself by taking part in the gulling of Sir Jacob, though she does it with reluctance. But later in the book disguise exemplifies the aristocracy's power of claiming privilege, and doffing responsibility. Pamela realizes that she has been recognized at the masked ball when, dressed as a Quaker lady, she is approached by a 'Presbyterian Parson', 'who bad me look after my *Musidorus* – So that I doubted not by this, it must be somebody who knew my Name to be *Pamela*' (IV, p. 95). The jostling fictions of Christian sects and romance characters here represent the instability of reference produced by disguise. Much later it is to prove that this same 'Presbyterian Parson' is Mr Turner, who has forged a letter purporting to show that Mr B. is living with Pamela's rival: 'he it was, as I guessed, that gave me, at the wicked Masquerade, the Advice to look after my *Musidorus*' (IV, p. 146).

There is enough promiscuity of fiction-making in ordinary life, Pamela comes to feel, without nurturing it imaginatively by means of romance. *Pamela II* is, in large measure, an attempt to control the romance qualities of *Pamela I*, as well as (as Terry Castle has recently observed) the social implications of Pamela's rise. The immovability of privilege, the capacity of power groupings constantly to realign themselves and yet to produce the same privileges as before, are examined in Mr B.'s behaviour as lover, husband, father, and possibly polygamous man. Pamela may not suckle her own child; servant-girls continue to be tempted – Pamela has not saved them all, as the story of Polly (denied the temptation of a romance name and afforded only a humdrum reduction of Pamela) shows.

At the end of the whole book, Pamela converses with three young women, one of whom, Miss Stapylton, is much under the influence of the 'Flowers of Rhetorick, pick'd up from the *French* and *English* Poets, and Novel-writers' (IV, p. 425). Miss Stapylton asserts that 'there are many beautiful Things, and good Instructions, to be collected from Novels, and Plays, and Romances, and from the poetical Writers particularly'. Without denying this wholly, Pamela rounds on romances and disengages her experience from them. Despite her disapproval of them she seems well acquainted with their tropes:

> there were very few Novels and Romances, that my Lady would permit me to read; and those I did, gave me no great Pleasure; for either they dealt so much in the Marvellous and Improbable, or were so unnaturally inflaming to the Passions, and so full of Love and Intrigue, that hardly any of them but seem'd calculated to fire the Imagination, rather than to inform the Judgement. Tilts and Tournaments, breaking of Spears, in Honour of a Mistress, swimming over Rivers, engaging with Monsters, rambling in Search of Adventures, making unnatural Difficulties, in order to shew the Knight-Errant's Prowess in overcoming them, is all that is requir'd to constitute the Hero in such Pieces. And what principally distinguishes the Character of the heroine, is, when she is taught to consider her Father's House as an inchanted Castle, and her Lover as the Hero who is to dissolve the Charm, and to set her at Liberty from one Confinement, in order to put her into another, and, too probably, a worse.

This is not quite the temper of *Arcadia*, though one can find passages like it. But Pamela's invention of romance scenarios has lodged within it the seed of Clarissa's predicament. Clarissa's initiating actions mimic the romance which her reason eschews.

Sidney argued that the business of the poet is to provide the energy of virtuous action and to persuade readers and writers to examine themselves: 'they that delight in Poesy itself should seek to know what they do, and how they do; and especially look at themselves in an unflattering glass of reason.' The special attribute of poetry, says Sidney, is that 'therein a man should see virtue exalted and vice punished – truly that commendation is peculiar to Poetry, and far off from History.' Sidney's wry comment poses the problem that Richardson struggles with throughout *Pamela; or, Virtue Rewarded*: how to reconcile the poetry and the history of human affairs. Or, as Woolf counterposed the possibilities latent in *Arcadia* and realized in *Pamela*:

> Will it keep to simple lines and great masses and the vast landscapes of the epic? Or will it look closely and carefully at what is actually before it? Will it take for its heroes Dametas and Mopsa, ordinary people of low birth and rough natural speech, and deal with the normal course of daily human life?

Mr B. sarcastically calls Pamela a '*speaking picture*' a phrase he seems to have gleaned, inappropriately enough in the circumstances, from Sidney's *Apology for Poetry*. Sidney, in the passage from which the phrase comes, argues that the philosophers' learned definition – 'be it of virtue, vices, matters of public policy or private government' – must be 'illuminated or figured forth by the speaking picture of poetry'.[19] Pamela is 'the speaking picture' of imaginative virtue. Despite her reluctance to disturb, her presence judges the 'private government' of Mr B.'s household. The work demonstrates how virtue, vice, public policy, and private government can be challenged by renaming and recategorizing: this serving-girl is not Mopsa but Pamela, and her story is as much Protestant epic as Arcadian romance.

NOTES

1 Virginia Woolf, *The Common Reader*, second series (London, 1935), pp. 40, 49–50.
2 The possible connection with Sidney's *Arcadia* was broached by earlier historians of the novel, such as J.J. Jusserand, *The English Novel in the Time of Shakespeare* (London, 1890), and Ernest A. Baker, *The History of the English Novel* (New York, 1929), but Maurice Evans writes in his introduction to the Penguin edition of 1987 that *Arcadia*'s 'influence on the work of both Fielding and Richardson is unmistakable, though still largely unexplored' (p. 9).
3 William Merritt Sale, in *Samuel Richardson: Master Printer* (Ithaca, NY, 1950), p. 204, argues on the basis of the printer's ornaments used that Richardson printed the introductory matter for volume I (books I and II of *Arcadia*); none of volume II (books III, IV, and V of *Arcadia*); the whole of volume III (a 'sixth book' to *Arcadia* by R.B. and all other of Sidney's works). T.C. Duncan Eaves and Ben D. Kimpel, in *Samuel Richardson: A Biography* (Oxford, 1971), p. 47, say simply that 'the output of his press during the rest of the 1720s … is not especially distinguished. The most literary items are the works of Sir Philip Sidney (1724 and 1725).'
4 *The Works of the Honourable Sir Philip Sidney, Kt., in Prose and Verse*, 14th edn, 3 vols (London, 1724), vol. III, p. 6.
5 See Sir Philip Sidney, *Arcadia*, ed. Maurice Evans, Penguin English Library (Harmondsworth, 1977), pp. 10–13.
6 *The Cyclopaedia of Names*, ed. B.E. Smith (London, 1894), already notes the class challenge in Richardson's appropriating of the princess's name for a serving-girl. *The Oxford Dictionary of English Christian Names*, ed. E.G. Withycombe (Oxford, 1977), comments that Sidney seems to have invented the name, that the great vogue of *Pamela* 'led to its being sometimes used as a christian name', and cites Fielding (p. 238). See also Eaves and Kimpel, op. cit., pp. 116–17.
7 *The Plays of Richard Steele*, ed. Shirley S. Kenny (Oxford, 1971), pp. 233–4; p. 238.
8 Jacob Leed, 'Richardson's Pamela and Sidney's', *AUMLA: Journal of the Australasian Universities Language and Literature Association*, 40 (1973), pp. 240–5.
9 *Arcadia*, vol. II, p. 857. I have, for clarity, silently corrected two misprints. All further references in this essay are to the 1724 edition, cited above.
10 *Pamela or, Virtue Rewarded*, Shakespeare Head Edition (Oxford, 1929), vol. IV, p. 319. All further references to *Pamela II* are to this edition.
11 *Pamela, or Virtue Rewarded*, ed. T.C. Duncan Eaves and Ben D. Kippel (Boston, Mass., 1971), p. 252. All further references to *Pamela I* are to this edition.
12 *The Correspondence of Samuel Richardson*, ed. Anna Barbauld, 6 vols (London, 1804), vol. I, pp. lxxiv–lxxv; quoted in Alan McKillop, *Samuel Richardson: Printer and Novelist* (North Carolina, 1936, 1960), p. 42.

13 Margaret Anne Doody, however, makes a strongly argued case for reading *Pamela* as pastoral. See her introductory essay to the Penguin edition (Harmondsworth, 1980).

14 Sir Philip Sidney, *An Apology for Poetry, or The Defence of Poetry*, ed. Geoffrey Shepherd (Manchester, 1973), p. 116.

15 *The Complete Works of Geoffrey Chaucer*, ed. F.N. Robinson, rev. edn (London, 1966), p. 86, ll. 150–64.

16 *Compact Oxford English Dictionary* (Oxford, 1971), p. 321. It also cites 'H. Smith, *Prep. Marriage* 157 God forbad the people to weare linsey wolsey, because it was a signe of inconstancie.'

17 *The Divine Weeks and Works of Guillaume de Saluste, Sieur du Bartas, translated by Joshua Sylvester*, ed. Susan Snyder (Oxford, 1979), vol. I, pp. 317, 336 (first translated by Sylvester in 1592 and printed in eight further editions by 1641). This is a protestant epic of encyclopaedic erudition and considerable sensuous delight which hopes to give an example sufficient to wean other poets from 'Ovids heres' and 'Pagan poets' topics. 'Sufficient rich in selfe-invention', poets such as Spenser, Daniel, and Drayton should seek divine topics. For himself, Du Bartas prays 'O furnish me with an un-vulgar style' (p. 317).

18 See Terry Castle's excellent analysis of *Pamela II* in *Masquerade and Civilisation* (London, 1987).

19 Sidney, *Apology for Poetry*, pp. 111, 107. Volume III of Richardson's 1724 edition of Sidney includes the *Apologie*, and his acquaintance with *ut pictora poesis* would be most probably from English sources.

4

RICHARDSON, MILTON, AND THE STATUS OF EVIL

Milton is a crucial presence in that debate between the merits of modern and ancient writers which repeatedly occupied the eighteenth century. In *Sir Charles Grandison* Harriet Byron engages in argument with the pedantic Oxford man, Mr Walden:

> A little encouraged; Pray, Sir, said I, let me ask one question – Whether you do not think, that our Milton, in his *Paradise Lost*, shews himself to be a very learned man? And yet that work is written wholly in the language of his own country, as the works of Homer and Virgil were in the language of theirs: – And they, I presume, will be allowed to be learned men. (I, 13, p. 76)[1]

Mr Walden replies that Milton is 'infinitely obliged to the great antients'; Harriet counters that his use of their mythology is 'a condescension . . . to the taste of persons of more reading than genius' and that *Paradise Lost* is the type of modern achievement built on the progressive learning of the past: Milton as much excels Homer 'in the grandeur of his sentiments, as his subject, founded on the Christian system, surpasses the pagan' (p. 77). Harriet is here clearly acting as the mouthpiece of her author, and indeed Richardson's social and literary circumstances made it inescapable that he should defend the position of the 'moderns'. He was not a man of classical learning and, as his acutely sensitive social consciousness forever reminded him, he was not a member of the 'world'. But the debate had in any case particular force for the novelists, since the form they were evolving found no sanction among the ancient literary kinds.

Fielding confidently and half humorously approximated *Tom Jones* to the kinds in which he had been educated by calling it a 'comic epic poem in prose'. Richardson, having claimed that *Pamela* was based on fact, changed his ground in *Clarissa* and declared that his new novel was less a history than a dramatic narrative, less a romance than a tragedy. He may have been seeking to remove *Clarissa* from the charges of vulgarity levelled against *Pamela*, but he was also analysing the special quality of *Clarissa* when he wrote in the Postscript that it was a tragedy of a new kind:

> [The author] considered that the tragic poets have as seldom made their heroes true objects of pity, as the comic theirs laudable ones of imitation: and still more rarely have made them in their deaths look forward to a *future hope*. And thus, when they die, they seem totally to perish. Death, in such instances, must appear terrible. It must be considered as the greatest evil. But why is death set in such shocking lights, when it is the universal lot? (IX, 309)

Richardson implies in the Postscript to *Clarissa* that he is writing Christian tragedy – whose cosmology must include heaven and hell as well as earth, and where acts and their consequences unroll far beyond the bounds of human society. The spirit, if not the machinery, of such a work would seem to have some kinship with epic. And, as religious tragedy, it will necessarily be both exemplary and intro-spective. Richardson seeks to 'investigate the great doctrines of Christianity under the fashionable guise of an amusement' (Postscript, p. 309). At first sight it may look as if there is something merely retro-spective about Richardson's attempt to relate *Clarissa* to the august mode of religious tragedy. But, although the *formulation* postdates the novel, the novel itself is instinct with the struggle to express intensely realized human experience in terms of values which transcend the human. On the level of myth, the book may be read as the reversal of the Fall: Eve is again tempted by the devil and this time rejects temptation; her integrity cannot be penetrated even by violence. But the poignant significance of the book depends on the recognition that Clarissa is both an example and *herself*; she is particular – not every woman raised to perfection. Lovelace categorizes her coarsely ('Is she not a woman?') instead of acknowledging her adamantine identity, and it is this which destroys the lives of them both.

In his attempt to infuse Christian experience into a literary form Richardson had constantly before him the pre-eminent 'modern', John Milton. Roughly a hundred years before Richardson wrote, Milton had set out to 'justifie the wayes of God' through a transformed epic and had used the once-fashionable amusement of the masque to express 'the sage / And serious doctrine of Virginity' in terms akin to those Richardson was to employ in *Clarissa.*

It is not unexpected that Richardson, who shared Milton's Puritan background, should have *Comus* in his mind when he came to write a book in which the central ethic of chastity is treated as absolute and unassailable. Most of the keywords in Richardson are morally ambivalent and his books explore and play upon the ambiguities of words like 'honour', 'freedom', and 'person'. But chastity – both the state itself and, by moral extension, as the type of integrity – was an absolute for Richardson. The form of his work – an extended prose study centred in psychological and social analysis – makes it a far more compellingly difficult idea than it was in the allegorical, essentially playful form of the masque. The parallels between *Comus* and *Clarissa* are clear and interesting, and they lead us on to understand the moral and artistic problems which Richardson set himself by attempting religious art in a form centred upon minutely examined human experience.

The parallels are both narrative and verbal: Comus, surrounded by his rout of transformed beings, tempts the lost and imprisoned Lady not only through the senses but through the splendour of language, through argument and intelligence. The Lady, protected by the power of her virtue, perceives the disparity between the glory of his words and the meanness of his deeds. Lovelace is characterized by the exuberance of his language, which is set against the intelligent sobriety of Clarissa's; Lovelace has his own delusive rout – more horribly animal than that of Comus because more clearly human:

> The old dragon straddled up to her, with her arms kemboed again – her eyebrows erect, like the bristles upon a hog's back, and, scouling over her shortened nose, more than half-hid her ferret eyes. Her mouth was distorted. She pouted out her blubber-lips, as if to bellows up wind and sputter into her horse-nostrils; and her chin was curdled, and more than usually prominent with passion. (VI, II, p. 74)

Milton's imagery of light, 'the Sun-clad power of Chastity' is taken up by Richardson and repeatedly used:

> Vertue could see to do what Vertue would
> By her own radiant light. (*Comus*, ll. 373–4)

Clarissa's beauty and virtue blaze upon Lovelace 'as it were, in a flood of light, like what one might imagine would strike a man, who born blind had by some propitious power been blessed with his sight all at once, in a meridian sun' (V, 24, p. 196).

Like Comus, Lovelace finds himself repeatedly baulked by the power of virtue. Comus says:

> I feel that I do fear
> Her words set off by som superior power;
> And though not mortal, yet a cold shuddring dew
> Dips me all o're. (ll. 800–3)

Lovelace writes:

> upon the point of making a violent attempt ... I was checked at the very moment, by the awe I was struck with on again casting my eye upon her terrified but lovely face.... O virtue! virtue! ... what is there in thee, that can thus against his will affect the heart of a Lovelace! – Whence these involuntary tremors, and fear of giving mortal offence? (IV, 33, p. 178)

But the parallels do not carry right through. Richardson is attempting something more intransigent than a masque where the characters may become their innocent selves again at the end. For Clarissa, there are no brothers to save her – indeed, her brother is her enemy. There is no rescue. She is raped. Her freedom is the freedom of her mind, her chastity is her inviolate will, and her deliverance, death and salvation.

Richardson assumes that his readers, like himself, are closely familiar with Milton's work, so that he can rely on verbal echoings which reverberate at a half-conscious level in the reader's mind and affect his or her judgement. In *Clarissa* Richardson appropriates *Comus* and *Paradise Lost* to his own complicated purposes. It is far more than a question of simple borrowing: it is something closer to Milton's own way of transforming whatever mode he worked in. Milton works through poetic religious allegory: Adam and Eve are fully, or merely, human only after the Fall. Satan's motivation and self are explored with a psychological complexity which brings out his kinship with tortuous, fallen man. But he remains always a superhuman figure. His degeneration and fall are expressed in terms of emblem and allegory: he ends, like a failed actor, to the hisses of his serpentine angels. The element of fairy-tale remains. We cannot be shown his destruction in terms of *action*, for he remains part of the moral cycle of the world.

Richardson, on the contrary, is working outward from human figures and attempting to invest them with the transcendental force of good and evil. He begins, not with a moral pattern which can be dramatized in human terms, but with a young woman living in her father's house, sipping tea, receiving clandestine letters, feeding her poultry. Whereas Milton could assume his readers' foreknowledge that Satan is evil and then magnificently demonstrate how turbulent, many-sided, and intricate are its manifestations, Richardson engages in an exploration of the acts and motives of an attractive human being, Lovelace. The exploration gradually brings home to the reader the extent of Lovelace's destructive will towards evil – through the evidence of his letters, which show consciousness at work in a way which is akin to Satan's soliloquies, but less dramatically formalized and retrospective. To Lovelace himself the process of recording gradually reveals (always a little too late) how inescapably he has committed himself to evil *in action*. We are shown his degeneration through events, not allegory; but these events begin in their turn to acquire an allegorical meaning. (For example, Lovelace finally obtains the marriage licence on the morning of the day he rapes Clarissa.) The intensity of Richardson's psycho-religious penetration, and the degree to which he could carry his readers along with his meaning, depend, to a significant extent, on the presence of Milton within his work – a presence invoked by parallelisms and echoes and always assumed as part of the moral and artistic nature of his world.

Early in his career Richardson, it seems, objected to the virulence of Milton's prose works, but in his later letters 'the glorious Milton' is the type of literary excellence.[2] Milton became doubly Richardson's hero: he was a modern, unassailably learned, writer writing in English. He offered a glorious literature fraught with moral purpose. Confined as Richardson was almost entirely to English literature, Milton shone out for him with peculiar lustre. In *Comus* Richardson could find Christian allegory, in *Paradise Lost* a Christian epic dramatized in characters whose relation to the human is never lost despite their scale. In Satan he found the grand example of his human villain, Lovelace.

The first direct linking of his own work with that of Milton occurs in a letter to George Cheyne, of 31 August 1741, which shows a characteristic mingling of self-justificatory intelligence and disingenuousness. He defends the erotic element in *Pamela* (which he describes as 'deep scenes') by reference to Milton, speaking of one kind Anonymous Gentleman, who has in a Letter vindicated these very Scenes, and has pointed out in Milton (To whose *Paradise Lost* possibly that were not so necessary) Passages full as strong if not stronger, because mine were mingled wth. Horror, and Censure against the lewd Attempter of Chastity. These are, as the Gentleman has pointed them out (and says they have been generally applauded) Book IV, Line 492 – Book VIII, Line 500, &c – Book IX, Line 1035, &c – And Book VIII, Lines 50, 54, 55, 56, 57.[3]

All the passages cited are accounts of the married bliss of Adam and Eve, ending with the description of their first guilty intercourse after the Fall. Milton is nobly praising full married love, and it is certainly true that only in the passage from Book IX is there any 'Horror, and Censure'. Richardson's argument that his own work is 'less strong' because it is directed against 'the lewd Attempter of Chastity' unpleasantly bypasses the crucial point: *Pamela* was then, and has since been, objected to because of its prurience. Richardson mingles detailed description with the *frisson* of the forbidden. Nevertheless, the suggestion by this 'kind anonymous gentleman' that Milton provided a model for mingled 'warmth' and moral teaching may well have continued to work in Richardson's mind until it finds far richer issue in *Clarissa*.

Milton offered to the eighteenth century a poetic diction quite unlike any to be found elsewhere in English. This diction echoes through Richardson's work, sometimes elevating the personal struggle of Lovelace and Clarissa by a reverberation of the clangour of the opponents in *Paradise Lost*, sometimes ironically deflating the pretensions of a speaker by suggesting to the readers a nobler sphere of action.[4] The heroic and the mock-heroic are equally invoked. When Lovelace makes his first attempt to rape Clarissa at the time of the fire, he finds himself like Satan about to tempt Eve:

> That space the Evil one abstracted stood
> From his own Evil, and for the time remain
> Stupidly good. (*Paradise Lost*, IX, 463–5)

I sat suspended for a moment: by my soul thought I, thou art, upon full proof, an angel and no woman. (V, 16, p. 106)

Her presence, he later says, 'half-assimilates me to her own virtue', though, 'Miss Howe says, I am the *devil*. – By my conscience, I think he has at present a great share in me' (IV, 48, p. 298).

Lovelace's career of vengeance, seduction, immediate success, and ultimate defeat approximates to that of Satan in *Paradise Lost*, and the parallel is sharpened through echoes of Miltonic language. Here is Lovelace encouraging his followers to obey his plan of action:

> And let me add, that you must attend to every minute circumstance, whether you think there be reason in it, or not. Deep, like golden ore, frequently lies my meaning, and richly worth digging for. The hint of *least* moment, as *you* may imagine it, is often pregnant with events of the *greatest*. Be implicit. Am not I your general? Did I ever lead you on that I brought you not off with safety and success? – Sometimes to your own stupid astonishment. (IV, 4, p. 38)

The speech moves from parallels with the Infernal Debate to actual impersonation. First comes the loosely imagistic allusion to 'golden ore', which Mammon found in hell (*Paradise Lost*, I, 678–720) and which created Pandaemonium, 'the high Capitol / Of Satan and his Peers' (I, 756–7). Then the language shifts: 'Am not I your general? – the earlier allusion has prepared the reader and in the rest of the passage a parallel is suggested with Satan's speeches to Beelzebub (I, 157–90) and at the end of the Infernal Debate (II, 430–66). Lovelace, half consciously, has been hurried on by the associations of his words towards assuming Satan's style and stance. The reader, perhaps scarcely more consciously, hears the Satanic echo and acknowledges the parallel.

Anna Howe calls Lovelace and his accomplices 'a set of infernals! And he is the Beelzebub' (IV, 44, p. 249). It is a parallel which Lovelace himself at the beginning of his enterprise does not overlook. But with his delight in assuming various identities he assumes it is a role he can doff at will, like a demon at a masquerade. Only gradually is it borne in on him that he is becoming, not even the devil himself, but the devil's instrument. The mordant humour of his career – a humour as grim and massive as Milton's at the expense of the fallen angels – is that he believes himself free, dedicates his career to 'libertinism', and finds himself more and more ensnared by his own devices, imprisoned by the roles he has assumed. Belford tells him that he has become the machine of his inveterate enemy, James Harlowe, and the devil's agent.

Lovelace's delight in disguise and in the invention of characters – a delight quite in excess of the demands of the plot – may be to some extent drawn from the anecdotes concerning the Earl of Rochester. Lovelace quotes from Rochester's *Valentinian*, and the easy wit and learning of Lovelace's epistolary style seem to owe something to Rochester's *Familiar Letters*, published in 1699. Equally, the passion for disguise makes of him an existential hero constantly fashioning and refashioning a personality for himself, while at the same time he reveals the pathological extent of his ontological insecurity (in R.D. Laing's term) by his dread of 'acting out of character', that is, ceasing to be a rake. But, although the historical and the psychological interpretations seem to me to be equally valid and illuminating, it is clear that Lovelace's power of disguise was used by Richardson *particularly* as a parallel linking him again to Satan. Like Satan, he is a failed 'actor'. What is emblem in Milton becomes actuality in Richardson. Satan has the power of specious appearances:

> now a stripling Cherube he appeers
> Not of the prime, yet such as in his face
> Youth smil'd celestial. (*Paradise Lost*, III, 636–8)

Clarissa cries: 'O Madam, you know him not! He can put on the appearance of an angel of light; but has a black, a very black heart.' (V, 26, p. 232). And a little earlier she writes:

> O why was the great fiend of all unchained, and permitted to assume so specious a form, and yet allowed to conceal his feet and his talons, till with the one he was ready to trample upon my honour, and to strike the other into my heart! – And what had I done, that he should be let loose particularly upon me! (V, 21)

The parallel is brought into the open when Lovelace captures Clarissa in Hampstead. Lovelace throughout the book quotes constantly from a variety of authors – for example, in one letter, he invents a play, quotes Terence and *Hudibras*, and with splendid effrontery explains his theft of a letter in terms of his literary enthusiasm which makes him burn to see what Clarissa has written: 'loving narrative letter-writing above every other species of writing and admiring your talent that way' (IV, 21, p. 116). However, he rarely quotes Milton directly. But in this scene he gleefully describes himself emerging from his disguise as an old man, like Satan restored to his own form – and with typical self-conceit adds his own parodic version of Milton:

I saw it was impossible to conceal myself longer from her, any more than (from the violent impulses of my passion) to forbear manifesting myself. I unbuttoned therefore my cape, I pulled off my flapt slouched hat; I threw open my great coat, and like the devil in Milton (an odd comparison though!) –

> I started up in my own form divine,
> Touch'd by the beam of her celestial eye,
> More potent than Ithuriel's spear! (V, 23, p. 197)

Lovelace's self-satisfaction and ultimate stupidity – the stupid blindness of conceit – is ironically suggested by the unmentioned context of the incident he cites, which Richardson expects us to recall without conscious effort: Satan has assumed the form of a toad and is found by the angels 'close at the eare of *Eve*':

> Assaying by his Devilish art to reach
> The Organs of her Fancie, and with them forge
> Illusions as he list, Fantasms and Dreams ...
> Vain hopes, vain aimes, inordinate desires
> Blown up with high conceits ingendring pride.
> (*Paradise Lost*, IV, 801–3, 808–9)

This is Lovelace's aim throughout the novel. Clarissa tells him a little later in this scene: 'Ever since I knew you ... I have been in a wilderness of doubt and error.'

There is a more immediate narrative parallel in the suggestion of a triumphant *coup de théâtre* with which Lovelace and Satan return to their own shapes. In each case the disclosure has in fact been forced upon them. Clarissa recognized Lovelace's voice; Ithuriel touched Satan with his spear:

> for no falsehood can endure
> Touch of Celestial temper, but returns
> Of force to its own likeness: up he starts
> Discoverd and surpriz'd. (*Paradise Lost*, IV, 811–14)

Satan expects the obedient angels to recognize in him the splendour of an archangel, but the young cherub Zephon scornfully tells him that his shape is changed, his brightness diminished:

>   abasht the Devil stood,
> And felt how awful goodness is, and saw
> Vertue in her shape how lovly, saw, and pin'd
> His loss. (*Paradise Lost*, IV, 846–9)

The process of degradation has begun, and as Book IV ends Satan flees murmuring, not daring to stand battle with the angels, having seen 'his mounted scale aloft'. Lovelace appears to be more successful – he has, after all, recaptured Clarissa – but the Miltonic reference of the incident acts as an ironic reassurance to the reader. We out-top Lovelace's vision, remembering what is in store in *Paradise Lost* for Satan, whom Lovelace has invoked as parallel:

>   read thy Lot in yon celestial Sign
> Where thou art weigh'd, and shown how light, how weak,
> If thou resist. (*Paradise Lost*, IV, 1,011–13)

This kind of rare forward-looking parallel is particularly gratefully felt by the readers of *Clarissa*, where we are engrossed in the moment-by-moment living out of the action and where the work stretches endlessly before us. I suspect that it is less often boredom which makes people stop reading *Clarissa* than emotional exhaustion – a sense of invasion. There seems no space beyond the book for us to retain *ourselves*; no omniscient author allows us to share his manipulation of the plot. The book contains two opposed patterns: the imposed, factitious, theatrical plotting derived from the machinations of Lovelace; the streamy, inchoate nature of suffering – a total responsiveness to experience – derived from Clarissa. The pattern derived from Lovelace is easier and more pleasant for the reader to follow, but, as in *Comus*,

> all [his] magic structures rear'd so high,
> [Are] shatter'd into heaps o're [his] false head. (ll. 798–9)

In part, the extreme length of *Clarissa* is necessary to Richardson in order to wean us from Lovelace: the initial attraction of intelligent irresponsibility at first elates the reader with Lovelace's own sense of freedom and it is only gradually that the practical jokes grow wearisome and the relentless gaiety is recognized as a psychopathic symptom. The subdued Miltonic allusions and the invoking of Milton's narrative as in the scene analysed provide the reader with a stable structure of judgement which is related to the world of the novel but independent of it.

Milton and Richardson each involve the reader in a process of dramatic instruction. The progress of Satan and of Lovelace is to be for us a gradual disillusionment which will make evil recognizable. Each is shown at his most attractive in the early part of the work; and in each case unwary readers have succumbed to the attractions of intelligence, determination, and courage present in evil. The sheer scale of *Clarissa* – a matter not simply of length but of the potency with which good and evil are seen struggling in the work – makes it not ridiculous to discuss it in the same breath as *Paradise Lost*. Richardson may even be said to have evolved his own form of the epic; it is epic like that of Milton in which the moral import of the work overarches any single adventure, but, like tragedy, it is always ultimately concerned with the expressive humanity of the people he shows us.

The poignancy of *Clarissa* in part derives from the double function of the characters: they are both examples and individuals. Clarissa becomes a saint, but she is not a redemptress; she withstands temptation, saves her own soul, but cannot save mankind, not even the particular man she loves. Lovelace is wicked but he is not Satan or even simply a rake; he suffers and dies a man. Each is isolated in his individuality, locked in the process of circumstance, of daily life. Richardson orders an art which gives to the fate of the ordinary individual, acting within a minutely observed society a grandeur of emotion and expression only previously attained in English literature by tragic princes or by Milton's epic religious art.

NOTES

1 All page references are to *The Novels of Samuel Richardson in Twenty Volumes* (London, 1902). The order of reference runs: volume, letter, page. The text for the quotations from Milton is *The Poetical Works of John Milton*, ed. H. Darbishire (Oxford, 1952–5).

2 See Mrs Barbauld's edition of Richardson's *Correspondence*, 1804 (Mrs Barbauld also notes the *Comus* parallel). Aaron Hill wrote to Richardson, 1 June 1734:

> It pleases me, but does not surprise me at all, that your sentiments concerning Milton's prose writings, agree with those I threw out, under influence of that back-handed inspiration, which his malevolent genius had filled me with, as I drew in the bad air of his pages. I know your good nature too well, to suspect it of esteem for an object so remotely unlike and unequal.

For praise of Milton, see *Selected Letters of Samuel Richardson*, ed. J. Carroll (Oxford, 1964), pp. 98, 176.

3 *Letters*, p. 50.

4 Anthony Kearney in 'Pamela: the aesthetic case', *A Review of English Literature*, VII (1966), p. 80, comments on the Miltonic echoes in *Pamela*.

5

CARLYLEAN TRANSPORTS

One of the pleasures for the visitor to Greece is to discover words that in English are rarified, engaged there in everyday activities: so postboxes may have different slots for 'esoteric' and 'exoteric' letters, that is, for inland or overseas; removal vans are labelled 'Metaphorikon', transports. Reading Carlyle gives something of the same pleasure of substantiating: abstract words become concrete; metaphors perform homely dramas. These performances generate new kinships between ideas. Realization cuts across boundaries and challenges categories. So the Carlylean transports of my title are not only those of euphoria and hyperbole (certainly marked characteristics of his writing). The transports are also the transcategorial activity of extended metaphor: the rumble of removal vans across country, bearing a heterogeneous clutter of household goods into new places where they will be disposed in new arrangements, arrangements which call our attention to what has been unobserved because taken for granted. In Carlyle's writing, moreover, not only goods but people are moved.

Carlyle was greeted by his contemporaries as a philosopher and a historian; yet his methods were not those of logical argument, and his translation and selection of source material was sometimes extravagantly interpretative. He preferred the oceanic to the measuring-line. He dislimned boundaries. He disturbed the authority of the present. He questioned current categories and even the activity of categorizing itself. He acknowledged only a few capacious and, in his understanding, irreducible orders.

In her unsigned *Leader* review in 1855 George Eliot prefaced a discussion of Carlyle with an analogy from mathematics, whose 'highest aim' is to 'obtain not *results* but *powers*, not particular solutions, but the means by which endless solutions may be wrought'.[1] By this move she elegantly bypassed a critical dead end which has beset much discussion of Carlyle's writing: namely, whether it is his aims and views or his manner of conveying them that matters most. George Eliot's emphasis on the obtaining of *powers* conjoins activism and reflection, politics and writing, system and application.[2]

In this essay I shall examine the powers Carlyle obtained and their effects in other writing of his time. I shall suggest also how these methods led to a writer who was seen as a radical in the 1830s and early 1840s appearing as an arch-reactionary by the early 1850s. Clearly, such changes have much to do with the writer's response to particular historical events – for example, the Governor Eyre controversy. But that response was itself under the sway of the powers of argument and representation that he had elaborated.

Carlyle rejects the methods of analysis, though he worked in genres where such methods have been of paramount importance: philosophy and history. He writes across generic constraints, and his early dispraise of Dugald Stewart has in it an awkward recognition of comradeship: Stewart, he wrote, early in his career, 'has done me hurt. Perpetually talking about analysing perceptions, and retiring within oneself, and mighty improvements that we are to make – no-one knows how – I believe he will generally leave the mind of his reader crowded with disjointed notions and nondescript ideas – which the sooner he gets rid of, the better!'[3]

Carlyle's student reading at Edinburgh University was in mathematics, physics, Greek, logic, and moral philosophy. In his biography of Carlyle, Fred Kaplan points out that he was taught by 'the well-known proponent of the Scottish school of practical idealism, Thomas Brown, who had just succeeded the famous Dugald Stewart.'[4] John Rosenberg, in his important study, *Carlyle and the Burden of History*, suggests that Carlyle 'belongs to what Isaiah Berlin calls the "Counter-Enlightenment"'. Rosenberg points out that 'Carlyle's picture of the European cultural climate in the late eighteenth century is remarkable for its inclusion of the popular and local movements that existed alongside or in opposition to the dominant intellectual culture of the Enlightenment.'[5]

Carlyle combines a feeling for popular movements and popular language with metaphysical concerns. Critics differ as to how extensive was his knowledge of German philosophy, and of Kant in particular. In the most thorough recent study of Carlyle's acquaintance with German thought Rosemary Ashton argues that Carlyle's 'knowledge of Kant was slight. He probably did not get beyond the 150th page of the *Kritik der reinen Vernunft*.' However, this section is the 'transcendental Deduction of the Concepts of Pure Understanding' which, as Ashton herself points out, leads to Kant's deduction of the categories.[6] So Carlyle had tussled with philosophical categorial problems even if he was worsted by them.

As I have argued in my introduction, such balked reading may be a more powerful pressure in continuing thought than the perfect, resolved reading which allows ideas to pass unobstructed into agreement. The desire to understand, the baffled will to proceed, and the uncertainty about Kant's value combine to make Kant a vigorous figure within Carlyle's intellectual dramas. He wrote in his journal in 1823: 'I wish I understood the philosophy of Kant. Is it a chapter in the history of human folly or the brightest in the history of human wisdom? Or of both mixed? And in what degree?'[7] Carlyle was more at home with Schiller than with Kant, but the continuing *trouble* he had with Kant (which later affected his antagonistic relationship with Coleridge) meant that German philosophy is a gripping and thwarted element in his writing.

His own work crossed back into German thought. Nietzsche seized on the 'undigested' in Carlyle's imagination in his hostile epigram: 'Carlyle, or pessimism after undigested meals, – John Stuart Mill, or offensive lucidity.'[8] But Peter Stern, in his characterization of Nietzsche's writing, well brings out what Carlyle and Nietzsche had in common in their apposition of literature and philosophy:

> In challenging ... the dichotomy of 'scientific' *versus* 'imaginative', or again the antitheses between 'concept' and 'metaphor', 'abstract' and 'concrete', Nietzsche is at the same time intent on challenging these divisions in our areas of knowledge-and-experience and that fragmentation of knowledge which he (together with other nineteenth century thinkers, men like Marx, Carlyle and Matthew Arnold) saw as one of the chief blights of modern Western civilization.[9]

Carlyle sought not so much to resolve as to jostle our areas of 'knowledge-and-experience': that was the way in which he challenged categorial divisions.

George Eliot continues her discussion of Carlyle by emphasizing his vitality in the work of other writers of the time:

> It is an idle question to ask whether his books will be read a century hence: if they were all burnt as the grandest of Suttees on his funeral pile, it would be only like cutting down an oak after its acorns have sown a forest. For there is hardly a superior or active mind of this generation that has not been modified by Carlyle's writings; there has hardly been an English book written for the last ten or twelve years that would not have been different if Carlyle had not lived. The character of his influence is best seen in the fact that many of the men who have the least agreement with his opinions are those to whom the reading of *Sartor Resartus* was an epoch in the history of their minds.[10]

George Eliot opens the passage with a Carlylean jarring of materials from Hinduism and from English national self-consciousness (suttee and oaks). Each metaphor becomes instantly the site of a parable drama; the first is a hyperbolic fantasy (all Carlyle's widowed books burned on his funeral pyre). The reader's unfigured knowledge that there are other copies of the books is first excluded from the metaphor but then naturalized in the image of the cut-down oak and it sprouting acorns. George Eliot's parodic method captures the way in which Carlyle's metaphors form instantaneous dramas rather than simply concretions. This method produces fantasy, as Todorov describes it: interpretative hesitation is prolonged. The reader vacillates between possible degrees of participation. The plainness of George Eliot's succeeding sentences takes some of its force from the initial sketched-in transformative fantasies of burning and growing.

Crucial in the George Eliot passage is the perception that Carlyle's presence might be strongest where there is least agreement. This adumbrates the argument that I shall advance: Carlyle's style demands the reader's resistance, and draws energy from that resistance. The reader is to be not only spiritually and intellectually involved, but bodily too. The struggle with the reader is a struggle to collapse stable categories. Indeed, one of the difficulties in approaching Carlyle is the rapacity of the style, which seems sometimes set to devour the reader. The tension between writing and reading in his work is often closer to quarrel than to contemplation, but the reader's affirmative distrust is essential to Carlyle's productivity. Emma Darwin put it plainly in a letter to Jessie Sismondi:

He fascinates one and puts one out of patience. He has been writing a sort of pamphlet on the state of England called 'Chartism'. It is full of compassion and good feeling but utterly unreasonable. Charles keeps on reading and abusing him. He is very pleasant to talk to anyhow, he is so very natural, and I don't think his writings at all so.[11]

'I don't think his writings at all so': the *unnaturalness* of Carlyle's writing style challenges the discursive, the political, the 'commonsense' communities of his time. Above all, he challenged classificatory systems and their status as nature. If, as Darwin later asserts in *The Origin of Species* 'morphology is the very soul of natural history',[12] Carlyle's seeking out of new likeness and difference disturbs previously 'natural' congruities and enclosures.

In his *History of English Literature*, translated in 1879, the French critic and observer Hippolyte Taine characterized Carlyle's procedures as wanton and promiscuous: he 'writes always in riddles' and 'confounds all styles, jumbles all forms, heaps together pagan allusions, Bible reminiscences, German abstractions, technical terms, poetry, slang, mathematics, physiology, archaic words, neologies. There is nothing he does not tread down and ravage.'[13] Taine's accusation suddenly expands its scope beyond questions of language in that last sentence: 'There is *nothing* he does not tread down and ravage.' Carlyle's barbarian exuberance leaps across boundaries, heaping the spoils of language together in such a way that analysis is confounded, and social as well as discursive categories are in disarray. His is a manner of argument hard to represent without mimicry, as Taine's characterization of it (and mine too) here demonstrates.

Carlyle's own complaint about Dugald Stewart's philosophical work was realized by pressing upon the word 'field' so as to address this same question of boundaries. In 'The state of German literature' he comments on the search for the '*Urwahr*, the Primitive Truth'. Stewart's writings, Carlyle argues in a footnote,

> are not a Philosophy, but a making ready for one. He does not enter on the field to till it; he only encompasses it with fences, invites cultivators, and drives away intruders: often (fallen on evil days) he is reduced to long arguments with the passers-by, to prove that it *is* a field, that this so highly prized domain of his is, in truth, soil and substance, not clouds and shadow.[14]

Carlyle makes concrete the word 'field' shifting its signification from 'specialization' to 'land'. He offers an absurdist narrative vignette of Stewart leaning over the fence of his untilled field to argue with passers-by whether it is substance or shadow. The fantasy anecdote makes several points for Carlyle at once: language is an untrustworthy discriminator, since it can serve two opposed senses with equal sobriety (field); Stewart is laying claim to property (even, perhaps, though this is not said outright, enclosing common land). Stewart's error, Carlyle suggests, lies in the effort to contain and categorize, to *prove* rather than *till*. Instead of preparing the soil for growth, he has concentrated on describing the circumference of his possession. Carlyle is determined to tramp down the encompassing fences. This activity can be viewed as vandalism or as liberation.

Metaphor, translation, chiasmus, heterogeneity of reference: such are the linguistic modes by which Carlyle transports the reader from the fixed grid of here and now. Recent theoretical writing has given us a confirming vocabulary with which to describe Carlyle's enterprise. Indeed, his work provides almost too copiously yielding an example of Bakhtin's dialogic imagination and the carnivalesque. Carlyle's own description of the writing of Jean-Paul Richter in 1827 sets out what seems like a substitute self-description. Emphasizing the fundamental humour of Richter, with its sportive disproportioning of the taken-for-granted, he writes:

> nay, we have Time and Space themselves playing fantastic tricks: it is an infinite masquerade; all Nature is gone forth mumming in the strangest guises ... he oversteps all bounds, and riots, without law or measure. He heaps Pelion upon Ossa, and hurls the universe together and asunder like a case of playthings. (*Miscellaneous Essays*, I, p.18)

'Calm down' may be the response one inclines to when confronted with this grandiose and antic baby, claiming the universe as his plaything, acting out his language games as if they were without consequences. Carlyle's own writing oscillates between enthusiastic participation in such games and a canny, wisecracking deflation of them. In *Past and Present* he realizes the disproportion of *laissez-faire* in a humorously ungainly image which uses some of the same material as his characterization of Jean-Paul Richter; 'No great Nation can stand on the apex of such a pyramid; screwing itself higher and higher; balancing itself on its great-toe' (p. 230). As fictive editor he presents

Teufelsdröckh's visionary rewriting of the social topography of London in *Sartor*: Monmouth Street 'at the bottom of our own English "ink sea"' becomes for Teufelsdröckh 'a Mirza's Hill, where, in motley vision, the whole Pageant of Existence passes awfully before us with its wail and jubilee, mad loves and mad hatreds, church-bells and gallows-ropes, farce–tragedy, beast–godhead, – the Bedlam of Creation.' The 'editor' comments dourly on these self-cancelling opposites: 'To most men, as it does to ourselves, all this will seem overcharged'. (*Sartor*, p. 234).

More instructive than the comparison with Bakhtin, because further from Carlyle's own terms, is Todorov's work on fantasy, with its emphasis on the prolonged moment of hesitation between interpretations, its recognition that this makes fantastic effects evanescent – and its reminder also that fantasy's removal of limits 'represents an experience of limits'.[15] Carlyle's attitude to categorization suggests that he yearned for and feared illimitability.

Carlyle's method is not that of analysis but that of expansion. Like a microscope, hyperbole characterizes by opening up the grain and inviting the reader to survey the new particulars revealed. Carlyle demonstrates that few categories are eternal: 'Alas, *Forever* is not a category that can establish itself in this world of Time. A world of Time, by the very definition of it, is a world of mortality and mutability, of Beginning and Ending' ('Chartism', *Miscellaneous Essays*, V, p. 389). In Carlyle beginning and ending need not come in that order or, indeed, in sequence at all. Dialogism and synchronism, or, as he might more robustly say, dog's dinner and gallimaufry, are his method. He disturbs categories of near and far, interior and exterior, past and present. In the title of *Past and Present* the apparently neutral copula, *and*, is made to do several sorts of works: yoking, contrasting, synchronizing. His conflicted relation to organicism is an outcome of his determination to disrupt the belief in the present as either more absolute or more 'real' than the past.

Carlyle likes to have things several ways and for this purpose he projects multiple personae in his works. So in his editorial persona he can describe with wan relish Teufelsdröckh's extremes of interpretation. The canny editor is jostled against Teufelsdröckh and Sauerteig, inhabiting them and disowning them at once: 'To bring what order we can out of this Chaos shall be part of our endeavour' *Sartor*, (p. 33). The example of chaos just offered has been that of a book like a hot meal without courses flung in a single container. This 'mad banquet' breaks some of the fundamental categorial taboos that the anthropologist Mary Douglas has since articulated:[16]

> the book distresses us like some mad banquet, wherein all courses had been confounded, and fish and flesh, soup and solid, oyster-sauce, lettuces, Rhine-wine and French mustard, were hurled into one huge tureen or trough, and the hungry Public invited to help itself. (*Sartor*, p. 33)

This wayward and literally dis-gusting banquet demands the reader's sense-participation, but ambiguously. We are held hesitating between an olfactory and an abstract reading, tasting the contradiction of wine and mustard, the inward slide of oyster-sauce hampered by the need to crunch lettuces. Simultaneously, distress is held at bay by an awareness that this is metaphor outperforming itself, that the words are signs, not sense-instructions, and signs describing a book. Teufelsdröckh challenges genre: 'in that labyrinthic combination, each Part overlaps, and indents, and indeed runs quite through the other' (p. 33).

Sometimes there seem to be too few containers in Carlyle's own language-kitchen. The intermingling of categories, like all colours mixed together on a palette, produces mud. But then we remember that Teufelsdröckh signifies, in English, devil's dung.

Without making of Carlyle a single origin it is yet extraordinary to see the diversity of his effect on other writers of his time. He is a transformative presence, deeply affecting writers as various as Elizabeth Gaskell and Gerard Manley Hopkins. Nor is this necessarily a matter of a liberal concurrence with reformist views. Carlyle's specific contribution to creativity is, rather, a concern with the politics and poetics of *articulation*. In an earlier essay I have argued that Elizabeth Gaskell's articulation of regional and working-class speech-styles responded to Carlyle's realizing of the silence of the workers, a silence which he refused to broach. Rather, he offered as substitute for it biblical quotation, the presence of silent and intelligent bodies, and the destabilizing of social hierarchy by the activity of metaphor.[17] Carlyle was of value both to 'spasmodic' poets like Richard Hengist Horne in *Orion* (1843) and to activists such as Thomas Cooper, the Chartist poet, who dedicated to him his poem *The Purgatory of Suicides* written in prison in 1844. He appears within fictions as a radical figure, questioning the structures of society though without proposing an alternative social programme. In Charles Kingsley's *Alton Locke: The Tailor Poet* (1850) he is figured as a Scots bookseller, and in George Meredith's *Beauchamp's Career* (1876) his writing is the basis for the figure of Dr Shrapnel. Shrapnel is, as it were, Carlyle reinvented out of Carlyle's words; his name expresses the uncontrollable scattering and fragmenting by whose means Carlyle's ideas spread abroad, and hints also at the dangerously fragmentary nature of the ideas themselves.

Carlyle provided his contemporaries with the means of crossing limits. When other Victorian writers sought a language which would express intimacy transgressing the ordinary bounds of knowledge, Carlyle could provide it: 'If we had a keen vision and feeling of all ordinary human life, it would be like hearing the grass grow and the squirrel's heart beat, and we should die of that roar which lies on the other side of silence.'[18] In this famous sentence from *Middlemarch* (1871–2) can be heard traces of Wordsworth, Huxley, and the editor's address in *Sartor*: 'O thou philosophic Teufelsdröckh that listenest while others only gabble, and with thy quick tympanum hearest the grass grow!' (p. 235). That sentence in Carlyle comes immediately after the description of the 'supernatural Whispering-gallery', where the '"Ghosts of Life" rounded strange secrets in his ear'. George Eliot develops the latter image also in *Middlemarch*. Another passage in *Sartor* moves within the lines of Matthew Arnold's 'Stanzas from the Grande Chartreuse': 'how shall we domesticate ourselves', writes the editor, 'in this spectral Necropolis, or rather City both of the Dead and of the Unborn, where the Present seems little other than an inconsiderable Film dividing the Past and the Future?' (p. 240).

> Wandering between two worlds, one dead,
> The other powerless to be born,
> With nowhere yet to rest my head,
> Like these, on earth I wait forlorn.[19]

Each of these verbal echoes is concerned with thresholds of perception: that is, with the relations between bodily reach and spectral manifestation. It was in this border country of the senses and the imagination that Carlyle's writing suggested new possibilities. As Todorov puts it: 'The supernatural may sometimes originate in a figurative image, maybe its ultimate extension. We shift, in this case, from hyperbole to the fantastic.' The loosening of the bounds set between living and dead is essential to Carlyle's task as he conceived it, both as historian and as social reformer: we see it in his favoured words such as 'apparition' and 'phantasm'.[20] The yet more speculative relation between present and future is the other face of that concern with temporal kinships.

The method Carlyle chose was fleetingly to realize possible worlds, figurative and ephemeral. He realized metaphors; out of that enacted realization emerged, for reader and for writer, further emotional and intellectual implications. His style provokes animistic description. His words sniff the air; his syntax is a rabbit warren; his questions clutch the reader. The psychodrama of Carlyle's work finds its centre in the struggle with the reader. Carlyle's writing is, in itself, activity; and that activity seeks to bring to pass further forms for itself in the future *acts* of the reader. Reform is enjoined, but so are despair and laughter. Problematically, Carlyle's most pessimistic urgings may produce comfort as much as disquiet. At times lambasted and abused, the reader is yet simultaneously placed at the source of authority, vivifying change by the act of participation. The parallel with Dickens is clear; people and objects exchange places freely in Dickens's language. Metaphor has generative powers: it spawns figures. It disturbs hierarchy: it declares hidden relations.

Equally clear is the enabling power of Carlyle's language in quite a different writer, Gerard Manley Hopkins. Hopkins parodied the effortfulness of Carlyle's style, his straining towards prophecy.

> But his writings are, as he might himself say, 'most inefficacious-strenuous heaven-protestations, caterwaul, and Cassandra-wailings'. He preaches obedience but I do not think he has done much except to ridicule instead of strengthening the hands of the powers that be. Some years ago when he published his Shooting Niagara he did make some practical suggestions, but so vague that they should rather be called 'too dubious moonstone-grindings and on the whole impracticable-practical unveracities'. However I am afraid some great revolution is not far off.[21]

With anguish Hopkins observed the same effects in his struggle with language. Present participles are valued as perpetuated acts but live on the edge of the adjectival:

> Of the rolling level underneath him steady air, and striding
> High there

83

Under pressure nouns become verbs:

> Brute beauty and valour and act, oh, air, pride, plume here
> Buckle![22]

Nouns must *act* as much as *be*. Here the style draws on Carlyle's energy. So too may Hopkins's forming of dissonant compound words, each element straining against the other: 'Spent Pegasus down the stark-precipitous air'.

The imaginative liberation of Carlyle's language for his contemporaries was expressed in this shifting of parts of speech so that new relations could be formed. Another upheaval he produced in his own writing was the ricochet across discourses of particular words, such as 'property'. Metaphor's shifts of scale brought into question set hierarchies of reference.

Carlyle's declared value for silence, in the midst of a zealously productive text, privileges the quietly scanning eye of the reader. Our silence becomes a proper mode of response and moreover allows us, dramatically, to fulfil the role of the socially excluded, whose silence Carlyle, perhaps sentimentally, idealized. At the same time, the reader is at the centre of the power-house of change promised by Carlyle's own linguistic practice. No wonder the effect is to absolve rather than to implicate damagingly in the abuses he uncovers.

The reader is exempted from full guilt, but driven to see things anew. This is achieved by multiplying our possible roles within the text, by means of personae and variety of address, while at the same time sustaining the intimacy of the reader/writer conjunction. This conjunction, expressed as I/thou, allows Carlyle freedom to break across most other categorial enclosures, and in particular the separated categories of past and present. The reader/writer relationship, which is one of immediacy and participation, always has a paradoxical time-lag in it. The present is already past when it is inscribed and packeted as book. Carlyle comments on the delusiveness of past tense, with its editing out of anxiety and its symptoms:

> For indeed it is a most lying thing that same Past Tense always: so beautiful, sad, almost Elysian-sacred, 'in the moonlight of Memory', it seems; and *seems* only. For observe, always one most important element is surreptitiously (we not noticing it) withdrawn from the Past Time: the haggard element is of Fear! Not *there* does Fear

dwell, nor Uncertainty, nor Anxiety; but it dwell *here*; haunting us, tracking us; running like an accursed ground-discord through all the music-tones of our Existence; making the Tense a mere Present one. (*The French Revolution*, IV)

For Carlyle, the struggle with tenses is the struggle with history, and with contingent alternatives and futures. What Todorov calls 'the perpetual present' which is the ideal of narrative is here chequered by consciousness of history: the *presentness* of the past can be recuperated only as writing, not as event. Yet, the past *is* present too, but objectified as landscape and architecture, inscribed as law, and enacted as class culture. 'It is all work and forgotten work, this peopled, clothed, articulate-speaking, high-towered, wide-acred World' (*Past and Present*, p. 164).

Topography has value for Carlyle because it gives visible evidence of survival in transformation – past people are metamorphosed into trees, fields, achieved structures, which live alongside *now*. So not vestiges but bodily transformations matter most to him: the hand not seen, but shaping with its plough the curve of the field; the foot solidifying the path. Repetition becomes more than a rhetorical trope: it becomes a good part of his topic. The redundant precision of his recollected past is collected in material form as a field, a book, a city. The question raised is how to make a fresh future out of – and not at the mercy of – the past.

The significant absence for Carlyle in our historical imagining of the past is the human individual outside the upper echelons of influence.[23] This loss can never be retrieved, but it can be realized *as* loss. The poignancy of this lack is focused by the occasional emerging of a single figure momentarily into the light of description. In his essay on 'Biography' Carlyle dwells on Clarendon's references to the poor man from whom the fleeing King Charles obtained clothes, and who brought His Majesty 'a piece of bread and a great pot of buttermilk.' Carlyle moves the scene into the present tense, focuses intently on the labourer, his rarity as written presence, and on his contemporaries, lost to record and memory:

How this poor drudge, being knocked-up from his snoring 'carried them into a little barn full of hay,' which was a 'better lodging than he had for himself;' and by and by, not without difficulty, brought his Majesty 'a piece of bread and a great pot of buttermilk,' saying candidly that 'he himself lived by his daily labour, and that what he had brought him was the fare he and his wife had:' on which nourishing diet his Majesty, staying upon the haymow, 'feeds thankfully for two days'; and then departs, under new guidance, having first changed clothes, down to the very shirt and 'old pair of shoes,' with his landlord; and so, as worthy Bunyan has it, 'goes on his way, and sees him no more.' Singular enough, if we will think of it! This, then, was a genuine flesh-and-blood Rustic of the year 1651: he did actually swallow bread and buttermilk (not having ale and bacon), and do field-labour: with these hobnailed 'shoes' has sprawled through mud-roads in winter, and, jocund or not, driven his team a-field in summer: he made bargains; had chafferings and higglings, now a sore heart, now a glad one; was born; was a son, was a father; toiled in many ways, being forced to it, till the strength was all worn out of him; and then – lay down 'to rest his galled back,' and sleep there till the long-distant morning! – How comes it, that he alone of all the British rustics who tilled and lived along with him, on whom the blessed sun on that same 'fifth day of September' was shining, should have chanced to rise on us; that this poor pair of clouted Shoes, out of the million million hides that have been tanned, and cut, and worn, should still subsist, and hang visibly together? (*Miscellaneous Essays* IV, pp. 14–15)

The making of the shoes and the swallowing of the buttermilk bring home the presence of that long-past body, but they offer only slight evidence concerning the long-past *person*. The haunting absence of the unknown ordinary men and women of history will later move Jude the Obscure, whose own designation seems to owe something to Carlyle's enlargement of people's history.

The time-lag between writer and reader is always part of their relationship, as is the perpetual remaking of the past as a realized present in writing. This paradox imposes curtailing conditions when the writing is seeking change specific to a historical moment. Carlyle's avoidance of described solutions – an avoidance which troubled some of his contemporaries – is one way out of the impasse. Insisting on the simultaneity of reading and writing as sense-experiences is another: this Carlyle does by producing bodily effects even while noting that these are conjured by signs alone. The reader's sense-experience *while reading* is brought to our attention. In this way synchrony with the initial activity of the writer writing is emphasized. Sense-experience is also used to challenge linguistic categories; most important is his insistence on sound.

His method of establishing relations and limits is as much auditory as argued: privileging the sounds – the sensed components – of words is a challenge to the plumbline of logic. *Invocation* becomes a phase of argument. Samuel Beckett has spoken of his own adherence to 'fundamental sounds (no joke intended)' and has claimed that those sounds are all that he can be held responsible for.[24] Without centring so closely in as does Beckett on sounds alone (breathing, silence, speeded up and syncopated voices), Carlyle is none the less pre-occupied with the body in language.

His insistence on the aural is in part the outcome of his skills as a translator. He is well aware of the indeterminacy of translation: not only is more than one translation of the sense of a word possible, but the change in sound-values alters irremediably the import of utterances. Language is yoked into its local society of speakers and listeners. Carlyle's manner of studding his text with German and with Latin words and phrases renders for the reader the difference from their own of the communities out of which this experience sprang. The untranslated phrases help to measure the length of the imaginative leap needed to move such knowledge into the reader's and the writer's homely present. One aspect of the auditory in his work is to assert the *unheimlich* in the activity of translation. But there are further implications in his silent oratory.

The opening of the chapter on *'Laissez-faire'* in 'Chartism' runs: 'Events are written lessons, glaring in huge hieroglyphic picture-writing, that all may read and know them' (p. 368). Hieroglyphics, to transfer a famous phrase of George Eliot's, are ideas 'wrought back to the directness of sense'. Carlyle uses consonance and alliteration to realize simultaneously the meaning of 'hieroglyph' for the scanning eye and inner ear of the reader: 'glaring in huge hieroglyphic'. Auditory elements of the word 'hieroglyphs' are presaged and fragmented in the sounds of the sentence before the word itself is reached. The enunciation of 'hieroglyphs' transforms them: 'glare' to 'glyph', 'hu' to 'hie', 'glare' to 'hier'. The reader's mind shadowily performs the task of speech, labouring with the fricatives and plosives. All these reading events (here foregrounded) are ordinarily successfully asimilated by the reader without pausing to analyse them, and therefore without defence against their effects.

Often in Carlyle's writing a perturbation is set off between the claims of the auditory and the semantic. He emphasizes the wap and buzz within which sense struggles and finds its form. This is not a matter of onomatopoeia necessarily, in which sound mimics sense. It is, rather, a matter of the seemingly autonomous patterns of produced sound, which may have slight or even *no* relevance to signification. Thus Carlyle's rhetoric questions whether sound is exterior to sense, simply its clothing – or whether it is, rather, the fundamental linguistic experience, challenging the rule-bound orders of syntax and semantics. Carlyle certainly enjoys the flagrant congruities of non-sense. He even makes of them a new level of argument: that our intellectual understanding can be made actual only through the senses. Thereby he offers another challenge to analysis, but not in the service of synthesis. *Incongruity* and disequilibrium are intensified by this method of foregrounding the auditory in his language.

At the outset of *Sartor Resartus* the narrator sets his proposed work in line with other theoretical writing, claiming (ironically as it will prove) a congruity between his project and that of established order-seeking and rule-bound undertakings: 'have we not a Doctrine of Rent, a Theory of Value; Philosophies of Language, of History, of Pottery, or Apparitions, of Intoxicating Liquors?' (p. 4). The misleading auditory closeness of 'History' and 'Pottery' (in particular the identity of sound in the last syllable and the shift of the 'o' across syllables) seems to pair or sequence them: history, the story of the past; pottery, the plastic evidence of an often shattered past. Then comes 'Apparitions', its sounds suggesting a fugitive anagram of pottery, its sense at the impalpable opposite extreme from the tactile of pots, literally untouchable. Last in the list is 'Intoxicating Liquors' with their vision-inducing and personality-changing powers – and their bathos as climax to a list of philosophical studies. What order of enquiry, Carlyle is suggesting, can be inclusive enough to enclose all these undertakings? He ends the paragraph and begins the next with a hint: a play across the significations of tissue: body, cloth, and argument.

Carlyle's disturbing of categories produces new antinomies, many of them reiterated across his works. These antinomies often counterpose concepts from quite diverse linguistic levels and systems: the quack and the phoenix; the baby and the patriarch; reason and the ocean; fact and impossibility; the body and the future. Carlyle's equivalences challenge assumed relations and denature kinship: 'impossible' here equals *laissez-faire*; the inarticulate, the truth; silence, the body; forgetting, recovering. Philosophical problems, as Wittgenstein remarks, do indeed arise when language goes on holiday. Semantic relations take their energy from sound-links in this prose. The carnivalesque aspect of Carlyle's mismatching, his emphasis on misrule and *das umgekehrte Erhabene* (the inverted sublime), expresses new insight poised on the borderline of the absurd: 'What worship, for example, is there not in mere washing.' Absurdity is represented as holy: silly and *selig*. Carlyle either shifts words rapidly across discursive boundaries (words such as 'tissue', 'property', 'fact', 'goose') or forces us obsessionally to devote our attention to a humdrum object newly remarked. At such junctures we may recall Wittgenstein again: 'we may indeed fancy naming to be some remarkable act of mind, as it were a baptism of an object.'[25]

Even Carlyle's use of the word 'fact' declares its fealty to orders of value other than those we might expect from the way in which 'fact' functions in utilitarian writing in the same period. 'Fact' in Carlyle is closer to *fait* or feat: the thing done, the act accomplished. It sustains a strong presence of discovery and process. The term 'biography', similarly, is invested with an intensely paradoxical significance: it is life-writing, history authenticated by means of the individual bodily instance and therefore preoccupied with death. *Writing life* is Carlyle's magical and conflicted enterprise. *Sauerteig* or leaven is Carlyle's favoured persona. His method is closer to that of romance than of realist fiction: his writing world is one of infinite availability. Language brings things to hand. Metaphors displace and bridge at need. The effect is of synchronicity: the return of the repressed and of the expressed, at once.

Such largesse is dangerously fulfilling to reader and writer. It seems, for the time, to absolve us from the determining historical and material conditions that are Carlyle's declared concerns. The freedom to breach enclosures and to break open categories may produce social change, or only intellectual sogginess. Its suspensions may satisfy the reader without inducing further activity. Creative prolongation of uncertainty is important for Carlyle, but recurrence becomes for him a comforting form of limit. Indeed, part of the force of his imagination rests in his creative greediness: once things are imagined, he never lets them go. He never gets rid of anything or relegates it to a lumber-room of the mind; instead, it emerges in a new form or is repeated after the reader has forgotten it.

*   *   *

One exception to Carlyle's breaking open of categories is notable. A strain in Carlyle's style which is never discussed, though much responded to by his contemporaries, is its ungainly eroticism. His syntax is typified by an effortful reaching towards climax – a climax deflected and often forgotten in the hurly-burly of intervening concerns. To Carlyle 'manly' is the fullest term of praise, 'manfully' the type of human action: 'Why was our life given us, if not that we should manfully give it?' (*Past and Present*, p. 174). Women play small part in the events of Carlyle's work, though few are likely to forget the forlorn Irish widow who helplessly infects with typhus those who have refused to acknowledge their kinship to her (*Past and Present*, p. 186). Of course, locutions such as 'manly' and 'manfully', supposedly inclusive concepts like 'fellow-man', are taken for granted in the historical period within which Carlyle wrote and cannot be invoked as conclusive evidence for his excluding attitude to women.

What is striking, however, is that Carlyle can write about fear, about food, about forgetting, but never directly about sex or sexual love. In the concluding sentence to the chapter 'Old clothes' in *Sartor Resartus* he shifts the description of writing a book rapidly and grotesquely across submarine conception, and ejaculation, to reach the neat and bounded image of the 'Egg of Eros.'

> Might we but fancy it to have been even in Monmouth Street, at the bottom of our own English 'ink-sea', that this remarkable Volume first took being, and shot forth its salient point to his soul, – as in Chaos did the Egg of Eros, one day to be hatched into a Universe! (p. 235)

When he images mythic birth and growth it comes about not through sexual congress but in the self-consuming self-renewal of the female 'World Phoenix':

> Little knowest thou of the burning of a World Phoenix, who fanciest that she must first burn-out, and lie as a dead cinerous heap; and therefrom the young one start-up by miracle, and fly heavenward. Far otherwise! In that Fire-whirlwind, Creation and Destruction proceed together. (p. 236)

The phoenix is autonomous and single. Unusually, in a writer generally concerned to break across categories, his images of a female principle emphasize intactness.

Carlyle's writing seeks to produce bodily confusion as well as intellectual uncertainty. For that reason, laughter, which, like blushing, runs across intellectual, emotional, and physical categories, becomes the touchstone for human *being*: 'the fewest are able to laugh, what can be called laughing, but only sniff and titter and snigger from the throat outwards; or at best, produce some whiffling husky cachinnation, as if they were laughing through wool' (*Sartor*, p. 32). The onomatopoeic here lets us experience the sound 'from the throat outwards'. The *inside* of the reader's body is brought into activity. This method has a particular significance in *Sartor Resartus*, whose subject is 'the tissue of all tissues': human bodies and their clothes. Clothes reach far inward, Carlyle suggests, not only mantling the person, but as close as language to substance: 'how often does the Body appropriate what was meant for the Cloth only!' (p. 232). Clothes make for social distinctions: in naked sleep all are equal. The 'poor bare forked creature', the 'two legged animal without feathers', is distinguished as king or hod-carrier by clothes (Lear haunts the undertones of this language: 'A dog's obeyed in office'). Clothes are semiotic systems, to be celebrated and distrusted. The drive of the argument forces Teufelsdröckh back to one stable meeting-point: 'For whether thou bear a sceptre or a sledge-hammer, art thou not ALIVE; is not this thy brother ALIVE?' (p. 230).

This insistence on *life* as an ultimate criterion and category controls Carlyle's idea of history. Here, one of the major points of difficulty is reached: Carlyle believes in change, disbelieves in continuity or permanence. He grasps the social construction of the body and its changed manifestations over time. Yet he wishes, above all, to assert the fundamental congruity – or, at least, interpretability – of past and present by means of sense arousal. 'We touch heaven, when we lay our hands on a human body' (*Sartor*, p. 232). He reminds the reader that all interpretation of past events will be falsified if the presence of *fear* is forgotten.

In *The French Revolution* he astutely pinpoints how easy it is to be magnanimous in long retrospect, or when engaged in the safe activity of reading: 'Reader, thou hast never lived for months, under the rustle of Prussian gallows-ropes.' Even knights-errant, he points out, usually slew the giant they conquered. The passage continues:

> The French Nation, in simultaneous, desperate dead-pull, and as if by miracle of madness, has pulled down the most dreaded Goliath, huge with the growth of ten centuries; and cannot believe, though

his giant bulk, covering acres, lies prostrate, bound with peg and back thread, that he will not rise again, man-devouring; that the victory is not partly a dream. Terror has its scepticism, miraculous victory its rage of vengeance. (XIV, p. 82)

In this description Goliath merges into Gulliver and then into the Giant of *Jack and the Beanstalk*. The reader's childhood fears are called up in the form of stories heard early in life. All past is present: fear knows no bounds of distant and present. The prone body of the possibly resurgent giant is criss-crossed with multiple cultural allusions which call up long-buried alarms. The hyperbolical scale of the imagined enemy body here conjures up the barely repressible power of kingship, a power felt as much in English literature and history as in the crisis of the French Revolution.

In the emphasis that critics have placed on Carlyle's debt to the Germans, with their sombre humour and fantastic hyperbole, too little attention has been paid to his invocation within his own style of English writing, particularly that of the seventeenth century. The effects Carlyle produces are achieved by cross-hatching Jean Paul and Thomas Browne, ricocheting between Teufelsdröckh and King Lear. Thomas Browne wrote that 'I love to lose my selfe in a mystery to pursue my reason to an *oh altitudo*.'[26] For Browne, this acceptance of mystery results in an attitude of incandescent resignation; for Carlyle, though, mystification unsettles the current ordering of the world.

> Brother, thou art a Man, I think; thou art not a mere building Beaver, or two-legged Cotton-Spider; thou hast verily a Soul in thee, asphyxied or otherwise! Sooty Manchester, – it too is built on the infinite Abysses; overspanned by the skyey Firmaments; and there is birth in it, and death in it; – and it is every whit as wonderful, as fearful, unimaginable, as the oldest Salem or Prophetic City. Go or stand, in what time, in what place we will, are there not Immensities, Eternities over us, around us, in us. . . . itself ought to pause a little and consider that. (*Past and Present*, p. 283)

Demystifying has little political value for Carlyle. His drive towards revolutionary change is fuelled as well as retarded by his fear of what he makes in imagination. The drive of his writing is fuelled too by the mystery of the future. The unforeseeable outcome of change is a source of pleasure and terror in Carlyle's writing. The struggle with tenses is the struggle with history. The often cumbersome intervening asides, the staying of his sentences with exclamation points or questions to which no answer is given, dramatize the encumbered straining towards control and towards chaos, the twin sirens of his politics. Authoritarianism and violent anarchism both allure him.

Delaying any collapse into one or the other, however, is the buried text of *King Lear*, whose fragments haunt Carlyle's argument: Lear tearing off his clothes in the storm, becoming such a bare forked creature as thou art; Lear, faced with destitution, for the first time identifying with the poor: 'Oh, I have ta'en too little thought of these!'; 'Poor Tom's a cold.' The discovery of the human body beneath the trappings of king and fool, the reduction of humankind to its physical needs, brings with it the counter-recognition of the need for *difference*, for individuation beyond 'merest necessities'. Carlyle writes into his sentences the play's denaturing of nature, its plumbing of suffering. *Lear, Hamlet*, and *The Tempest* (with its flattering role of Prospero) are the plays of Shakespeare that Carlyle skeins into his discourse with almost unmarked recall. Each of these plays is preoccupied with differing concepts of reason.

A more troubling cultural complicity is imposed on the reader in 'Occasional discourse on the nigger question', where Caliban is made to serve Carlyle's purposes. Here the *enfant* Carlyle with his universal playthings has become terrible indeed. The vatic 'unspeakable' proves, when it is spoken, to be unspeakable in another sense. The reader/writer dispute is formalized in a mannered way in 'The nigger question', a way which signals unease, and causes it too. The discourse is, we are told at the outset, 'delivered by we know not whom' (no longer, as in *Sartor* is it just a question of Weissnichtwo but now of Weissnichtwem) (*Miscellaneous Essays*, VI, p. 171). The account comes via the reporter Dr Phelim MQuirk, whose assumed Irish 'unreliability' further destabilizes the authority of the text. This allows Carlyle to shrug off responsibility for the essay's diatribe in favour of slavery and against liberalism and the ballot box. The reader's indignation is theatricalized and undermined by the interposed italicized accounts of the audience's behaviour:

> [*Here various persons, in an agitated manner, with an air of indignation, left the room; especially one very tall gentleman in white trousers, whose boots creaked much. . . .*] (p. 178)

That gentleman 'in white trousers' enigmatically enters the hall again (his boots still creaking despite his efforts at silence) before the lecture is over, leaving us awkwardly uncertain whether his earlier exit was the result of ideology or bladder trouble. The effects of this essay are deliberately scandalous, working against the reader's assumed predilections and largely against the expectations derived from the earlier figure of 'Carlyle' himself. This time the persona is nameless: no baptism is possible.

The problem that Carlyle has created for himself is that his doing away with fine-drawn categories leaves him with too many lists, too few controlling orders, and those few too diffused for scrutiny. He therefore holds ultimate authority himself. His positive categories resolve into the human body, the ocean or unconscious, Godhead, silence, and work. In 'The discourse of history' Barthes affirms that 'the sign of History is no longer the real but the intelligible'.[27] In Carlyle's work the challenge to categories and the multiplying of 'reality effects' produces, at last, the *unintelligible*. The past is shown as baffling and enigmatic: enigma is, one might say, a condensation of irreconcilable realities to the degree that they have an appearance of strict form. The present in his writing is baffling because unformed, *in*formed with uncertain interpretations.[28] The future is unperformed, and so evades interpretation. Towards the end of his career, therefore, he can scornfully bundle together black Caribbeans, unemployed seamstresses, the Irish, and aristocrats as all equally and blameably work-shy. Another latent category now also very clearly defines itself – that of race. His image of the communality of mankind is figured in the image of white male Europeans – workers, bourgeoisie, or aristocrat maybe; but white and masculine. Earlier in his writing life, he crossed his own boundaries, assimilating blacks and women. But the tendency was assimilation rather than expansion of categories – and that eventually produces an imaginative retrenchment.

Instead of fantasy, as a hesitation shared by reader and character within the text, in *Latter Day Pamphlets*, for example, the authority of the writer positions him ahead of us in time. We are caught as readers within the loop of his retrospective and authoritative assertions. There is no arguing with him. The unconscious and the body prove to be privileged categories which allow no denial. Yet, to do him justice, Carlyle, continues to need the reader's distrust of him as well as the reader's acquiescence. The strifeful, disequilibrated style wrestles for our belief. At the start of his last enormous enterprise, the *History of Frederick the Great*, the image he uses for his enterprise is that of revivifying a drowned body.

> The French Revolution may be said to have, for about half a century, quite submerged Friedrich, abolished him from the memories of men; now on coming to light again, he is found defaced under strange mud-incrustations, and the eyes of mankind look at him from a singularly changed, what we must call oblique and perverse point of vision. (I, pp. 8–9)

The father lies full fathom five and comes to the surface again subject to mischievous glances askance. Carlyle then spends nine volumes seeking to revive him and to make the reader capable of looking on him directly. In the very last paragraph of the book, worsted, Carlyle returns to the submarine imagery of his opening. Now whole nations are in the belly of the whale: 'blinded, swallowed like Jonah, in such a whale's belly of things brutish, waste abominable (for is not Anarchy, or the Rule of what is Baser over what is Nobler, the one life's misery worth complaining of)' (X, p. 271).

Inversion of the high and low, the collapse of categories, which earlier promised so much fresh possibility, has here become for Carlyle the suffocating enclosure of the whale's undigested swill. It is a nightmare outcome for his jubilant trampling down of boundaries – the revenge of the categories indeed, a parable spelt from Sibyl's leaves:

> a rack
> Where, selfwrung, selfstrung, sheathe and shelterless' thoughts
> against thought in groans grind.[29]

The prolonged struggle with the reader yet sustains Carlyle to the end: 'Meanwhile, all I had to say of him is finished: that too, it seems, was a bit of work appointed to be done. Adieu, good readers; bad also, adieu' (X, p. 272). The embedded iambic pentameters ('all I had to say of him is finished' and 'a bit of work appointed to be done') set the reader's rhythmic memory to work. Metrics sustain meaning, or so Carlyle hopes. The bared last line emphasizes balance on either side of the heavily marked silence of the caesura. Good readers and bad readers are twin aspects of Carlyle's needed symbiosis. He invites us to read against the grain of the 'natural' and naturalized. He provokes us, also, to read athwart his own writing: the reader's resistance is the enabling force which makes his writing. The quirkiness of the opposites disturbs the formulaic address 'Good reader', making of it no phatic utterance but one that combines ethical and aesthetic categories. The good reader, as much as the bad, opposes the writer. (We may remember how Dickens used some of the same effects a little later, at the close of chapter 47 in *Bleak House*, where he breaks apart the toastmaster's invocation into 'Right Reverends and Wrong Reverends' in his apostrophe at the death of Jo. The climax is the iambic pentameter, 'And dying thus around us every day.')

Carlyle's breaking up of categories and his method of expanding rather than analysing went historically alongside other disequilibrating thought-systems. In accustoming the imagination to the creative forces of unevenness and imbalance, his writing contributed to the possibility of new formulations far removed from his own. Darwin read each of his books as it appeared, with enthusiasm and sometimes rage.[30] Other scientists such as Tyndall and Proctor responded to him. We may do well to consider, last, the relations of his writing beyond reformist politics, ethics, and historiography. In 1857 Herbert Spencer wrote a letter to Tyndall about the new physics, and the implications of the second law of thermodynamics.

> That which was new to me in your position ... was that equilibration was death. Regarding, as I had done, equilibration as the ultimate and *highest* state of society, I had assumed it to be not only the ultimate but also the highest state of the universe. And your assertion that when equilibrium was reached life must cease, staggered me.[31]

Tyndall's side of the argument owes its theoretical formulation to Helmholtz. What George Eliot called the 'powers' that Carlyle discovered helped to prepare the imagination in England for this other fundamentally disturbing German idea too.

NOTES

1 *Leader*, 27 October 1855, pp. 1,034–5; collected in *Essays of George Eliot* ed. Thomas Pinney (London, 1963), pp. 213–15, and in *Thomas Carlyle: The Critical Heritage* ed. Jules P. Seigel (London, 1971), pp. 409–11.

2 Even among critics who have done valuable work on Carlyle we see the impasse when the 'literary', the 'philosophical', and the 'political' in Carlyle's production are disjoined: in his pioneering work *Sartor Called Resartus: The Genesis, Structure, and Style of Thomas Carlyle's First Major Work*

(Princeton, NJ, 1965), G.B. Tennyson set up a matter/manner contrary: 'since Victorian readers accepted *Sartor* primarily as a moral document, it is small wonder that scholarly emphasis has fallen on Carlyle's ideas and their sources. ... But Carlyle's ideas commend themselves to the reader not because of their philosophic rigor and clarity, but because of their compelling literary manner. That manner is of the essence' (p. 5). George Levine in 'The use and abuse of Carlylese', in *The Art of Victorian Prose* (Oxford, 1968), p. 101, opens his essay by asserting the counter-position: 'The attempt to turn Carlyle into an "artist", to preserve his writing as literature, would have been for him the worst of all imaginable fates.' For an invaluable historical-political reading of Carlyle, see Philip Rosenberg, *The Seventh Hero: Thomas Carlyle and the Theory of Radical Activism* (Cambridge, Mass., 1974).

3 Quoted in David A. Wilson, *Carlyle till Marriage (1795–1836)* (London, 1923), p. 110.

4 Fred Kaplan, *Thomas Carlyle: A Biography* (Cambridge, 1983), esp. pp. 30–2, 96.

5 John Rosenberg, *Carlyle and the Burden of History* (Cambridge, Mass., 1974), p. 33.

6 Rosemary Ashton, *The German Idea: Four English Writers and the Reception of German Thought 1800–1860* (Cambridge, 1980), esp. pp. 91–9. See also René Wellek, *Immanuel Kant in England 1793–1838* (Princeton, NJ, 1931).

7 Thomas Carlyle, *Two Note Books*, ed. C.E. Norton (New York, 1898), p. 114. The entry dates from 1823.

8 Friedrich Nietzsche, 'Skirmishes in the war with the age', in *The Twilight of the Idols*; quoted in Crane Brinton, *Nietzsche* (New York, 1965), p. 81.

9 Peter Stern, *A Study of Nietzsche* (Cambridge, 1979), p. 201.

10 See note 1 above.

11 Barbara and Hensleigh Wedgwood, *The Wedgwood Circle 1730–1897* (London, 1980), p. 238.

12 Charles Darwin, *The Origin of Species (1859)*, ed. John Burrow (Harmondsworth, 1968) p. 415.

13 H.A. Taine, *History of English Literature* (London, 1879), pp. 648–50.

14 *Thomas Carlyle's Collected Works*, Library Edition (London, 1869–70), *Critical and Miscellaneous Essays*, vol. I, p. 92. All page references in the text of this essay are to this edition.

15 Tzvetan Todorov, *The Fantastic: A Structural Approach to a Literary Genre* (Ithaca, NY, 1975), pp. 77, 93.

16 Mary Douglas, 'Deciphering a meal', in her *Implicit Meanings: Essays in Anthropology* (London, 1975), pp. 249–75.

17 Gillian Beer, 'Carlyle and *Mary Barton*: problems of utterance', in Francis Barker, David Musselwhite, *et al.* (eds), *1848: The Sociology of Literature* (Colchester, 1978), pp. 242–55.

18 George Eliot, *Middlemarch*, ed. W.J. Harvey (Harmondsworth, 1965), p. 227.

19 'Stanzas from the Grande Chartreuse', *The Poetical Works of Matthew Arnold*, ed. C.B. Tinker (Oxford, 1950), p. 302.

20 Todorov, op. cit., p. 93. Terry Castle makes a number of striking points

about the terms 'phantasmagoria' and 'apparition' in Carlyle's work in an as yet unpublished paper.

21 *The Letters of Gerard Manley Hopkins to Robert Bridges*, ed. Claude C. Abbott (Oxford, 1955), p. 27, 2 August 1871.

22 'The Windhover: To Christ our Lord', *The Poems of Gerard Manley Hopkins*, ed. W.H. Gardner and N.A. MacKenzie (Oxford, 1970), p. 69.

23 For a stimulating discussion of nineteenth-century historiography (though not of Carlyle), see Stephen Bann, *The Clothing of Clio: A Study of the Representation of History in Nineteenth Century Britain and France* (Cambridge, 1984).

24 In a short film seen at the National Portrait Gallery.

25 Ludwig Wittgenstein, *Philosophical Investigations*, vol. I (Oxford, 1963), p. 19c: 'This is connected with the conception of naming as, so to speak, an occult process. Naming appears as a *queer* connexion of a word with an object. For philosophical problems arise when language goes on holiday. And here we may indeed fancy naming to be some remarkable act of mind, as it were a baptism of an object.'

26 Thomas Browne, *Religio Medici and Other Works* (1643), ed. L.C. Martin (Oxford, 1964), p. 9.

27 Roland Barthes 'The discourse of history', trans. Stephen Bann, *Comparative Criticism Yearbook*, ed. Elinor Shaffer, no. 3 (Cambridge, 1981), p. 18.

28 Tzvetan Todorov, 'The quest of narrative', in his *The Poetics of Prose* (Oxford, 1977), p. 132. See the introductory essay to this volume.

29 *The Poems of Gerard Manley Hopkins*, p. 98.

30 Darwin's reading lists record his reading of Carlyle's works as they appeared throughout the 1840s. The very different tone of his comments on Carlyle's work in his late *Autobiography* suggests Carlyle's changed cultural meaning in the intervening years. For an excellent discussion of the friendship between Carlyle and Darwin and its intellectual significance, see Fiona Erskine, 'Darwin in London', Open University PhD thesis (1988).

31 Herbert Spencer, *Life and Letters*, ed. David Duncan (London, 1908), p. 104. See the discussion of this passage in relation to nineteenth-century ideas of degeneration in Daniel Pick, 'The conception and descent of degeneration 1848–1914', Cambridge PhD thesis (1988).

6

CIRCULATORY SYSTEMS: MONEY, GOSSIP, AND BLOOD IN *MIDDLEMARCH*

In *Middlemarch* George Eliot was writing a 'domestic epic', an oxymoron which would express the shared aspirations and rituals of a society, would give space to the most intense emotions and deepest moral questions, but, as the qualifier 'domestic' indicates, would be set on the level of family, inside houses, among ordinary circumstances – in the West Midlands rather than on the plains of windy Troy. Fluctuations, subtle movements, currents, shifts, slides, and alterations are emphasized in her early account of the society over time; so too are changes in proximity:

Old provincial society had its share of this subtle movement: had not only its striking downfalls, its brilliant young professional dandies who ended by living up an entry with a drab and six children for their establishment, but also those less marked vicissitudes which are constantly shifting the boundaries of social intercourse, and begetting new consciousness of inter-dependence. Some slipped a little downward, some got higher footing: people denied aspirates, gained wealth, and fastidious gentlemen stood for boroughs; some were caught in political currents, some in ecclesiastical, and perhaps found themselves surprisingly grouped in consequence; while a few personages or families that stood with rock firmness amid all this fluctuation, were slowly presenting new aspects in spite of solidity, and altering with the double change of self and beholder. Municipal town and rural parish gradually made fresh threads of connection – gradually, as the old stocking gave way to the savings-bank, and the worship of the solar guinea became extinct, while squires and baronets, and even lords who had once lived blamelessly afar from the civic mind, gathered the faultiness of closer acquaintanceship. (p. 122) [1]

This process of *familiarization* was to be one not of reduction – the mock-heroic – but of intensification: the tragic. She was well aware of the absurdities that would be impressed on the reader by such closeness to the normal. Defamiliarization is a procedure of englamouring the humdrum: it allows the reader a magical distance from what has seemed ordinary. In *Middlemarch* the commentary sometimes wryly draws the reader's attention to the awkwardness of hymning the everyday, or prying out the passionate implications of moneydealings. 'Who was ever awestruck about a testator, or sang a hymn on the title to real-estate?' (p. 336). 'Testators' and 'real estate', words from the discourse of legal dealings; 'awestruck' and 'hymn', words from religious and ritual discourse: the two distanced repertoires are set awkwardly in juxtaposition here. As so often, when we meet one of those moments of awkwardness, or facetiousness, in the narrative of George Eliot's work, we are made aware of gaps of judgement and feeling over which language will not seamlessly spread itself. These gaps are indicative and symptomatic of shared suppressions, not the writer's only. Just as we should always pay attention to Dorothea's uncle, Mr Brooke, we should respond to these moments of embarrassment, which register disturbance, and loosen our assumptions.

The writing is not simply mirroring society, as a 'classic realist text'. Rather its discursive twists and turns set up turbulences which unsteady these reflections. This effect is intensified, as I shall show, by the ironic abrasions produced by the double time of the novel. The referential circle between the time of production and first reading – the 1870s – and the time of enactment, forty years earlier, is never quite a closed system. The unwritten time between the two, which is the time of George Eliot's own life and of all her emotional, political, and intellectual involvement, disturbs the apparently reflective surface of the work. As later readers we may too placidly level the text and miss the circulating energies within it, which declare themselves both temporally and discursively.

Middlemarch is concerned with bringing to the surface the implicit values by which people live their lives: within the plot the medium of evaluation is, over and over again, money. The quarrels in the book all have as a trigger money: whether these be between Lydgate and Rosamond, Mary Garth and Featherstone, Mr Brooke and his tenants, or even Dorothea and Casaubon. Since the establishment of the novel as a major form of fiction, there has been an easy slippage between the discourse of narration and the discourse of finance. Even

100

'utterance' had a trading meaning in the Middle Ages (and still does in specialized City and legal circles): utterance is bringing goods for sale; it requires a buyer as well as a seller for its meaning, an addressee as well as an addresser. 'Telling' likewise moves freely to and fro across counting and retailing, and retailing means both selling in small lots and retelling a story. The same slippage occurs in 'an account'. *Credit* and *crediting* is the tightest conjunction of significations. We are allowed credit if our standing is good; we credit a story if we believe in its consistency or inclusiveness; we behave creditably; we perform discreditable acts and find ourselves out of credit.

Trust is at the basis of credit; distrust is provoked by discreditable actions. Reputation, therefore – as we all still read daily in the news-papers – is essential to bargains struck and to permitted delays in payment. Reputation is essential to to a person's value in the community. The loss of reputation is intrinsic to the loss of money in many situations. So gossip is not just a matter of background chorus but the agent of change. Gossip in novels is often discussed as if it were simply a way of conveying information to the reader, or provided a background of authentic popular chat and comedy: giving veri-similitude, and a foil for the distinguished main personages. On the contrary, gossip is *a medium of transaction* and, once it has been gener-ated, it is hard to control its consequences. The world is 'a huge whispering-gallery' (p. 449), we are told in *Middlemarch*. Whispering galleries may offer us clear secret messages or the turgid *brouhaha* of crossed communications.

In a work begun at the time that George Eliot was finishing *Mid-dlemarch* in 1870, Walter Bagehot analysed *Lombard Street: A Description of the Money Market*. He was writing in the light of the panic of 1866 which brought about the crash of the great City bank of Overend, Gurney & Co. ('Ten Years ago', he wrote, 'that house stood next to the Bank of England in the City of London.') George Eliot was writing *Middlemarch* in the period just after that crash. Money and gossip were much in people's minds. Bagehot gives a generic description of the onset of financial panic:

At first, incipient panic amounts to a kind of vague conversation: Is A.B. as good as he used to be? Has not C.D. lost money? and a thousand such questions. A hundred people are talked about, and a thousand think – 'Am I talked about, or am I not?' 'Is my credit as good as it used to be, or is it less?' And every day, as a panic grows, this floating suspicion becomes both more intense and more diffused; it attacks more persons, and attacks them all more virulently than at first. [2]

'A kind of vague conversation', 'a hundred are talked about but a thousand wonder' about their reputation. Many of the crises in the later part of *Middlemarch* are brought about by that conjunction of money-matters and gossip which we call crediting or discrediting.

George Eliot suggests that *writing*, as opposed to spoken communication, may give us access to the full understanding of the machinations of the past. Writing is a dangerous act – the letters between Mr Bulstrode and Mr Joshua Rigg Featherstone cannot be unwritten.

> Who shall tell what may be the effect of writing? If it happens to have been cut in stone, though it lie face downmost for ages on a forsaken beach, or 'rest quietly under the drums and tramplings of many conquests', it may end by letting us into the secret of usurpations and other scandals gossiped about long empires ago: – this world being apparently a huge whispering-gallery ... so a bit of ink and paper which has long been an innocent wrapping or stopgap may at last be laid open under the one pair of eyes which have knowledge enough to turn it into the opening of a catastrophe. To Uriel watching the progress of planetary history from the Sun, the one result would be just as much of a coincidence as the other.
>
> Having made this rather lofty comparison I am less uneasy in calling attention to the existence of low people by whose interference, however little we may like it, the course of the world is very much determined. (p. 448)

Again, George Eliot discomposes her own writing here as soon as it is achieved. She suggests that these high comparisons have prepared for the invasion of a more disagreeable truth: 'the existence of low people by whose interference, however little we may like it, the course of the world is very much determined.' Her writing, by its vacillation between registers, superficially *discredits* itself but, by such uneasy jostling, sways the reader to believe in its inclusiveness, its power of tracking 'those invisible thoroughfares' which are 'the first lurking-places of anguish, mania, and crime, that delicate poise and transition which determine the growth of happy or unhappy consciousness' (p. 194). That half-sentence comes at the end of her description of Lydgate's scientific enterprise, which is implicitly that also of the novelist, by means of the double meaning of 'invention' and 'relation' here: 'that arduous invention which is the very eye of research, provisionally framing its object and correcting it to more and more exactness of relation'.

In the previous chapter we have been told of the initiating moment in Lydgate's imaginative commitment to science. As a schoolboy he has reached down from a high shelf some dusty volumes of a Cyclopaedia.

> The page he opened on was under the heading of Anatomy, and the first passage that drew his eyes was on the valves of the heart. He was not much acquainted with valves of any sort, but he knew that *valvae* were folding doors, and through this crevice came a sudden light startling him with his first vivid notion of finely adjusted mechanism in the human frame. A liberal education had ... left his imagination quite unbiassed, so that for anything he knew his brains lay in small bags at his temples, and he had no more thought of representing to himself how his blood circulated than how paper served instead of gold. (p. 173)

Lydgate approaches anatomy through classical language: he enters through the metaphor of folding doors and discovers, by means of William Harvey, the primary circulatory system – the circulation of the blood. The narrative supplements his metaphor with another circulatory system (and a system of substitution) which Lydgate has not considered: the circulation of money, in which paper is substituted for gold.

This substitution was itself relatively novel at the period in which *Middlemarch* is set, and provides one of the many markers within the text for the first 1870s readers to measure (and adjust) the organization and assumptions of their world against the relatively recent but largely vanished world of the community she describes in the West Midlands in 1828–32. I shall return to this question of the ironic poise of 1870/1830 and its expression by means of money-values, organization of banking, and gold versus paper. Let us first, though, dwell on the reference to Harvey here. William Harvey was the first to establish, early in the seventeenth century, in 1628, that the 'blood moves in a circle, flowing from the heart through an impulse by the force of which it is driven through all the fibres of the arteries; thereafter, from all parts, in a continuation of the flow, it returns in succession through the veins, which absorb and remove it.'[3] The importance of the folding doors, or valves, as Harvey pointed out, was that they prevented the blood running back. Its only way was forward: 'with it moving on in full flood, you will be able to see and feel by touch both systole and diastole'.

In *Middlemarch* we are invited in the 'Prelude' to observe the history of man, and how the mysterious mixture behaves 'under the varying experiments of Time'. The work is strikingly synchronic and forward-moving. The flow of inexorable onward movement is never reversed. We learn about the characters' pasts, certainly, but through the activity of their present – there is no turning back. The folding doors close behind; the heart constantly transmits blood: the narrative pulse spreads through many veins simultaneously but always forward.

In *Middlemarch* the intellectual activities of the characters drive backwards, to the Key to all Mythologies, the primitive tissue, but the book's own activity is that of diversification, and setting alongside, of sequence and consequence. The 'idea of the single centre' or the 'one form' is always set at odds with the book's own values, though seen as the source of much passionate enquiry. Harvey's work, therefore, may have a special value for the project of *Middlemarch*. He changed the conception of the heart from being the *source* of heat and blood to being a *machine for propelling* and transmitting the blood; the move is from single source to system. Harvey insists: 'Nor is the heart, as we think, like a sort of burning coal or brazier or hot kettle, the source of heat and blood, but rather the blood, as being the warmest part of all in the body, gives to the heart (as to all the other parts) the heat which it has received.' In *Movement of the Heart and Blood in Animals* he asserts: 'the heart's one role is the transmission of the blood, and its propulsion, by means of the arteries to the extremities elsewhere.'[4] At the time of its publication, Harvey's work was viewed as having dangerous political implications, removing kingly authority from its central and originating role as the heart of the communal body, and emphasizing instead the equal value of the whole system.

The body is itself a circulatory system; so is money, so is gossip. Apart from Lydgate, the other characters in the book are not much interested in the activity of their own bodies – though fever and the recurrent return of typhoid and typhus are made part of the plot. Lydgate's research is on fever; he first visits the Vincy's to treat Fred when he has typhus; the hospital which Bulstrode helps to fund will advance Lydgate's research; and it is at a meeting to discuss the funding of a graveyard outside the town for the latest victims of a new typhoid epidemic that Bulstrode is denounced and his and Lydgate's fortunes reach their nadir. Lydgate dies prematurely of diphtheria. This emphasis on epidemics may have called to mind another circulatory system to the first 1870s readers: that of the drainage system which Chadwick's work had managed to establish between the setting and the writing of the book. But that system is not, so far as I have traced, remarked on in *Middlemarch*.

There is, however, a further circulatory system, much connected both with money and with gossip, which does mark the historical moment of the work. That is the coming of the railways. That development is always on the periphery of the characters' concerns, demonstrating how little we understand in the moment the crucial forces of change in a community and in its relations with other communities. The Liverpool and Manchester Railway opened in 1830. In the twenty years after that, 6,000 miles of track carrying about 1 million passengers was laid. In 1750 the journey from London to Edinburgh took as much as ten days; by train in 1830 it took 50 hours; by 1850, $17\frac{1}{2}$ hours; by 1855, $13\frac{3}{4}$ hours. This change in ease of interconnection would, of course, have been vivid to George Eliot's first readers. In *Middlemarch* we are reading of the last period in which it would be possible for a man like Bulstrode confidently to bury his past, or for a community like Middlemarch quite so confidently to believe itself the middle of the world – the heart of England. Middlemarch as a community behaves as if it were a closed system; but reading opens it.

The tight ironic relationship between the first readers in the 1870s and the 1830s setting is seen clearly if we dwell for a moment on some of the inventions which occurred between the setting and the composition of *Middlemarch*, bringing with them, in some cases, immediate and profound changes of sensibility. Of these, two are medical discoveries: anaesthesia came into British medical practice soon after it was first used in America in 1846, allowing much more exact and complicated surgery; and, of even more universal significance because of the effect on mother-and-child survival rates, and therefore on family structure, antiseptics were beginning to be accepted. In 1865 Lister treated a boy with a broken shin and suppurating skin with carbolic acid. The wound soon healed, whereas previously most wounds had festered and the chief cause of death in England in the 1850s was from such infection.

Such inventions occupy the space between setting and reader.

George Eliot refers in *Middlemarch* to another of the medical inventions which had just begun to be used: we can observe how up-to-date Lydgate is by his use of the stethoscope and his diagnosis of 'fatty degeneration' of Featherstone's heart as well as his understanding of Casaubon's heart condition. The stethoscope was very slow to enter practice even after its invention in 1819, because 'signs' removed from the body, such as drops of blood and faeces, were analysed in isolation and a general physical examination was not conducted. The stethoscope, in contrast, gives access to the body's systems and allows the action of heart and lungs to be heard. The emphasis now falls on systems rather than objects. I emphasize for a particular reason this cluster of inventions. Two other inventions reinforced the 1830s interest in systems of circulation – Faraday's 1831 discovery of the electric charge and invention of the transformer, and Fourneyron's success with the water turbine in 1827.

These intervening inventions bring home to us the different set of relations between reader and text which operated in *Middlemarch's* initial meaning. It made for a harsher and more tightly sprung rebound upon the reader. In my recent book on George Eliot, I have argued this point at large in relation to women's education and the Victorian women's movement.[5] Now, in the late twentieth century, much in *Middlemarch* has acquired a somewhat pastoral glow. But in the novel's immense and detailed length there is no escape from 'the various blows, clashings, motions, by which things severally go on' (p. 328). The reference here can be taken to be to machinery, or even to hand-to-hand fighting, though the subject George Eliot is here describing is *gossip*: gossip about the flirtation of Lydgate and Rosamond. Rosamond is sharply reminded by her aunt of the connections between reputation, gossip, and a woman's value – which here means, quite crudely, her monetary value, her prospects:

'I am not engaged, aunt.'

'How is it that every one says so, then – that it is the town's talk?'

'The town's talk is of very little consequence, I think,' said Rosamond, inwardly gratified.

'Oh, my dear, be more thoughtful; don't despise your neighbours so. Remember you are turned twenty-two now, and you will have no fortune: your father, I am sure, will not be able to spare you anything. Mr Lydgate is very intellectual and clever; I know there is an attraction in that. I like talking to such men myself; and your uncle finds him very useful. But the profession is a poor one here.'...

'Mr. Lydgate is not a poor man, aunt. He has very high connections.'

'He told me himself he was poor.'

'That is because he is used to people who have a high style of living.'

'My dear Rosamond, you must not think of living in high style.' (pp. 330–1)

Rosamond, we are told elsewhere, was not mercenary: 'she had no wicked plots, nothing sordid or mercenary; in fact, she never thought of money except as something necessary which other people would always provide' (p. 301). That insouciance proves in the end to be blameable (though as later readers we are likely to resist blaming Rosamond for what the conditions of her life make so probable).

Within the work Rosamond's happy ignorance is set over against Dorothea, who is always 'thinking about' money and worrying about how best to use it. She addresses her troubled husband in the middle of the night thus: 'I have been thinking about money all day – that I have always had too much, and especially the prospect of too much' (p. 409). Her generously ill-judged plan is that Casaubon should give money to Will Ladislaw instead of to her, by way of recompense for the disinheriting of Will's grandmother on her marriage to a poor Polish teacher disapproved of by the family because he earned his own bread. Casaubon has been finely compensatory to Will, but never amply so; he has given him an allowance, supported his education, and believes that the allowance he has given entitles him to prevent Will taking paid work in the low capacity of journalist on Mr Brooke's paper – because this will lessen Casaubon's name in the district. Again, the 'knot intrinsicate' of reputation and money occurs, though here in a different sequence. Money defines how people are regarded by the community, and language becomes a form of currency.

Fred was conscious that he would have been yet more severely dealt with if his family as well as himself had not secretly regarded him as Mr. Featherstone's heir; that old gentleman's pride in him, and apparent fondness for him, serving in the stead of more exemplary conduct – just as when a youthful nobleman steals jewellery we call the act kleptomania, speak of it with a philosophical smile, and never think of his being sent to the house of correction as if he were a ragged boy who had stolen turnips. In fact, tacit expectations of what would be done for him by Uncle Featherstone determined the angle at which most people viewed Fred Vincy in Middlemarch. (p. 266)

In this passage, class interests protect the 'youthful nobleman', by substituting 'kleptomania' for stealing. 'Jewellery' and 'kleptomania' are paired in discourse, as are rags, turnips, and stealing. Monetary 'expectations' show gossip determining a person's worth and standing.

Wage-earning in the book is the great social divide. Will's mother had expressed her independence by earning her living as an actress; Will wants to earn his living likewise, since, we are told, his only capital is his brain. The Garth's are a family of wage-earners: Mrs Garth by teaching; Mary Garth as housekeeper and, if obliged to be so, schoolteacher; Mr Garth as land agent. This wage-earning sets them apart from all the other characters in whom our interest is invited and allies the narrative with them. The writing of this great novel is, after all, a wage-earning project as well as a major intellectual and emotional one. One can feel here the influence perhaps of George Eliot's great friend, Barbara Bodichon, with her insistence that every human being should work, and that the dependence of women on fathers and brothers is a form of endless servitude. Moreover, Bodichon strongly took the view that middle-class women should ask for *wages*, not content themselves with philanthropic good works – and that bears on Dorothea's dilemma.

In the first chapter of the book we see the division of the jewels between Dorothea and Celia, a scene which brings into play a great number of symbolic questions about value – aesthetic, monetary, moral, and religious. The second chapter is essentially a discussion of political economy – though this phrase is used by the men in the scene to bat Dorothea on the head whenever she makes suggestions for the redistribution of wealth or the rehousing and better employment of the ordinary people of the community.

'Surely,' said Dorothea, 'it is better to spend money in finding out how men can make the most of the land which supports them all, than in keeping dogs and horses only to gallop over it. It is not a sin to make yourself poor in performing experiments for the good of all.'

She spoke with more energy than is expected of so young a lady, but Sir James had appealed to her. . . .

'Young ladies don't understand political economy, you know,' said Mr. Brooke, smiling towards Mr. Casaubon. 'I remember when we were all reading Adam Smith. There is a book, now. I took in all the new ideas at one time – human perfectibility, now. But some say, history moves in circles; and that may be very well argued; I have argued it myself.' (p. 39)

Change involves expenditure; does history move safely in circles? Adam Smith's *The Wealth of Nations*, Humphry Davy's *Agricultural Chemistry*: these are the works from which the book's argument takes its starting-point, and we are made immediately aware of Brooke's timid meanness in the management of his lands – a matter that will become crucial to his reputation when he puts himself forward for Parliament as a Reform candidate.

How to use wealth? What do do with money? How to come by money? These are important issues in the work and bear an extraordinary degree of moral complexity. The main sources of money represented are wealth inherited by descent; land management; hoarding; and banking. Gambling is a side diversion, though also a moral marker. Another tight knot of reputation and money is blackmail – an aspect of George Eliot's interest which Alexander Welsh's recent book has examined in detail.[6] But blackmail is only the most hostile form in which society catches the individual by the tail: family pressure, keeping up appearances, doing what the neighbours expect of people in your social class and financial circumstances: all these are modes by which the individual is made aware of the endoubled senses of 'worth'. How, then, to discover value independent of finance, and to gauge human worth according to criteria not wholly economic? That is a humanistic level of the book's enquiry, but the work is hardheaded about the extent to which the individual can ever disengage from the toils of evaluation and the toils of money.

Independence for the three main women characters is to a great degree bound up with money; 'an independence' for a woman means, at that period, a sum of money left specifically to her and therefore not under the control of her father or her husband. At the centre of *Middlemarch* is the book called 'The Dead Hand': the dead hand is 'mortmain' and a commission in 1855 had sought to revise its powers. 'Mortmain' allows posthumous control by the testator over the use to which the property is applied. The dead hand is, therefore, the will (in both senses) of Featherstone and Casaubon reaching out to reshape the life of those left behind and to change the circulation among them.

Dorothea is, in these terms, Casaubon's 'property'. Both men write more than one will. In Casaubon's late addition, if Dorothea marries Will she will forfeit her inheritance. Featherstone in his later will leaves everything to his illegitimate son Rigg and nothing to his relatives, including Fred Vincy. That is the will which Mary Garth will not destroy (knowing nothing of its content). Featherstone offers her gold and notes to fulfil his last dying wish, but she obdurately refuses, bent above all on keeping her life and reputation in integrity. She is paid to watch over Featherstone, not to connive with him. She fears that others would interpret her intervention as dishonesty. This would wreck her usefulness to her family – but, far more, it would wreck her self.

Mary has to live for a while with the consequences of her action. Fred does not inherit the £10,000 he has anticipated, so they cannot marry. Fred, moreover, has already brought her family to the edge of ruin by losing the £160 for which her father had issued a promissory note. The gap between the two sums serves as a ruler of the span of wealth in the book. Caleb, we are told, with all his reverence for 'business', has no knowledge of finances. He cannot handle capital; he will work without pay; he is interested only in the use-value, not the exchange-value, of work. Indeed, Caleb runs close to being the perfect example of Goldman's description of the homology between novel and hero in *Towards a Sociology of the Novel*. But Caleb does not go uncriticized. His wife must give up to this debt the money she has set aside for her son's education; Mary must leave home to find a job. Here, 'prospects' are immediate, and blighted. Mary, obliged to undertake the tedious work of double-hemming handkerchiefs for Rosamond Vincy's wedding because she needs the pay, is sharp-eyed about the nature of need: Rosamond, she quips, 'can't be married without this handkerchief' (p. 345).

Mary's escape from poverty, however, comes about in the end by means of her father's *reputation*: his honesty and professionalism lead Sir James Chettam to invite Caleb Garth to take over the management of his and Mr Brooke's estates. Mr Brooke is persuaded to allow new management of his estates because his standing for Parliament has brought to light his parsimony to his tenants. The 'closeness' of Brooke and of Featherstone is measured alongside each other. Dorothea, as willing to reorganize other people's finances as her own, has spoken out to Mr Brooke about the management of his estates, but it is the confrontation with his drunken tenant, Dagley, which at last drives

Mr Brooke to realize, humiliated, that pub talk is unstoppable.

> I'll hev my say – supper or no. An' what I say is, as I've lived upo'
> your ground from my father and grandfather afore me, an' hev
> dropped our money into't, an' me an' my children might lie an'
> rot on the ground for top-dressin' as we can't find the money to
> buy, if the King wasn't to put a stop. (p. 431)

We cannot control what our neighbours say. Gossip brings brutally
into the open the unacknowledged and may force us to examine our
unconsidered actions.

Mary's lot is recovered, but it reminds the reader of alternative
outcomes. She does not have to leave home to take the excellent wage
of £35 a year, 'and extra pay for teaching the smallest strummers the
piano'. Her father can, in stalwart comfort, provide a basic income
for the family. With the management of the two estates he will earn
£400; Dorothea's own income, apart from what she shares with
Casaubon, is £700 per annum; Fred bought a horse for £80, took
surety from Caleb Garth for £160, and stood to inherit £10,000; the
landowners' interests are so considerable that they are never even
translated into money sums. The book is set before the penny post,
and that other circulating system, the postal service, brings heavy
burdens of payment to the recipient of letters: to the Garths, 'nine
costly letters, for which the postman had been paid three and two-
pence' (p. 434).[7]

Even without attempting to translate the incomes of this community
into the monetary values of our own day we are given evidence within
the book of the relative values placed by society on differing trades
and social positions. Rosamond's misunderstanding of what being
'poor' or living in a fine way might mean is linked to the chronic
ignorance of the value of money in which she has been genteelly
reared. Her education has made her into a Victorian ideal of a lady,
bait to catch a rich husband. She is intensely vulnerable, because she
does not have money of her own, has no arts of household management, no discrimination concerning costs, no understanding of people
who have other than monetary value, and a simple idea of perfect
appearance which is the only measure she can use. At the end of the
book, wryly, she is given her reward when, after Lydgate's death, she
marries 'an elderly and wealthy physician': 'She made a very pretty
show with her daughters, driving out in her carriage, and often spoke
of her happiness as "a reward" – she did not say for what' (p. 893).

Dorothea, equally trammelled by ignorance, but always seeking answers, misapplying her generous inclinations, seeking the human meaning of political economy in building cottages, renewing the estate, and, at last, in acknowledging and asserting her own desires, expresses all this in a leap of passion towards Will. He is willing to let her go because he has no income:

> 'We shall never be married.'
>
> 'Some time – we might,' said Dorothea, in a trembling voice.
>
> 'When?' said Will, bitterly. 'What is the use of counting on any success of mine? It is a mere toss up whether I shall ever do more than keep myself decently, unless I choose to sell myself as a mere pen and a mouthpiece. I can see that clearly enough. I could not offer myself to any woman, even if she had no luxuries to renounce.'...
>
> 'Oh, I cannot bear it – my heart will break,' said Dorothea, starting from her seat, the flood of her young passion bearing down all the obstructions which had kept her silent – the great tears rising and falling in an instant: 'I don't mind about poverty – I hate my wealth.'...
>
> 'We could live quite well on my own fortune – it is too much – seven hundred-a-year – I want so little – no new clothes – and I will learn what everything costs.' (pp. 869, 870)

'Learning what everything costs' has large meaning in this novel: it involves learning what everything costs to others as the consequence of actions, as well as to the individual.

The inextricability of community interests is given its other form in the figure of Bulstrode, the banker, for whom religious and financial discourses are not separate, but who feels within his own secret past the difficulty of giving them so full an accord. At the centre of Christian theology is 'redemption' – a word that signifies retrieving an object from a pawnbroker or, later, exchanging paper money or cheques for gold. It is out of those financial parables that the sense of Christ's redemption of the world is obtained. Bulstrode is the town's banker: the man who can see into all pockets, though not into all hearts. Again, George Eliot has shrewdly selected as her narrative nexus a topic of the late 1820s which will reinforce the ironies for 1870s readers. In 1825 there had been a panic like that of 1866. Between the two came Peel's great 1844 Act which reorganized banking practices in England. At the end of the 1820s the West Midlands, as it happened, had more banking per head of population than any other area: one bank for 12,000 people as against 17,000 in London. The Bank of England and the London City banks were supplemented by the country banks, of which there were only a handful in 1750 but around 800 in 1810 and a good many more by the peak of 1825. The capitalization of such banks was surprisingly low, an average of £10,000 – the same sum, we recall, as Fred was likely to inherit from Featherstone. Moreover, they were unit banks, without branches, lodged close within the single community. Not only industrialists but shopkeepers, lawyers, and other relatively small capitalists could set up as bankers. In 1825–6 sixty country banks failed.

As Rondo Cameron explains in *Banking in the Early Stages of Industrialization*, banks were particularly needed in country districts:

> in agricultural areas, in particular, for safe repositories for idle funds. Finally, but by no means of minor significance, the deficiencies of the coinage, the need for a local circulating medium ... led to the use of token coins, paper currency, which soon took on the characteristics of bank notes.[8]

So we are in the period where the transfer from metal to paper is taking place, where the promissory or symbolic character of money has come to the fore, and where the community is very much at the mercy of one banker – who, like the heart, is not the centre but the agent of the flow of the community's relations, their credit. We see now, I think, more clearly why in the passage I quoted at the outset George Eliot sets 'paper and gold' alongside the action of the heart and the valves (p. 173).

Bulstrode has 'made good', but his past, in the person of Rigg, returns to dog and break him. What breaks him most is his willingness to implicate himself in the muddied and unscrupulous act. Here Mary Garth acts as his counter-representative, as throughout this book people fleetingly and shiftingly act as the shadow selves of each other. She stood out, remained intact, let the money pass away. Bulstrode and, in some measure, Lydgate are compromised; and in this tight community, before the coming of the railway, the penny post, the telegraph service, it is the gossip – the talk of *neighbours* – which sets the price on people.

Or almost so. For George Eliot shows that it is possible to escape that crude valuation – the repetitive formulaic stories of gossip which can only ever imagine simple motives and simple outcomes to stories, which give a censorious glamour to misunderstood misery. Mrs Bulstrode, faced by her husband's scandal, tries to discover what has happened. It is only her brother who will tell her, after her anguished series of visits to her hinting friends. The theme of jewels, their symbolic meaning strangely interconnected with commercial values, reappears. The parcelling out of the jewels in the first scene with Celia and Dorothea is here replaced, in the magic of narrative, by Mrs Bulstrode's taking off all her jewels and finery and descending to her husband: 'Look up, Nicholas'. Mr Bulstrode becomes Nicholas, and not old Nick, redeemed from despair by his wife's love. In the monetary discourse of the book this scene is distinguished by its directness and intimacy. It ends with a silent reference to gossip: 'She could not say, "How much is only slander and false suspicion?" and he did not say, "I am innocent." '

This is no simple resolution. The next chapter opens with the creditors leaving Rosamond and Lydgate's house. His bankruptcy is of the heart as well as the purse. But, again, his willed affection can sustain the couple forward and Dorothea can release him from his debt to Bulstrode, taking on the role of creditor for his thousand pounds. By doing so, she gives him credit. She proves her trust in him, and thereby begins the slow process of recovery. It is with the weight of all this that Dorothea begins to learn 'what everything costs'. Her great plans come to nothing direct. 'Many who knew her, thought it a pity that so substantive and rare a creature should have been absorbed into the life of another, and be only known in a certain circle as a wife and mother' (p. 894). Instead of standing distinct, she is 'absorbed' and *known in a certain circle*. She is a transmissive presence.

Circulation is part of the fictionality of this fiction: the degree of interconnection still leaves out many and much in the life of Middlemarch and yet requires nearly 900 pages. The old notion that *Middlemarch* is constructed as a series of parallels misses the underlying metaphor which energizes the book's movement. Is the novelist, then, the banker – or the heart – the machine of circulation, propelling characters and urging time forwards? Certainly, a difficulty in the writing of fiction is how to delay or divert the drive towards conclusion which is simultaneously set up by telling a story. Linearity is not the project. The double time of this work means that for the first readers a circle of reference and allusion was formed which ran around the circuit of 1830–1870–1830. Multiple interrelated systems and circulations, even loops, are additionally needed to divert the reader's rapacity for ending.

One of George Eliot's strengths as a writer, however, is her power to get outside her controlling narrative metaphors. Circulatory systems are not the only model in the work. The labyrinth, the tree, and the river with its tributaries are all also present as metaphor.[9] The coursing of the blood through the body has a certain diagrammatic similarity to these metaphors, but they suggest other outcomes. At the end of the work we are left with two possibilities: Dorothea Brooke, we are told, is spent – or spends herself – in many irrigating tributaries. Brook becomes river, but a nameless river: 'her full nature, like that river of which Cyrus broke the strength, spent itself in channels which had no great name on the earth. But the effect of her being on those around her was incalculably diffusive' (p. 896). The river enters estuary and then sea, its waters irretrievably mingled. The metaphor of expenditure does not here rely on the idea of exchange.[10] Dorothea's son, in contrast, re-enters the Middlemarch community and inherits Mr Brooke's estate. He becomes part of the world of entail and descent which in this work is equivocally, but finally benignly, viewed as affording a needed continuity. The emphasis of the book's conclusion, however, is on the cost of individual experience: expenditure, not entail.

NOTES

1 All references are to the Penguin English Library edition of *Middlemarch*, ed. W.J. Harvey (Harmondsworth, 1965). Page references are given in parentheses at the end of quotations in the main text. The 'solar guinea' became extinct in 1813 and was replaced by the sovereign. George Eliot is here providing a chronology which frames precisely her chosen period of 1828–32.

2 Walter Bagehot, *Lombard Street: A Description of the Money Market* (London, 1873), pp. 12, 49. Bagehot suggests that social order itself is based on a fictional form of credit: 'Queen Victoria is loyally obeyed – without doubt, and without reasoning – by millions of human beings. If those millions began to argue, it would not be easy to persuade them to obey Queen Victoria, or anything else. Effectual arguments to convince the people who need convincing are wanting. Just so, an immense system of credit, founded on the Bank of England as its pivot and its basis, now exists' (p. 68).

3 William Harvey, *The Circulation of the Blood and Other Writings*, trans. K.J. Franklin (London, 1963), pp. 170–1.

4 ibid., pp. 175, 39–40.

5 Gillian Beer, *George Eliot* (Brighton, 1986), especially pp. 147–99.
6 Alexander Welsh, *George Eliot and Blackmail* (Berkeley, Cal., 1986).
7 For a very helpful account of how to translate money-values, see David Holbrook, 'What was Mr Darcy worth?', *The Cambridge Review* (December 1984), pp. 219–21.
8 Rondo Cameron, *Banking in the Early Stages of Industrialization* (Oxford, 1967), p. 24.
9 For discussion of these metaphors, see Gillian Beer, *Darwin's Plots* (London, 1983), pp. 149–80.
10 Something closer to the imagery of thermodynamics discussed by Michel Serres in *Zola: Feux et signaux de brume* (Paris, 1975) enters here.

7

BEYOND DETERMINISM: GEORGE ELIOT AND VIRGINIA WOOLF

In this essay I want to look at the particular patterns of intelligibility implied by determinism and to think about ways in which the dominance of deterministic organizations of experience in the later nineteenth and earlier twentieth centuries bore upon women, and in particular upon two writers: George Eliot and Virginia Woolf. In the course of the argument I hope to demonstrate some of the ulterior or alternative patterns created by the two novelists. These fictive patterns question, dilate, or surpass the deterministic ones which were so vigorous a part of their intellectual and emotional upbringing. To put it at its simplest: can the female self be expressed through plot or must it be conceived in resistance to plot? Must it lodge 'between the acts'? Virginia Woolf said that she could not make up plots and George Eliot that conclusions are at best negations. At the end of *Middlemarch* George Eliot writes of Dorothea's two marriages:

> Certainly those determining acts of her life were not ideally beautiful. They were the mixed result of young and noble impulse struggling amidst the conditions of an imperfect social state, in which great feelings will often take the aspect of error, and great faith the aspect of illusion. For there is no creature whose inward being is so strong that it is not greatly determined by what lies outside it.[1]

Here the conditions of an imperfect social state bear in upon young and noble impulse, changing its aspect and cramping its powers without obliterating its nature. The ironic transformation of 'great' into 'greatly' registers this diminishing and enclosing: 'great feelings', 'great faith', 'greatly determined'. The passage also brings out an issue which I should clarify at the outset. The determinants of gender, upbringing, heredity, class, and historical period are all constituent elements in our experience. The idea of determinism is newer, and is in itself perhaps the most powerful single determinant of the past hundred years. It is with the system-making powers of this idea and their bearing on women's experience that I am chiefly concerned.

Determinism is a comparatively recent word. The first instance noted by the *Oxford English Dictionary* is 1846. In 1844 it was still possible for Marx to see free, conscious activity as man's species-characteristic, a view he was not to hold for long. So George Eliot wrote at a time when determinism was still a fresh idea which seemed to promise the possibility of a knowable world without godhead. For Virginia Woolf it is a pattern associated with her father's generation, and with the authority of a male-organized world. Before determinism, necessity required, or Fate struck. In the idea of Fate the apparent autonomy of the human being is interrupted by Fate's interventions, and individuals prove to be part of a plot not of their own making. But Fate's interventions are selective; determinism is all-inclusive. In determinism autonomy is extinguished and 'the consciousness of freedom rests chiefly upon an oblivion of the antecedents to our choice'. That quotation from William Thomson's *Oxford Essays* (1855) illustrates how already the idea of pre-consciousness or even of the unconscious was becoming a needed element in the definition of determinism. Freud's analysis of the role of the unconscious in conscious motive extended the area of the determined and made it impossible for consciousness ever fully to encompass or control it.

The *Oxford English Dictionary*'s earliest instance emphasizes the rationalism of the deterministic idea; Hamilton Reid contrasts the two schemes of necessity, one that of 'brute or blind Fate', the other 'rational Determinism'. In all the early instances there is a suggestion that, although the individual may be inattentive to the sources of his own state, determinism represents a knowable order which is to be preferred to the aberrant and unscrupulous interventions of 'brute Fate'. Fate reverses or propels, is an external force. Determinism implies an inherent and irreversible order capable of including all phenomena. The Freudian concept of overdetermination emphasizes the multiple pathways by which one arrives at the same place. The individual is directed into a restricted time, space, and activity. Although she cannot know all the conditions that have brought her there, they are, according to this arrangement of experience, ineluctably present, intertwined and matted so thick that there is no space, no interruption, no moment which can escape from sequence.

Determinism emphasizes relations, but relations fixed in a succession which more and more acutely delimits and characterizes. It is a process we recognize in *Middlemarch*'s melancholy.

The all-inclusiveness which is essential to deterministic organization of experience means that any method of seeking escape from its omnivorous powers will be cast as wish-fulfilment, impossibility, something freakish and fitful, something delusory. Feelings take the aspect of error and faith the aspect of illusion. So all such assertion of apparently other perceptions – the indeterminate, the reversible, the reality of that which might have been, the multiplicity of the future, the moment broken away from sequence, broken away from relations, fear without object, lack without object – is seen as second-order experience, doomed and negative. It is perceived as either failing to recognize the laws which underlie apparent heterogeneity or as merely fancifully ignoring them. Virginia Woolf in her essay on George Eliot explores the nature of desire in George Eliot's women:

> In learning they seek their goal; in the ordinary tasks of womanhood; in the wider service of their kind. They do not find what they seek, and we cannot wonder. The ancient consciousness of woman, charged with suffering and sensibility, and for so many ages dumb, seems in them to have brimmed and overflowed and uttered a demand for something – they scarcely know what – for something that is perhaps incompatible with the facts of human existence.[2]

Virginia Woolf does not specify what those facts may be, though she says that George Eliot had too strong an intelligence to tamper with them. As so often in her critical writing, she draws back, leaving only that 'perhaps' to suggest an alternative view of possibilities. In the ordering of her fiction she is bolder. Indeed, both these writers are more exploratory in the ordering of their fiction than in polemics. They work askance from the expected rather than confront it.

I have written up to now of determinism as a concept in a way which might be held to bear on both men's and women's idea of the self. Of all the figures who gave energy to the concept of scientific determinism Darwin is the most influential. In *The Origin of Species* (1859) he wrote that chance is the name we give to 'as yet unknown laws' – a passage which trawls the future back into the deterministic net. In *The Origin of Species* the radical insistence that transformation *has* occurred and species *do* change disguised for a time the equal insistence upon order, upon things being inevitably as they are because

119

of their antecedents, upon a gradualistic process so extended as to be always beyond the horizon of the individual human life. In *The Descent of Man* (1871) the emphasis upon the determined and the irremediable is much more marked. If women have a quarrel with Darwin, this study, with its use of anthropological even in preference to biological evidence, must be its source. Eliza Gamble, indeed, challenged Darwin's reading of the evidence in her book *The Evolution of Woman: An Inquiry into the Dogma of her Inferiority to Man*, published in 1894. In *The Descent of Man* Darwin concentrates on sexual selection as one of the controls in evolutionary process. He wished to emphasize that random mutation was not the sole, or indeed the dominant, mechanism in man's development. Darwin bases his argument on a fixed notion of sexual distinction. 'Man is more courageous, pugnacious and energetic than woman, and has a more inventive genius. His brain is absolutely larger, but whether or not proportionately to his larger body, has not, I believe, been fully ascertained.'[3] Writing at exactly the same time George Eliot comments ironically in the 'Prelude' to *Middlemarch* on society's reaction to women's yearnings:

> Some have felt that these blundering lives are due to the inconveneint indefiniteness with which the Supreme Power has fashioned the natures of women: if there were one level of feminine incompetence as strict as the ability to count three and no more, the social lot of women might be treated with scientific certitude.[4]

One of the still crucial issues of debate among theorists in the women's movement, such as Montrelay and Kristeva, drawing for example on Karen Horney, is whether biological determinism is a dangerous underlying element in our insistence on the distinctiveness of women's psychosexual understanding of the world. Darwin identified women with a position intermediate between child and man and used the analogy with the 'childhood of the race'. Extending the then current metaphor of the varying races as being at different points in the growth towards adulthood, he places women in the position of a less developed race, one closer to the childhood of humanity:

> It is generally admitted that with women the powers of intuition, of rapid perception, and perhaps of imitation, are more strongly marked than in man; but some, at least, of these faculties are characteristic of the lower races, and therefore of a past and lower state of civilization.

Moreover, he suggests that 'during manhood' men 'generally undergo a severe struggle in order to maintain themselves and their families; and this will tend to keep up or even increase their mental powers, and, as a consequence, the present inequality between the sexes.'[5] A passage like this clearly gives particular pungency to Virginia Woolf's ironic glance at the collapse of manhood at the discovery that the women servants (a neat condensation of terms) are getting along very nicely without his providing for them:

> He has been out all day in the city earning his living, and he comes home at night expecting repose and comfort to find that his servants – the women servants – have taken possession of the house. He goes into the library – an august apartment which he is accustomed to have all to himself – and finds the kitchen maid curled up in the arm chair reading Plato. He goes into the kitchen and there is the cook engaged in writing a Mass in B flat. He goes into the billiard room and finds the parlourmaid knocking up a fine break at the table. He goes into the bed room and there is the housemaid working out a mathematical problem. What is he to do? He has been accustomed for centuries to have that sumptuous mansion all to himself, to be master in his own house. Well of course his first instinct is to dismiss the whole crew. But he reflects that then he would have to do the work of the house himself, and he has not been trained to do it. – Nature has denied him certain (quite essential) gifts. He therefore says that these women servants may practise their silly little amusements in their spare time, but if he finds them neglecting the sacred duties which nature has imposed upon them he will do something very dreadful indeed.

> *I am the bread winner; how am I going to support a wife and family if my wife and family can support themselves? No, I will make it as hard as possible for my wife and family to support themselves because [I then hope they will give up doing it, and they will let me support them and it] for reasons which I need not go into but they have to do with the most profound instincts of my nature it is much pleasanter to support a wife and family, than to allow a wife and family to support themselves.*[6]

Darwin does acknowledge that educating women when they are close to adulthood might produce some changes:

In order that woman should reach the same standard as man, she ought, when nearly adult, to be trained to energy and perseverance and to have her reason and imagination exercised to the highest point; and then she would probably transmit these qualities chiefly to her adult daughters.

But for these effects to spread he notes that such women must, statistically, bear more children than their less educated sisters. Darwin is not without irony in his attitude to the relations between the sexes; of music in courtship, for example, he observes that:

Women are generally thought to possess sweeter voices than men, and as far as this serves as any guide, we may infer that they first acquired musical powers in order to attract the other sex. But if so, this must have occurred long ago, before our ancestors had become sufficiently human to treat and value their women merely as useful slaves.

However, he goes on to state that, in contradistinction to the idea of slavery, 'In civilised life man is largely, but by no means exclusively, influenced in the choice of his wife by external appearance.'[7] Therefore sexual selection will always emphasize the predominance of beauty over other characteristics. Significantly, Darwin assumes that among humans, as opposed to other species, it is always the men who do the selecting. The implication of his argument is that women's characteristics will be determined by their acceptability to men. It's a way of squeezing and defining the identity of women which George Eliot glances at ironically in one of the epigraphs for *Daniel Deronda* – a novel preoccupied with the conditions of the marriage market and inheritance:

What woman should be? Sir, consult the taste
Of marriageable men. This planet's store
In iron, cotton, wool, or chemicals –
All matter rendered to our plastic skill,
Is wrought in shapes responsive to demand:
The market's pulse makes index high or low,
By rule sublime. Our daughters must be wives,
And to be wives must be what men will choose:
Men's taste is woman's test. You mark the phrase?
'Tis good, I think? – the sense well winged and poised
With t's and s's.[8]

Women are shaped, like other natural matter, into forms 'responsive to demand'. The rancorous ironies generated by this situation spread throughout society and throughout this novel whose space and whose ellipses condense the pretensions of the present-day English upper-class assumptions into pilulous smallness.

It is in the context of such arguments – from zoology (women's brains are smaller), from social-evolutionary theory (women are fixed in a state analogous to that of less developed races), from sexual conditions (women must be wives and can become so only by representing what men value in them) – that the major determining argument about sexual distinction grows. Darwin's book appeared in 1871, just before *Middlemarch* was published. In the succeeding years George Eliot was at work on *Daniel Deronda*. Virginia Woolf selects the 1880s as the period on which she offers analytical intervening commentaries, revealing the oppression and denial internalized by a young middle-class woman in the 1880s. *The Pargiters* attempts to distinguish with tonic clarity between the socially determined elements in women's *understanding* of their experience, the constraints of that experience, and what is endemic to experience. Clearly there are some processes which are inescapable and irreversible: physical growth is one of them. Virginia Woolf comments in 'A sketch of the past':

> But somehow into that picture must be brought, too, the sense of movement and change. Nothing remained stable long. One must get the feeling of everything approaching and then disappearing, getting large, getting small, passing at different rates of speed past the little creature; one must get the feeling that made her press on, the little creature driven on as she was by growth of her legs and arms, driven without her being able to stop it, or to change it, driven as a plant is driven up out of the earth, up until the stalk grows, the leaf grows, buds swell. That is what is indescribable, that is what makes all the images too static, for no sooner has one said this was so, than it was past and altered.[9]

Here Virginia Woolf seizes upon the rapidity, the silently expanding kaleidoscope of childhood growth. The driving power of growth is an ungainsayable and successive element in experience – an experience which she ceases to recount here as she reaches puberty and the day of her mother's death. The particular organization implied by evolutionary theory and determinism borrows the idea of irreversible onward sequence from the experience of growth. It can't run

123

backwards, though it may include equally convergence and branching. Nor can it stay still. George Eliot wrote just after the appearance of Darwin's *Origin of Species*, 'But to me the Development theory and all other explanations of processes by which things came to be, produces a feeble impression compared with the mystery that lies under the processes.'[10] Though she tended in her early work to identify this mystery with origins, George Eliot never entirely does away with a sense of some slumberous and unchanging mystery outside – or, as she puts it, 'under' – process. I think it is possible to see the recrudescence of this sense as part of an attempt to move beyond determinism which is most subtly organized in *Daniel Deronda*.

But I would like first to look at the book in which she seems to be working most acceptingly within the confines of that which is determined: *The Mill on the Floss*. The onward movement in determinism has a particular implication for narrative. Our *understanding* of events must run in reverse order. We can understand the present only in terms of its past, which is seen as stable and irremediable. If Virginia Woolf emphasizes the unfurling and lapsing of time in her images of physical growth, George Eliot emphasizes the passionate slowness of childhood in *The Mill on the Floss*. Though the narrative is arranged like memory with crystal-clear episodes of recall, the book dwells upon the shaping elements of Maggie's emotional growth – within a particular small community for which George Eliot provides not only a full account of the present trading activities but a history of its past and an eponymous saint's story. Narrow as the society and environment are, George Eliot remarked in conversation that the conditions for a young girl in such a community in her youth were in fact far worse than she had shown them to be in *The Mill*. A series of episodes dramatizes the development and the starvation of Maggie's possibilities: there is a superabundance of intelligence and emotion which can find no answering form in its environment. Maggie's father ruminates: 'a woman's no business wi' being so clever; it'll turn to trouble, I doubt.'[11]

The organicist form of the *Bildungsroman* is invoked, with its emphasis upon the gradual assimilation of the young man (say, *Wilhelm Meister*) to his environment. In that organicist form we are left with a sense of both completion and disillusionment – the autocratic self acquiesces at last in the humdrum terms of its own surival within society. But *The Mill on the Floss* demonstrates that for the heroine, as opposed to the hero of *Bildungsroman*, there can be no such accommodation. (Kingsley makes a similar point about the proletarian hero of *Alton Locke* who must die at the book's end on the way to a new life abroad because there is no place for him in current society.) Death may become the only means of escape from the determining bonds of a particular society – especially is this so if the author subscribes intellectually to the idea of determinism. So at the end of *The Mill on the Floss* George Eliot reverses the novel's flow, allowing Maggie to escape the parsimonious anguish of a misunderstood life amidst a narrow community. Instead she sweeps back upon the flood waters over the scenes of her youth, over the Red Deeps to childhood, back to the Mill and her brother, to 'the strong resurgent love ... that swept away all the later impressions of hard, cruel offence and mis-understanding, and left only the deep, underlying, unshakable mem-ories of early union'.[12] The transformations of growth and development are reversed; the past is recoverable; Maggie appears as the active rescuer of her alienated brother Tom. When she had floated down the stream with Stephen Guest (set off from the community by his name) her will was in abeyance. At the end she is endowed with a kind of natural freedom. The chapter is entitled 'The final rescue', and the uneasiness which many readers feels with the conclusion is, I think, hinted at defensively in that address from author to reader: it is George Eliot who rescues Maggie from the grim, cramped future that the social determinism of the plot has seemed to make inescapable.

George Eliot chose always to imprison her most favoured women – Dinah, Maggie, Dorothea. She does not allow them to share her own extraordinary flight, her escape from St Oggs and from Middlemarch. She needs them to endure their own typicality. But at the end of *The Mill* her obduracy fails. She allows to Maggie the fulfilment of an infantile, passionate, incestuous recovery of love: 'In their death they were not divided.' The solution exceeds the book's terms because George Eliot permits to herself in addition that fulfilment of immersion and self-denial, the obliteration of self in familial love, which she steadfastly resisted in her own adult life. What we have in *The Mill* is an apparently deterministic order which in its conclusion whirls backwards into desire, instead of into understanding and ration-alization. George Eliot is fascinated by the unassuageable longings of her heroine. She allows them fulfilment in a form of plot which simply glides out of the channelled sequence of social growth and makes literal the expansion of desire. The river loses its form in the flood. This total dowsing of the self is an uncontrolled challenge to the idea of necessary sequence. It lacks bleakness, is even lubricious, and yet that sense of the inordinate and of full satisfaction which George Eliot creates in the conclusion does realize confused and passionate needs. For women under oppression such needs can find no real form within an ordering of plot which relies upon sequence, development, the understanding and renunciation of the past, the acceptance of the determined present. The end of *The Mill* is symbolic outcry. It goes outside the forms of social realism to which determinism is at that period so closely linked. Social realism later becomes for Virginia Woolf the enemy of the real.

So even in as early a novel as *The Mill* we can see George Eliot straining the idea of 'necessary sequence' which she at the same time found so reassuring. It seemed to imply secure pathways, channels for the 'persistent self', of which she wrote in *Middlemarch*: 'Strange, that some of us, with quick alternate vision, see beyond our infatuations, and even while we rave on the heights, behold the wide plain where our persistent self pauses and awaits us.'[13] The persistence of the self is important to her, but the idea of persistence admits also that of transformation in her work: 'Character is not writ in marble.' This sense of 'self' as the enduring core of being, capable of being the object of its own attention, is a surprisingly recent sense for the word. For George Eliot the topic is complicated by the high value she places upon self-abnegation. Maggie's self can be fully asserted only in death; in life she is striving for compliancy. George Eliot is preoccupied with the interplay of organism and medium, but in her work tragedy is generated out of the impassibility of the medium – the very slow rate at which society accepts change, particularly change of assumptions whatever the diversity of practice – so that a quick being like Maggie or Dorothea will be trapped in time, in a medium whose rate of change lags, and so forecloses their futures. Virginia Woolf too recognizes the 'immense forces society brings to play upon each of us' – but the image she uses to express this emphasizes the rapidity with which sensibility shifts:

> Consider what immense forces society brings to play upon each of us, how that society changes from decade to decade; and also from class to class; well, if we cannot analyse these invisible presences, we know very little of the subject of the memoir; and again how futile

life-writing becomes. I see myself as a fish in a stream; deflected; held
in place; but cannot describe the stream.[14]

'The present moment' is indescribable, or flat, she suggests at the
end of *Orlando*. Language, even at its most feverish, is writing its
own elegy and that of the experience which prompted it. It cannot,
therefore, escape the past. But it can select and compress the past,
surveying it instead of being embedded in it – and that is the function
of pastiche in both *Orlando* and *Between the Acts*. It is a form of
celebration and revenge simultaneously which allows her to rupture
the continuities of language by fixing our attention on them. *Orlando*
creates an order which shows the self as fantastically autonomous,
jubilantly intact through changes of gender, of nation, of historical
period. *Orlando* is play, coming immediately after *To the Lighthouse* and
its grave exploration of sexual polarities and of the self at the mercy
of its historical place in time. *Orlando*'s jesting reminds us of the *power*
of what it frees us momentarily from believing in: the determinants of
gender, individual ageing, history. Yet the suppression of such belief
has its own authority: it unravels accustomed patterns and suggests
other orders of possibility. The disjunction between the self and
history, the speeding up of time, creates an unreflective victory over
evolutionary determinism. The self in this book is clad in gender and
history and survives them.

Elaine Showalter in *A Literature of their Own* dismisses *Orlando* as
'tedious high camp', but this, I think, is because she is preoccupied
with her attack on androgyny. Indeed, she is impatient with all
Virginia Woolf's later books, which, she holds, 'show signs of a progressive technical inability to accommodate the facts and crises of
day-to-day experience'.[15] I do not believe that Virginia Woolf had lost
a technical ability she earlier commanded, but rather that she had
come to distrust the day-to-day as a sufficient register of reality. It
seems to me that Elaine Showalter, by concentrating her attention on
the polemical writing, has missed considering the narrative politics of
Virginia Woolf's reorganization of experience in a work like *The
Waves*. If Virginia Woolf moves away from facts and crises it is because
she denies the claim of such ordering to be all-inclusive. Escape is not
necessarily a form of retreat or failure. Escape can mean freedom and
the trying out of new possibilities after imprisonment. Similarly, in
her discussion of George Eliot, Showalter pays most attention to *The
Mill on the Floss*, where she tracks the fate of the 'feminine heroine',

and barely mentions *Middlemarch* or *Daniel Deronda*, which far more radically question assumptions about the limits of women's experience.

Julia Kristeva in *Polylogue* entitles one discussion 'La femme, ce n'est jamais ça'. She distrusts the new romanticism which places its belief in feminine identity – a practice which she sees as the inverse of 'phallocratisme'. She recommends 'cet aspect du travail de l'avant-garde qui dissout les identités, y compris les identités sexuelles'.[16] I shall return to this in the discussion of *The Waves*. Here she is in argument with, for example, Michèle Montrelay, whose 'Inquiry into femininity' in *L'Ombre et le nom* (1977) suggests that femininity is 'the blind spot' of the symbolic processes analysed by Freud. 'Two incompatible, heterogeneous territories co-exist inside the feminine unconscious: that of representation and that which remains the "dark continent".'[17] The themes of lack and absence become in Montrelay, as in Lacan, specific to women's primary psychosexual experiences, and hence to their art. Clearly such arguments draw upon Lacan's emphasis upon language as a pre-existing system which orders and constitutes the subject as the other, the object of desire, that which can never be fully known or realized through articulation.[18]

Without arguing a fully theorized case it is possible to see ways in which these suggestions do throw light upon the practice of the writers with whom I am concerned. But each of them is also held within a specific ideological situation related to determinism, and I think that it is important to understand the means by which, as writers who are women, they bring that dominant order into question. Neither of them is content to remain within the sanctuary of women's issues. Nor did they acquiesce in that form of imperialism which claims all reasoned modes of discourse as male and accords to the female lyrical interventions only. George Eliot, as Virginia Woolf remarked, reached beyond the sanctuary of womanhood into men's preserves and 'plucked for herself the strange bright fruits of art and knowledge' while not renouncing 'her own inheritance – the difference of view, the difference of standard'.[19] It is probably no coincidence that *The Mill on the Floss* and *To the Lighthouse*, the most autobiographic novels of their authors' careers, are also those which most emphasize the polarization of sex roles. *Daniel Deronda* and *The Waves* are the works in which they each explore to the furthest reach possible the relationship between plot and the self, and study ways of loosening the ties between them. One way of doing this is to destabilize the idea of origins. This

128

topic includes the relationship of writer and text, and I should like briefly to discuss that first.

George Eliot, with her massive, eloquent, and finely discriminate concern with intellectual issues, saw the question of origins in relation to evolutionary theory. She probably, like Lewes, perceived the theistic and patriarchal indications of Darwin's idea of 'the one form' and preferred the idea of the earth at the dawn of life as 'like a vast germinal membrane, every slightly diversified point producing its own vital form'.[20] After *Romola*, in which a succession of fathers and father-figures are killed and rejected, fathers are notably absent from her work (Caleb Garth has the appearance of a survivor from some other era). One kind of origin has lost its power for her. But there remains in *Middlemarch* the problem of the narrator who is also the originator, the maker. The narrator is a source of succession and of determining interpretation, accorded an objectivity which has been shown to be impossible through the study of the partial knowledge of the characters. Does she simply exempt her own creativity and presence from her distrust of origins and teleology? She attempts ways out of the dilemma – the use of 'we' as a form of address, multiplicity and variability of event. But 'she' remains a hidden alternative, one that is not offered, allowed, or mentioned within what appears to be the absoluteness of the book's ordering. Dorothea is permitted no transformation. She escapes from Middlemarch, not to create any substantive event, but to work through others. George Eliot, that figure of androgynous power for the 1870s, is inscribed within the work because of the presence of the author's name. Her surviving presence is part of the text, and she seems to stand, perhaps delusively, for ways out of the determinations of the book. In her case the organism did change medium. It's a dilemma which reminds us that the apparent all-inclusiveness of Middlemarch the town is a matter simply of its own pretensions. But it also suggests that the apparent all-inclusiveness of *Middlemarch* the book is dubious too and permits a doubtful optimism which runs counter to its own mordant study of entrapment.

In *Daniel Deronda* George Eliot renounces the advantages of her position as originator, determining sequence:

> Men can do nothing without the make-believe of a beginning. Even Science, the strict measurer, is obliged to start with a make-believe unit, and must fix on a point in the stars' unceasing journey when

129

his sidereal clock shall pretend that time is at Nought. His less
accurate grandmother Poetry has always been understood to start
in the middle.[21]

Time sequence is disrupted and the author's location is blurred. There
is no longer a gap between characters' discourse and writer's discourse.
Instead of the attribution of linear or arboreal sequence, time is
shuffled, overlapped, suspended. Origins become a theme, and are
thus brought into the area of that which may be questioned and
debated. But much of the imagery is proleptic, and second sight is a
reality in the consciousness equally of Gwendolen and of Mordecai.
Cycle, recurrence, the reversal of time and its suspension are all
admitted. The book's surface is clandestine. The characters dwell in
a formidable state of passivity amidst the buzz of unspoken obsession.
The two men in Gwendolen's life are notably passive: Deronda with
the passivity of the therapist and Grandcourt of the domineering. The
figure of the mother becomes the predominant source of emotion –
fathers simply do not count as origins in this text (even the Meyrick
family is dominated by the mother). Gwendolen's mother is her only
emotional concern beyond herself. Deronda's mother has liberated
herself from the demands of race, love, motherhood, in order to follow
her stupendous career as an opera singer; she appals and compels
Deronda. She is punished but indomitable:

'Oh – the reasons of our actions!' said the Princess, with a ring of
something like sarcastic scorn. 'When you are as old as I am, it will
not seem so simple a question – "Why did you do this?" People talk
of their motives in a cut and dried way. Every woman is supposed
to have the same set of motives, or else to be a monster. I am not
a monster, but I have not felt exactly what other women feel – or
say they feel, for fear of being thought unlike others. When you
reproach me in your heart for sending you away from me, you
mean that I ought to say I felt about you as other women say they
feel about their children. I did *not* feel that'.[22]

Mothers are no longer Madonnas – Gwendolen avoids being either.
Her triumph is that of barrenness; she does not conceive an heir to
Grandcourt. Moreover, George Eliot herself has renounced the role
of mother towards her creations which had so powerfully drawn her
earlier in her career. George Eliot lurks now in the periphrases of the
text, no longer retaining for herself some space unblemished by the

confusion of her characters' consciousness. This is signalled particularly by the way in which the ending abuts the present of herself and her first readers, permitting no retrospect from a vantage-point of intervening years. That structure would settle and confirm a deterministic reading. Instead we are left – perhaps unsatisfactorily – with Mira and Deronda sailing off to the east to make a then seemingly impossible Zionist state (heredity triumphs over environment); while Gwendolen is left indeterminate, no longer emotionally and sexually dependent on Deronda, sustained by the outflaring of her own fear and need. Her future is not mapped for us: it is hard to imagine any activist outcome for Gwendolen, but this time the woman has not drowned. She is still there, not George Eliot's favourite kind of woman but permitted to survive that too – insistent, febrile, positive, undetermined. The eliding of the distance between writer and text and at the same time the opening up of gaps within the text perturb any sense of necessary sequence. At the same time the emphasis upon heredity as Daniel discovers his Jewishness suggests a contrary issue. It is too easy since Macherey to praise fissures simply for being there, for wrecking any pretence at wholeness, and in *Daniel Deronda* George Eliot certainly mourns the loss of cultural integrity rather than accepting it; the book strives structurally for a unity its perceptions will not fully permit. But in the image of Gwendolen, not quite wrecked, surviving into a future no one has charted for her, we glimpse a woman who has survived the business of sexual selection. Her image of herself is no longer simplified into a hierarchy of what is acceptable. Gwendolen has come to care for her own heterogeneity.

> Now is life very solid or very shifting? I am haunted by the two contradictions. This has gone on for ever; will last for ever; goes down to the bottom of the world – this moment I stand on. Also it is transitory, flying, diaphanous. I shall pass like a cloud on the waves. Perhaps it may be that though we change, one flying after another, so quick, so quick, yet we are somehow successive and continuous we human beings, and show the light through. But what is the light?[23]

Virginia Woolf's books reject plot. Plot insists on origins, sequence, consequences, discovery, exclusion, and closure. She reads the formulation of experience as being essentially social, and conforming to the particular rigid structure of English society. Plot gives primacy to our acted parts. 'She was convinced that society is man-made, that the chief occupations of men are the shedding of blood, the making of money, the giving of orders, and the wearing of uniforms, and that none of these occupations is admirable.'[24] This insistence on occupation and action she saw as part of a patriarchal ordering and it is an element in her quarrel with Arnold Bennett in 'Mr Bennett and Mrs Brown'. For her Bennett was an example of a masculine world of fixity and determination. His naturalistic novels emphasize the details of daily life and delineate that which is internal through a record of the external. She wanted, in contrast, to 'stand further back from life'. 'The psychological novelist has been prone to limit psychology to the psychology of personal intercourse. . . . We long for some more impersonal relationship. We long for ideas, for dreams, for imaginations, for poetry.'[25] She wants a novel that will 'give the relation of the mind to general ideas and its soliloquy in solitude . . . the outline rather than the detail'. She distrusted what was called 'reality'; she sought to 'insubstantise'.[26]

At the time that she began writing *The Waves* Virginia Woolf experienced a particularly intense dislike of what she called 'this appalling narrative business of the realist'.[27] All the usual elements of plot are discarded or made peripheral: Bernard's marrige and four children, Louis and Rhoda's affair, Louis's career in the city, the imperial theme of the raj in India. We do in a veiled and unclimactic way know of all these things, but the book sloughs off most of the complexities of social thriving and personal possession. The characters exist alongside each other, partaking of each other's imagery, meeting at intervals in situations which reveal a hieratic dignity in their long acquaintance. The book substitutes rhythm for plot. It makes no pretence at the busy inclusiveness of social or scientific determinism. Instead it surveys tides, waves, phases of human life, which have their own inescapable forms but which require – and this, I think, is crucial – no prognosis, no concealment, no fixing and polarization by the writer. In other works Virginia Woolf allowed genealogy the role of plot: *Night and Day*, *The Years*. She liked to select for our attention rhythms which are not purely human rhythms (the turn of tides, of night and day, a day). But common to all her novels is the quietistic recognition of the single life-span.

The eschewing of plot is an aspect of her feminism. The avoidance of narrative climax is a way of getting outside the fixing properties of event. The effect of recurrences in *The Waves* is a kind of stasis. Immobility becomes as important as evanescence, and as much a challenge to deterministic plot. Moments are incandescent but do not transform. Doing without transformation means that perceptions abide and are not cast into irreversible succession. The characteristics of style replace plot. Virginia Woolf described the effect of Proust's style on her own desire to write:

> Oh if I could write like that! I cry. And at the moment such is the astonishing vibration and saturation and intensification that he procures – there's something sexual in it – that I feel I *can* write like that, and seize my pen and then I *can't* write like that.[28]

'Saturation' is the word that Virginia Woolf used to describe what she desired to produce in *The Waves*, 'a saturated unchopped completeness'.[29] The author is all-penetrative because expressed through style, not plot. In this way the question of origins is suspended. The style with its heightened sense-perceptions creates arousal without climax.

Arnold Bennett had earlier seen an 'utter absence of feeling for form' as typically feminine. Writing of George Eliot in his *Journals* he comments:

> Her style, though not without shrewdness, is too rank to have any enduring vitality. People call it 'masculine'. Quite wrong! It is downright, aggressive, sometimes rude, but genuinely masculine, never. On the contrary it is transparently feminine – feminine in its lack of restraint, its wordiness, and the utter absence of feeling for form that characterises it.[30]

This confident attribution of male and female characteristics to style is still to be found at quite a simple level in criticism of Virginia Woolf and should make one wary of easy polarizations which reproduce embedded assumptions about male and female character. James Naremore, for example, in *The World without a Self* (1973) complains that in *The Waves*

> There are times when Virginia Woolf seems untrue to her characters, making them all speak with a peculiarly feminine sadness and wonder, as when Bernard the child says 'The air no longer rolls its long, unhappy, purple waves over us', or when he excitedly declares 'Let us take possession of our secret territory, which is lit by pendant currants like a candelabra.' In neither case does he sound much like a child, but more especially he does not sound like a boy.[31]

133

But *The Waves* shifts attention away from polarized forms of sexuality (it was originally conceived as a multiple autobiography of a woman) – *not*, I would suggest, into the kind of vigorous androgyny that Herbert Marder argues for in *Feminism and Art*, where the old oppositions are preserved in a new form of marriage. He comments in this style on a quotation from *A Room of One's Own*:

> For if Chloe likes Olivia and Mary Carmichael knows how to express it she will light a torch in that vast chamber where nobody has yet been. It is all half lights and profound shadows like those serpentine caves where one goes with a candle peering up and down. (pp.145–6)

> Here Virginia Woolf sketches the movement toward liberation, as far as it has gone: the personal freedom that makes it possible for Mary Carmichael to be an artist; the economic independence that enables her to make use of her freedom; the ability to see women in relation to each other; the struggle to find a new style appropriate to new subject matter; the opening of hitherto obscure regions of women's minds. Undoubtedly the illumination of the cavern, the increase in self-knowledge, would bring women one step closer to androgyny.[32]

Virginia Woolf works rather through a dislimning of the edges of identity, an acknowledgement of how much of our life is to do with primary perceptual experience: not humanistic, but tactile, auditory – she called *The Waves* an 'abstract ... eyeless book'[33] – in which the self is in undetermined relations with objects, surface, heat and cold. These depend, only fitfully, on memory; they do not depend upon a current social system, or upon modes of order created by society, nor, she suggests, are they exclusively based upon gender (Naremore imagines a peculiarly deprived kind of boy child who is incapable of sniffing the candelabra of currants).

In *The Waves* we can observe some of the qualities shared by feminist and avant-garde writing, such as Kristeva commented on in her remark about the dissolution of identities, even sexual identities. But this community of practice should not lead us to assume that their motives are identical. *The Pargiters* reveals how much Virginia Woolf felt herself fixed in historical time, in the conditions of her own generation, because of her need to work through language, which imposes current social forms. She tells her imagination:

I cannot make use of what you tell me – about women's bodies for instance – their passions – and so on, because the conventions are still very strong. If I were to overcome the conventions I should need the courage of a hero, and I am not a hero.

I doubt that a writer can be a hero. I doubt that a hero can be a writer.[34]

To that extent Virginia Woolf lives in a determined situation. She does not tell about women's bodies but in *The Waves*, having driven out authoritarian narrative, she uses women's special experience of time as one or the two underlying orders of the book. The book accepts the common human condition of growth and ageing, while relying for its particular order on recurrence and cycle. The menstrual relationship to time is implicit in the tides, the recurring waves, the stilled episodes of reunion and dissolution.

Gender, in so far as it determines, always reminds us of our 'unacted parts'.[35] In many of Virginia Woolf's books, lack and absence are crucial to the form of the experience – and this theme may well have psychosexual bearings on her self as woman. Such explanation is, I think, valid but not all-sufficient. For the theme clearly has also to do with her individual experiences of early bereavement and her generation's experience of the Great War. In her earlier novels closure is assembled about an absence: Jacob, Septimus, Mrs Ramsay. What *does* seem to me to be specific to her situation as a woman is her insistence that relations other than enacted ones – other even than binary ones, such as that between man and woman – are essential to full life.

George Eliot saw the range of immanent worlds about us, and their ever-extending relationships, as ways out of the thickening and fixing properties of determinism. She drives her characters through plot and, in *Daniel Deronda*, out beyond it. Virginia Woolf avoids the condensations of plot, which to her imply the inevitability of an established order. She moves beyond the male–female polarization, not into androgyny, but into a sense of movement, lapsing, of identity flowing out into the moment. Neither George Eliot nor Virginia Woolf escaped entirely the assumptions of determinism, but each of them drew upon 'her own inheritance – the difference of view, the difference of standard', to test the patriarchal implications of the idea and to explore territories beyond it, seeking 'more knowledge and more freedom'.[36]

NOTES

1 *The Works of George Eliot*, Cabinet Edition (Edinburgh and London, 1878–80), *Middlemarch*, vol. III, p. 464. All references to her novels are to this edition.

2 Virginia Woolf, 'George Eliot', in *The Common Reader* (London, 1925), p. 217; collected in *Collected Essays*, vol. I (London, 1966), pp. 196–204.

3 Charles Darwin, *The Descent of Man, and Selection in Relation to Sex*, 2 vols (London, 1871) vol. II, pp. 316–17.

4 *Middlemarch*, vol. I, pp. 2–3.

5 Darwin, op. cit., vol. II pp. 326, 329–30

6 Virginia Woolf, *The Pargiters*, ed. M.A. Leaska, (London, 1978), pp. xlii, xliii; speech of January 1931. The second passage is a deleted section.

7 Darwin, op. cit., vol. II, pp. 329, 337, 338.

8 *Daniel Deronda*, vol. I, p.144.

9 Virginia Woolf, *Moments of Being*, ed. Jeanne Schulkind (London, 1976), p. 79

10 *The George Eliot Letters*, ed. Gordon Haight, 7 vols (New Haven, Conn., 1954–6), vol. III, p. 227.

11 *The Mill on the Floss*, vol. I, p. 20. George Eliot's remark is recorded in an unpublished letter in Girton College Library.

12 ibid., vol. II, p. 395

13 *Middlemarch*, vol. I, p. 231.

14 'A sketch of the past', *Moments of Being*, p. 80.

15 Elaine Showalter, *A Literature of their Own: British Women Novelists from Brontë to Lessing* (Princeton, NJ, 1977), p. 291.

16 Julia Kristeva, *Polylogue* (Paris, 1977), pp. 517, 519, 520.

17 Michèle Montrelay, 'Inquiry into femininity', trans. Parveen Adams, *m/f*, 1 (1978), p. 92.

18 See Jacques Lacan, 'The subject and the other: alienation', in *The Four Fundamental Concepts of Psychoanalysis*, trans. Alan Sheridan (London, 1977).

19 'George Eliot', in *The Common Reader*, pp. 217–18.

20 'Mr Darwin's hypotheses', *Fortnightly Review*, n.s., 4 (November 1868), p. 494.

21 *Daniel Deronda*, vol. I, p. 3.

22 ibid., vol. III, p. 127.

23 Virginia Woolf, *A Writer's Diary* (London, 1953), p. 141 (4 January 1929).

24 E.M. Forster, Rede Lecture (Cambridge, 1942); quoted in *The Question of Things Happening: The Letters of Virginia Woolf*, ed. Nigel Nicolson, vol. II (London, 1976) p. xviii.

25 Virginia Woolf, 'The narrow bridge of art' (1927), in *Collected Essays*, vol. II (London, 1966), pp. 225, 226.

26 *A Writer's Diary*, p. 57 (19 June 1923).

27 ibid., p. 139 (28 November 1928).

28 *The Question of Things Happening*, vol. II, p. 525.

29 *A Writer's Diary*, p. 164 (30 December 1930).

30 *The Journals of Arnold Bennett*, compiled by Newman Flower (New York, 1932), pp. 5–6.

31 James Naremore, *The World without a Self* (New Haven, 1973), p. 159.
32 Herbert Marder, *Feminism and Art* (Chicago and London, 1968), p. 124.
33 *A Writer's Diary*, p. 137 (7 November 1928).
34 *The Pargiters*, p. xxxix.
35 Virginia Woolf, *Between the Acts* (London, 1941), p. 179.
36 'George Eliot', in *The Common Reader*, p. 218.

8

THE VICTORIANS IN VIRGINIA WOOLF: 1832–1941

Where did Victorian writing go? What happened to those piled sentences of Ruskin's, those Carylean metaphors, the lyrical grotesqueries of Dickens, aspirated for the speaking voice but lodged between covers? One answer is that they went into the writing of Virginia Woolf – and some very strange things happened to them there.

In May 1882 Adeline Virginia Stephen was born into what she later described as that 'complete model of Victorian society', the family of Leslie Stephen, editor of the *Cornhill Magazine* and of the *Dictionary of National Biography*, literary essayist, mountaineer, and Victorian man of letters and intellectual *par excellence*.[1] In that same year of 1882 (the last of his editorship of the *Cornhill*) there appeared, among articles on 'The sun as a perpetual machine' and 'The world's end', an anomymous piece on 'The decay of literature', which looked back to the great days of Dickens and Thackeray, Elizabeth Gaskell and Kingsley, failed even once to mention George Eliot, and bemoaned the decline in novelistic achievement of the years between 1850 and 1880. The writer does unbend a little after observing that realism does not suit the English genius:

We can only say in the vaguest way that in the mental as in the physical world there are periods of sudden blossoming, when the vital forces of nature are manifested in the production of exquisite flowers, after which it again passes into a latent stage. ... Perhaps the Shakespeare of the twentieth century is already learning the rudiments of infantile speech, and some of us may live to greet his appearance, and probably ... to lament the inferiority of the generation which accepts him.[2]

138

If the writer of that essay had any immediate family hopes it might have been of his son Thoby, then rising two and 'learning the rudiments of infantile speech'. As it turned out, the gender and the model are wrong (Shakespeare is not quite the fitting comparison). Like Dombey and Son, Stephen and Son (for Leslie Stephen was the writer) proved to be Stephen and Daughter after all.

Leslie Stephen, who was born in 1832, died in 1904, only just outliving the Victorian age. He did not live to see the emergence of Adeline Stephen as Virginia Woolf, who in November 1928 mused in her diary: '1928-1832. Father's birthday. He would have been 96, 96, yes, today; and could have been 96, like other people one has known: but mercifully was not. His life would have entirely ended mine. What would have happened? No writing, no books; – inconceivable.' But despite the gloom of that judgement she realizes in the next paragraph that her own writing has changed her relationship to her parents, freeing them as well as her. The burden of the parental is laid aside and she can respond to the previous generation anew, as contemporaries: 'I used to think of him and mother daily; but writing the *Lighthouse* laid them in my mind. And now he comes back sometimes, but differently. ... He comes back now more as a contemporary.'[3] This process of resistance, exorcizement, transformation, and a new levelling relationship expresses also Woolf's relations with Victorian culture and writing.

The Victorians are not simply represented (or re-presented) in her novels (and in her last novels *The Years* and *Between the Acts* they are so with peculiar intensity); the Victorians are also *in* Virginia Woolf. They are internalized, inseparable, as well as held at arm's length. They are mimicked with an art of parody so indebted to its material that it sometimes, as in *Orlando*, seems at a loss to measure the extent of its own subversion or acquiescence. Wrestling with the angel in the house is a more protracted struggle even than that of the biblical wrestling match of Joseph and the angel.[4] For this angel is indoors, inside the self, a maternal figure whose worsting and expulsion might prove to have an intolerable creative cost. In *The Pargiters* Virginia Woolf acknowledges that dilemma and distinguishes the woman writer from the hero.

Virginia Woolf grew up a Victorian. She was already a young adult before the twentieth century. One of the tropes of modernism is its insistence on its own novelty, its disconnection from the past. 'In 1910 human nature changed', as Virginia Woolf asserted. But that assertion should not mislead us: Woolf did not simply reject the Victorians and their concerns, or renounce them. Instead she persistingly rewrote them. Surviving our parents is a hard lesson to learn (parent-texts as well as parent-people), but essential if we are to survive at all. One way is to ignore them, another way is elegy, a third is to liberate them so that they become elements in a discourse and an experience which, bound in their historical moment, they could not have foreseen. Rewriting sustains and disperses, dispels, restores, and interrupts.[5] These observations are essential to my current enterprise of tracking Woolf's argument with the culture within which she grew, out of which she grew, and which she never quite grew out of.

Virginia Woolf grew up imbued with the literary culture of late-Victorian life, familiar with the major writers as books, acquaintance, and, in some cases, kin. But she was always peripheralized education-ally. She had the run of her father's library, supplemented by the books he brought home for her from the London Library, but she did not – unlike her brothers – go to school or university. She rightly and profoundly resented this exclusion. She did not take part in the history of the women's colleges. She was never a student at Girton or Newnham and took a wry look at them only in her middle age. She had no experience of institutions. The school scenes in *The Waves* are as distant from her own autobiographical experience as are the university scenes. Writing to Vita Sackville-West, Woolf suggests that she has missed therefore, not learning, but the slapstick of ordinary experience: 'But then think how I was brought up; mooning about alone among my father's books; never any chance to pick up all that goes on in schools – throwing balls; ragging; slang; vulgarity; scenes; jealousy.'[6]

In her essay on Elizabeth Barrett Browning, the summary that Woolf offers of Barrett Browning's early life has an undertow of self-reference, a suppressed congruity from which she must break free.

> Her mother died when she was a child; she read profusely and privately; her favourite brother was drowned; her health broke down; she had been immured by the tyranny of her father in almost conventual seclusion in a bedroom in Wimpole Street.[7]

Virginia Woolf's mother died when she was 12; her brother Thoby died of typhoid on a visit to Greece; her health repeatedly broke down; and, although the tyranny was of a different kind, any reader of Stephen's *Mausoleum Book* and of Virginia Woolf's own accounts will recognize the tyrannical tenderness of the husband–father. It is not surprising that the Barrett Browning letters Woolf chooses to quote include one where Elizabeth Barrett Browning complains that her upbringing has made her too inward, too inexperienced in human nature. One task that Virginia Woolf set herself was necessarily that of how to escape from the education described by Aurora Leigh, Barrett Browning's first-person woman poet. Aurora remarks that women's rapid insight and fine aptitude are approved:

> As long as they keep quiet by the fire
> And never say 'no' when the world says 'ay',
> For that is fatal, – their angelic reach
> Of virtue, chiefly used to sit and darn,
> And fatten household sinners, – their, in brief,
> Potential faculty in everything
> Of abdicating power in it.[8]

The description seems more apt, perhaps, to Julia Stephen, Virginia's mother, or to Mrs Ramsay (in *To the Lighthouse*), than to Virginia herself. But she is obliged to repeat the rebellion already described in *Aurora Leigh* in the 1850s and to pry apart that fatal compacting of 'potential', 'abdication', and 'power'. This she had to do in her writing. 'Power' is a word she very rarely uses in her own work. Instead she peripheralizes many of the imposing categorizations of narrative and renders frail and absurd those claims to authority which emanate from family or past literature.

In his severe obituary of Leslie Stephen for the *Cornhill*, Frederic Harrison, after setting Stephen alongside the mid-Victorian masters, ends by emphasizing his limitations: he wrote without much poetry, only of literature; he was really only interested in the eighteenth and nineteenth centuries; he had no awareness at all of the Middle Ages and he was incorrigibly English in his preferences – never wrote of Dante or Molière or Goethe or other great European writers.[9] Woolf explored many of the writers who lay outside her father's sympathies: she had a particular responsiveness to the incandescent intelligence of Elizabethan and seventeenth-century language; she read Dante 'in the place of honour' while her mind was still red-hot at the end of each day's work on *The Waves*; probably she too did not read Goethe, to judge by the nature of her allusions to him.[10] Isa, in *Between the Acts*, is haunted by the line from Racine's *Phèdre*: 'Vénus toute entière à sa proie attachée'. But Woolf did not eschew her father's pleasures, reading Sterne particularly with admiration. To them she added the roll, the rise, the carol, the creation (though Hopkins is a poet she only twice and passingly refers to, however closely her feeling for the 'thisness' of things runs to his). All this is to say that she had a more shifting and scintillating sense of the fugitive presences of literature in our experience than had her father. Yet she shared the fascination of her parents' generation with 'Englishness', even if the definition differs.

Despite her abhorrence of the imperialism and patriarchy of English society past and present – and particularly of their forms as she experienced them in late-Victorian England – she is yet attracted by the idea of English history and of England. She tries to find a distance from which it will be possible to observe what is unmarred by dis-agreeable opinions or out-of-date politics, to find a language and a rhythm by which to measure what persists without faltering in land and people.

From our present vantage-point, which emphasizes the invention of tradition and the fictionality of all celebrated pasts, this enterprise may seem as romantically unprincipled as any imperialist dream, but it is nevertheless one to which Woolf brought the instruments of linguistic analysis and recall in all their refinement. To find a linguistic rhythm by which to express England without false patriotism she must work through parody and pastiche, fracturing and conjuring the verbal traces of the past – as we see particularly in *To the Lighthouse, Orlando, Flush, The Pargiters, The Years,* and *Between the Acts.* She works too, through what is communal: architecture, clouds, cows, street scenes. She is appalled by permanence when it is the permanence of heavy objects or relationships. She is heartened by the permanence of shifting and fleeting manifestations which recur: the day passing; cows bellowing; clouds; the sound of voices and of feet brushing the pavement; and writing, which again and again lends itself to fresh reading.

Looking back on her own early family life she emphasized its seeming permanence and bruising enclosure. The house 'seemed tangled and matted with emotion. ... It seemed as if the house and the family which had lived in it, thrown together as they were by so many deaths, so many emotions, so many traditions, must endure for ever. And then suddenly in one night both vanished.'[11] Loss and freedom became hard to distinguish. Everyday life, whose familiarity makes it seem permanent, vanishes even fecklessly, the heavy furniture more fleeting than the residual forces of emotion. In another passage Woolf expresses her relations to Victorian society in terms which invoke the Gradgrinds and the horseriders in Dickens's *Hard Times*, where Mr Gradgrind comes upon his children, 'his own metallurgical Louisa' and 'his own mathematical Thomas' 'abasing' themselves to peep into the circus tent. Woolf writes:

> I felt as a tramp or a gypsy must feel who stands at the flap of the tent and sees the circus going on inside. Victorian society was in full swing. George was the acrobat who jumped through the hoops and Vanessa and I beheld the spectacle. We had good seats at the show, but we were not allowed to take part in it. We applauded, we obeyed – that was all.[12]

The circus has here become the central image for society, instead of representing an alternative world of amusement and skill opposed to the regulated workaday one. In this passage Virginia Woolf first figures herself as tramp or gypsy, but then – more prosaically – as bourgeois spectator: 'we had good seats'. The peeping Thomas and Louisa have been given good seats at the circus and required to admire its self-congratulatory and competitive antics. Sissie Jupe was a worker in the circus family, but the Stephen daughters were kept outside the ring. By a rearrangement of Dickensian hyperbole Woolf condenses the garish Grand Guignol of family and public life as circus. This impacting yields a comic image of Victorian society at its exercise.

Woolf's writing, indeed, everywhere suggests that hyperbole was the principal stylistic and psychological mode of Victorian experience, despite its dowdy surface. It was manifested in their hubristic desire to run the world in imperialism, in their uncontrolled procreativity, and in the besotted plenitude of their natural world:

> And just as the ivy and evergreen rioted in the damp earth outside, so did the same fertility show itself within. The life of the average woman was a succession of childbirths. She married at nineteen and had fifteen or eighteen children by the time she was thirty; for twins abounded. Thus the British Empire came into existence; and thus – for there is no stopping damp; it gets into the inkpots as it gets into the woodwork – sentences swelled, adjectives multiplied, lyrics became epics, and little trifles that had been essays a column long were now encyclopaedias in ten or twenty volumes.[13]

Like, one may say, the assembled volumes of Leslie Stephen's *Dictionary of National Biography*, the nation's memorial boast of its curious and manifold distinction.

With hyperbole goes promiscuity, so that a statue of Queen Victoria is transmogrified by a sunbeam into 'a conglomeration . . . of the most heterogeneous and ill-assorted objects, piled higgledy-piggledy in a vast mound . . . seemingly calculated to last for ever'. 'The incongruity of the objects, the association of the fully clothed and the partly draped, the garishness of the different colours and their plaid-like juxtapositions afflicted Orlando with the most profound dismay' (p. 209). Woolf's technique is to display the obverse of the Victorian ideal intellectual fiction of *synthesis*. As she demonstrates, synthesis more often founders as clutter than discovers true relations. Its intellectual acquisitiveness becomes indistinguishable from material greed.

Yet the medium for the opening of her satire on the Victorian age in *Orlando* is a version of Ruskin's prose: Ruskin both represents the idealistic mode of Victorian polymathism and the Victorian response to the particular. Of Ruskin's writing she said elsewhere: '*Modern Painters* takes our breath away. We find ourselves marvelling at the words, as if all the fountains of the English language had been set playing in the sunlight for our pleasure, but it seems scarcely fitting to ask what meaning they have for us.'[14] In *Orlando* she takes up Ruskin's late sad vision of 'the storm-cloud of the nineteenth century' and interpenetrates it with the language of chapter 26 of *Modern Painters*, 'Of modern landscape'. The most striking thing about modern landscapes, argues Ruskin, 'is their *cloudiness*'.

> Out of perfect light and motionless air, we find ourselves on a sudden brought under sombre skies, and into drifting wind; and, with fickle sunbeams flashing on our face, or utterly drenched with sweep of rain, we are reduced to track the changes of the shadows on the grass, or watch the rents of twilight through angry cloud. . . . The aspects of sunset and sunrise, with all their attendant phenomena of cloud and mist, are watchfully delineated; and in ordinary daylight landscape, the sky is considered of so much importance, that a principal mass of foliage, or a whole foreground, is unhesitatingly thrown into shade merely to bring out the form of a white cloud. So that, if a general and characteristic name were needed for modern landscape art, none better could be invented than 'the service of clouds'.[15]

To Ruskin 'the service of clouds' brings with it the loss of '*stability, definiteness*, and *luminousness*, we are expected to rejoice in darkness, and triumph in mutability'. Woolf opens her chapter thus:

> The great cloud which hung, not only over London, but over the whole of the British Isles on the first day of the nineteenth century stayed, or rather, did not stay, for it was buffeted about constantly by blustering gales, long enough to have extraordinary conse-quences upon those who lived beneath its shadow. A change seemed to have come over the climate of England. Rain fell frequently, but only in fitful gusts, which were no sooner over than they began again. The sun shone, of course, but it was so girt about with clouds and the air was so saturated with water, that its beams were discoloured and purples, oranges, and reds of a dull sort took the place of the more positive landscapes of the eighteenth century. (p. 205)

Woolf sympathetically appropriates Ruskin's analysis, but to his afflicted, creatively agitated description she adds a single term: damp. Whereas in Ruskin's account words like 'flashing', 'drenched', 'angry' suggest the drama of extremes, Woolf continues her description thus:

> But what was worse, damp began to make its way into every house – damp, which is the most insidious of all enemies . . . damp steals in while we sleep; damp is silent, imperceptible, ubiquitous. Damp swells the wood, furs the kettle, rusts the iron, rots the stone. So gradual is the process, that it is not until we pick up some chest of drawers, or coal scuttle, and the whole thing drops to pieces in our hands, that we suspect even that the disease is at work. (pp. 205–6)

In Woolf's comic version of Ruskin the transacting words are 'insi-dious', 'silent', 'imperceptible', 'gradual'. Instead of turmoil and dash, she expresses the dowdiness of swollen continuity which at last, in a new hyperbole, simply 'drops to pieces in our hands': the traditional phrase attributed by the middle classes to hapless servant-girls who have broken valuable objects. Here, the (absurd) explanation is given: damp. The lexical play is extreme: objects have lost all weight ('we pick up some chest of drawers, or coal scuttle') even while they are permeated with chill damp.

So the passage functions as pastiche: she brings out the repressed humdrum 'damp', to supplement and undermine the mythic aggran-dized account of Victorian weather in Ruskin, what he later calls, quoting Aristophanes, 'the coronation of the whirlwind'. But the passage functions also as collusion and celebration. Ruskin attracts her as the writerly medium for expressing the Victorian age perhaps because of his antagonistic relationship to the powers of his society, as well as, I think, his capacity for self-contradiction. She opens her essay on Ruskin by enquiring, 'What did our fathers in the nineteenth century do to deserve so much scolding?', and she observes the teacherly tone which so often takes over from poet or prophet in Carlyle and Ruskin. But another reason for her responsiveness to Ruskin is his countervailing immersion in the specific: his joyous zeal in particularizing gives life to his writing in the modernist era, particularly to Virginia Woolf in her search for the 'moment', both evanescent and fully known. Ruskin's hyperaesthesia matched Woolf's own: his helpless openness to the sensory world alternated with a severe and minatory closing of the self against the follies and injustices of the age. He is askance from his generation, even while we take him as typifying much in Victorian literature and society. The fountainous and the crabbed alternated in his writing, often within a sentence.

Perhaps, too, Virginia Woolf appreciated the androgynous in Ruskin. He was never merely a patriarchal figure, though his fatal over-identification with women had results as disastrous to his happiness as his ignorant idealizing of them. It will be remembered that the Victorian husband of Orlando, Shelmerdine, is 'really' a woman, to the degree that she is 'really' a man. Seeking the woman's sentence, as Woolf did, she might have glimpsed it among the Victorians in the agglomerative, impressionistic, ranging movement of Ruskin's sentences. In her rewriting of that sentence she interrupted its hyperbolic drive, scissored its afflatus, and yet, as in *The Waves*, swam with its tide. His emphasis on change and sameness in his description of waves, and his metaphors, certainly accord with Woolf's project in *The Waves*:

> Most people think of waves as rising and falling. But if they look at the sea carefully, they will perceive that the waves do not rise and fall. They change. Change both place and form, but they do not fall; one wave goes on, and on, and still on; now lower, now higher, now tossing its mane like a horse, now building itself together like a wall, now shaking, now steady, but still the same wave till at last it seems struck by something; changes, one knows not how, becomes another wave.[16]

Fortunately, in the whimsical good sense of the unconscious, fathers can be mothers, and so in looking back through our mothers, as she says women must do, Ruskin may be among them. Perry Meisel, in *The Absent Father*, has made a case for Pater as her obliterated kin and I have argued the case for Darwin in the next essay.[17] There is no contradiction in such multiplicity. In literary relationships parents are not restricted to two, nor need their gender be stable. Moreover, they may be most valuable when they come back as contemporaries. Despite his moralism, Ruskin represents a world alive to Woolf, opposed to that of Arnold – a world of acute sensation, of passionate involvement with the anonymous life of unrecorded people: as she puts it, 'an eagerness about everything in the world'. His effects can sometimes even be seen, perhaps, in that condescension, the opening of *The Years* (though even here it is difficult to mark how far the plurals are parodic). Equally, though, he provides an example of 'impassioned prose' where there is nothing 'unfused, unwrought, incongruous, and casting ridicule upon the rest'. Seeking 'saturation' in her own writing in *The Waves*, she finds it in Ruskin, as she could find also a description of the action of waves which answers to her own need for the *permanently changing*, the untransformed.

The hyperbole in Ruskin's writing both amuses and empowers her; his feeling for detail lies alongside her own, yet it is distanced from hers by his nostalgic preference for the discrete and stable particularity of medieval observation, where acorns, fishes, faces, each are given their full record in the picture. Though this is Ruskin's declared preference, Woolf's writing has learnt more from the shifty evanescence of detail in Ruskin's prose, even while he seeks to analyse in fullest spectrum all the changes of colour and to list their sequences.

Ruskin's struggle to record and value 'life' though language, to render the visual world through the symbolism of letters, offered Woolf also a displaced understanding, a place from which to assess her own project. It would be a mistake to read the figure of Orlando as a self-portrait. Orlando is her hero-ine, not herself. Orlando is close to Vita Sackville-West and participates in the swashbuckling inertia of the landed classes who survive, not greatly changed by historical forces or even by simple onward movement of time. Virginia Woolf, on the other hand, is the writer whose hyperaesthesia forces her close into the welter of circumstance, and who controls that closeness by appropriating and recasting writing of the past as pastiche and celebration. In *Orlando*, in particular, her writing of others' writing is audacious. She can clutch, jettison, repossess those sombre, turgid sentences of the Victorians. The panache of *Orlando* helps her to break out of those 'seclusions' which she shares with Elizabeth Barrett Browning and which result, according to her description of Barrett Browning, in another form of hyperaesthetic hyperbole:

> The tap of ivy on the pane became the thrash of trees in a gale. Every sound was enlarged, every incident exaggerated, for the silence of the sick-room was profound and the monotony of Wimpole Street was intense. .... Ordinary daylight, current gossip, the usual traffic of human beings left her exhausted, ecstatic, and dazzled into a state where she saw so much and felt so much that she did not altogether know what she felt or what she saw.[18]

This reading of Elizabeth Barrett Browning seems self-admonitory; it certainly does not pay sufficient attention to the wit of *Aurora Leigh*. It is by means of wit that Barrett Browning channelled heightened observation into often caustic poetry, as in her account of the over-interpretative scrutiny of Aurora's slightest acts as the household waits upon the outcome of her rejection of Romney. The humour both of Barrett Browning and of Woolf becomes much more marked when read aloud. On the page the eye glides without incongruity from level to level of discourse. Read aloud, the same passage registers the awkwardness of a syntax which seeks to yoke unlike, the collusive asides muttered within the public sentence. It is in the light of her endangering kinship with Barrett Browning (the sensibility of the sick-room, the writer's recalcitrance too quick consumed, the unstaunched lyric effusion) that we should measure also Woolf's admiration for this poet who was a woman, and thereby trod across the categories of expectation, and who had for company her own creation, 'Aurora Leigh', a woman poet, and Flush, a spaniel. Virginia Woolf's choice of a dog as her second subject for biography, after the man/woman of *Orlando*, and before Roger Fry, has been a source of puzzlement, not to say embarrassment, to many of her professional readers.

In *Flush* Woolf finds a new means of measuring and limiting Victorian hyperaesthesia and hyperbole. Flush's doggyness means that the early Victorian age is experienced through different senses, its description made strange through hearing, touch, but particularly through smells. Woolf relishes the new configurations which emerge from the Browning letters when the encounters they record are re-perceived as a racy mixture of coarse and delicate textures yielding smells, scents, stench, odours. She brings out playfully the censored version of the past we usually accept as true by offering us supplementarily a smell repertoire. It is impossible, this method paradoxically suggests, to regain the physical welter of life. Even the subtle naming of smells cannot communicate their pungency:

> Mixing with the smell of food were further smells – smells of cedarwood and sandalwood and mahogany; scents of male bodies and female bodies; of men servants and maid servants; of coats and trousers; of crinolines and mantles; of curtains of tapestry, of curtains of plush; of coal dust and fog; of wine and cigars. Each room as he passed it – dining-room, drawing-room, library, bedroom – wafted out its own contribution to the general stew.[19]

The bourgeois world stinks and so does the world of the poor.

Flush, like Elizabeth Barrett, like Adeline Virginia Stephen, is a prisoner always on the edge of escape in Victorian bourgeois society. When he is stolen and his mistress goes to Whitechapel to rescue him, she sees for the first time the world of the poor:

> They were in a world where cows were herded under bedroom floors, where whole families sleep in rooms with broken windows; in a world where water is turned on only twice a week, in a world where vice and poverty breed vice and poverty. . . . They had come to a region unknown to respectable cab-drivers. . . . Here lived a woman like herself; while she lay on her sofa, reading, writing, they lived thus.

The next sentence reads: 'But the cab was now trundling along between four-storeyed houses again' (p. 89). This episode alone is shown through the eyes of Miss Barrett, rather than those of Flush, as though Woolf needed to move outside the arch device of the animal observer (whose subversiveness is limited by its quaintness) and to observe human chagrin more directly, though still through that securing and mocking device of the carriage-window within which the reader trundles safely though the dangers of Victorian London.

It would probably be too much to claim on Woolf's behalf any specific project in *Flush* of socially disquieting her reader about conditions still current in England. Rather, this small and lightly learned work suggests the fictionality of our imagined Victorian England, even by its use of documents and known personages. The spaniel's nose and eyes and ears yield us intimacies with the sensory material of that past world, but it remains fictional, irrecoverable. In her essay on 'Geraldine and Jane' (Geraldine Jewsbury and Jane Carlyle) Woolf presents a poignant appreciation of the impossibility of knowing other people fully. Knowing them across time in letters sometimes gives the illusion of full intimacy, but she ends by quoting Geraldine Jewsbury:

> Oh, my dear (she wrote to Mrs Carlyle), if you and I are drowned, or die, what would become of us if any superior person were to go and write our 'life and errors'? What a precious mess a 'truthful person' would go and make of us, and how very different to what we really are or were![20]

Virginia Woolf's method in her quasi-biographies is to suggest that we can know the past and its people best, not through opinions, but through textures, sounds, smells, sight (though rarely taste), through bodily impersonation – a method which, at the same time, shows up the absurd though necessary mismatch between writing and being. Her methods mock the ponderously achieved apparatus of the 'life and opinions' biography, and the assumption that the individual's success is the criterion for making record worthwhile, which is harboured by much Victorian biography.

Woolf enjoyed reading biography and, especially, autobiography. Her own method mocked the hagiographic style of many Victorian 'lives and letters', the summary accounting of the *Dictionary of National Biography*. She repudiated the insistence on action and event as the biographer's main resource. But she abjured equally the demystifying iconoclasm of Lytton Strachey. She liked delicately to bring to the surface mislaid lives, particularly those of women, excluded from historical record.

In her essay 'I am Christina Rossetti' she remarks on the fascination of reading biographies:

> Here is the past and all its inhabitants miraculously sealed as in a magic tank; all we have to do is to look and listen and to listen and to look and soon the little figures – for they are rather under life size – will begin to move and to speak, and as they move we shall arrange them in all sorts of patterns of which they were ignorant, for they thought when they were alive that they could go where they liked.[21]

The image of the controlling biogapher and the knowing reader surveying the belittled figures of the past 'sealed as in a magic tank' seems aimed at Lytton Strachey and his accounts of Victorian figures. Strachey, indeed, had remarked in a letter to Maynard Keynes in 1906 that the Victorian age was one in which people 'were enclosed in glass'. He adds: 'it's damned difficult to copulate through a glass case'.[22] Woolf suggests that the glass is a product of the biographer's distance and it is he, not his subjects, who finds it difficult to copulate. (Strachey's formulation revealingly suggests his balked desire sexually to invade his subjects.) In Woolf's judgement the biographer, like the realist novelist, claims too much authority – an authority which stifles their awareness of the spontaneity and aimlessness of life: 'as they move we shall arrange them in all sorts of patterns'. The joke at Strachey's expense grew sad when he died while she was in the midst of writing *Flush*, in which she demonstrates how to release the Victorians from the stodginess of self-approval without simply transferring that self-approval into modernist knowingness.

In 1929, in 'Women and fiction', she remarks that future women writers will 'be less absorbed in facts. ... They will look beyond the personal and political relationships to the wider questions which the poet tries to solve – of our destiny and the meaning of life.'[23] Woolf is seeking an impersonality which will not be alienation and a permanence which will not be stasis. Frederic Harrison, in his obituary of Leslie Stephen, singled out for praise Stephen's essay 'Sunset on Mont Blanc' (1873). The essay opens thus: 'Does not science teach us more and more emphatically that nothing which is natural can be alien to us who are part of Nature? Where does Mont Blanc end, where do I begin?'[24] This is certainly a grandiose and emphatic way of presenting the problem of the frontiers of identity. But put in less massive, less hyperbolic style it is a question that Woolf's writing, like that of her father, constantly poses. And Victorian scientific writing presented her, as much as him, with a language in which to muse upon such issues.

In *Mrs Dalloway* Peter meditates with whimsical recollection on Clarissa's possible thoughts, 'possibly she said to herself, as we are a doomed race, chained to a sinking ship (her favourite reading as a girl was Huxley and Tyndall, and they were fond of these nautical metaphors)'.[25] Let us take up the hint that this passage's allusion offers us and consider the reading that Woolf must herself have had in her background to make the point here. The problem of 'where Mont Blanc ends and I begin' was presented by Huxley in a way which seems much closer than Stephen's formulation to Virginia Woolf's language, with its rapid shifts of scale and perturbation between metaphor and substance. Huxley is arguing, against appearance, for 'community of faculty' between living organisms quite unlike in complexity and scale: between 'the brightly-coloured lichen' and the painter and botanist.

> Again, think of the microscope fungus – a mere infinitesimal ovoid particle, which finds space and duration enough to multiply into countless millions in the body of a living fly; and then of the wealth of foliage, the luxuriance of flower and fruit, which lies between this bald sketch of a plant and the giant pine of California, towering to the dimensions of a cathedral spire, or the Indian fig, which covers acres with its profound shadow, and endures while nations and empires come and go around its vast circumference. Or, turning to the other half of the world of life, picture to yourselves the great Finner whale, hugest of beasts that live, or have lived, disporting his eighty or ninety feet of bone, muscle, and blubber, with easy roll, among waves in which the stoutest ship that ever left dockyard would flounder hopelessly; and contrast him with the invisible animalcules – mere gelatinous specks, multitudes of which could, in fact, dance upon the point of a needle with the same ease as the angels of the Schoolmen could, in imagination.[26]

These alternations imply unity by proposing only diversities: 'what is there in common between the dense and resisting mass of the oak, or the strong fabric of the tortoise, and those broad disks of glassy jelly which may be seen pulsating through the waters of a calm sea, but which drain away to mere films in the hand which raises them out of their element?' The word 'pulsating', set with faintly shocking energy between words indicating stability and immovability ('disks', 'glassy', 'calm'), is typical of the imaginative allure of Huxley's style which here finds its point of intervention in the tactile: the hand enters the water and changes pulsating life to 'mere films'. The fibrous connectedness of bodily life and physical world, the recognition of other forms as our 'unacted parts', which inform this and other Huxley passages, may be compared to the language of self-discovery in the childhood section of *The Waves*: 'My body is a stalk'. Rhoda rocks her petals as boats in a basin:

On we sail alone. That is my ship. It sails into icy caverns where the sea-bear barks and stalactites swing green chains. The waves rise; the crests curl; look at the lights on the mastheads. They have scattered, they have foundered, all except my ship which mounts the wave.[27]

The 1927 commentary in *Orlando* ponders with some element of pastiche of the earnest enquiring Victorians:

even now (the first of November 1927) we know not why we go upstairs, or why we come down again, our most daily movements are like the passage of a ship on an unknown sea, and the sailors at the mast-head ask, pointing their glasses to the horizon: 'Is there land or is there none?'

Froude in his life of Carlyle describes the Victorian age as one with 'the compasses all awry and nothing left to steer by but the stars'.[28] 'A doomed race, chained to a sinking ship': Clarissa's supposed images of empire and of degeneration register the darkest thoughts of the Victorians about themselves – and of Virginia Woolf's quarrel with them. At the heart of that quarrel was her rejection of their masculinism, their Mont Blanc self-image.

But within Victorian scientific writing was to be found release from such glacial impersonality. It is signalled in that other favoured name in *Mrs Dalloway*: John Tyndall. Tyndall's principal scientific work was on radiant heat, and he wrote at large concerning the 'use of the imagination in science', not only in the essay of that title but in his lectures on light, on heat, and on sound. Waves compose the universe and are endlessly in motion, as light-waves, heat-waves, water-waves, sound-waves.

Darkness might then be defined as ether at rest; light as ether in motion. But in reality the ether is never at rest, for in the absence of light-waves we have heat-waves always speeding through it. In the spaces of the universe both classes of undulations incessantly commingle. Here the waves issuing from uncounted centres cross, coincide, oppose, and pass through each other, without confusion or ultimate extinction. ... Its waves mingle in space without disorder, each being endowed with an individuality as indestructible as if it alone had disturbed the universal repose.[29]

In such a theory individuality is indestructible, but part of an endlessly fleeting pattern of coincidental crossing of waves. Interpretation rather than interaction is emphasized, and motion and stasis are hard to distinguish. The individual particles remain, the form changes. As Tyndall wrote in *On Light* of wave-motion: 'The propagation of a wave is the propagation of a *form*, and not the transference of the substance which constitutes the wave.'[30] Thus we have simultaneously form and dissolution, onward motion and vertical rocking. The parallels with the community of life-histories in the *The Waves* are striking. The passage is worth quoting in full:

> The central difficulty of the subject was, to distinguish between the motion of the wave itself, and the motion of the particles which at any moment constitute the wave. Stand upon the sea-shore and observe the advancing rollers before they are distorted by the friction of the bottom. Every wave has a back and front, and, if you clearly seize the image of the moving wave, you will see that every particle of water along the front of the wave is in the act of rising, while every particle along its back is in the act of sinking. The particles in front reach in succession the crest of the wave, and as soon as the crest is passed they begin to fall. They then reach the furrow or sinus of the wave, and can sink no further. Immediately afterwards they become the front of the succeeding wave, rise again until they reach the crest, and then sink as before. Thus, while the waves pass onward horizontally, the individual particles are simply lifted up and down vertically. Observe a sea-fowl, or, if you are a swimmer, abandon yourself to the action of the waves; you are not carried forward, but simply rocked up and down. The propagation of a wave is the propagation of a form, and not the transference of the substance which constitutes the wave.

Tyndall, too, it was who in 'The use of the imagination in science' brought to public knowledge that the blue of the sky was distance, not colour; and this assertion of his provoked considerable hostility in the 1870s. We know that the Tyndalls were friends of the Stephens. More important, Tyndall's exercise of the imagination in the oceans of the universe continued to have meaning for Woolf through to the end of her writing life. Near the beginning of *Between the Acts* she describes the 'blue that has escaped registration' in words close to those of Tyndall.[31]

When we consider Virginia Woolf's relations to the Victorians we scant their meaning if we fail to recognize how widely imaginative was her continuous reading and her rewriting, how broad a knowledge she drew on. Victorian physics may have come more strongly to her mind again in the 1930s because of the intervention of Einstein's theories, which fascinated her, and her reading of Eddington and Jeans. I have discussed that probability elsewhere. The Victorian reading bases of her imagination were not simply expunged, outdated by modernist writing and science. They were, as probably, reawakened by such interventions.[32]

In *Between the Acts* Victorian England re-emerges as a not quite dislodged present, no longer represented, as in *The Years*, as past family and national history. Instead, *Between the Acts* is preoccupied with synchrony as a new form (perhaps the only feasible remaining form) for permanence. When she wrote this work Woolf was nearing 60 years old, closer in age to the old people in the book than the young. Isa looks 'at Mrs Swithin as if she had been a dinosaur or a very diminutive mammoth. Extinct she must be, since she had lived in the reign of Queen Victoria.'[33] As had Virginia Stephen.

In *Between the Acts* she shows the whole community of England poised, only half aware, on the brink of national disaster (it is an afternoon of mid-June 1939). In the village pageant the past is summoned up, in the form of caricature, celebration, and reminiscence, 'Home' and ''Ome' epitomize Victorian expansion and repression together.

> BUDGE. . . . Home, gentlemen; home, ladies, it's time to pack up and go home. Don't I see the fire (he pointed: one window blazed red) blazing ever higher? In kitchen; and nursery; drawing-room and library? That's the fire of 'Ome. And see! Our Jane has brought the tea. Now children where's the toys? Mama, your knitting, quick. For here (he swept his truncheon at Cobbet of Cobbs Corner) comes the bread-winner, home from the city, home from the counter, home from the shop. 'Mama, a cup o' tea.' 'Children, gather round my knee. I will read aloud. Which shall it be? Sinbad the sailor? Or some simple tale from the Scriptures? And show you the pictures? What none of 'em? Then out with the bricks.' (pp. 200–1)

Budge, the constable, guards 'respectability', 'prosperity', 'the purity of Victoria's land'. But it is 'going home': giving way like an old garment. Mrs Lynn Jones, watching the representation of Victorian family life, protests inwardly against the parody, but muses:

> Was there, she mused, ... something – not impure, that wasn't the word – but perhaps 'unhygienic' about the home? Like a bit of meat gone sour, with whiskers, as the servants called it? Or why had it perished? (p. 202)

Does the past simply 'go off', like a piece of meat, too closely connected to appetite to endure? Was the Victorian home particularly corruptible? Woolf here moves in on our irremediable confusions between language and body. She separates out for attention the word 'unhygienic', itself a Victorian coinage and crucial to the anxieties of that culture. So 'perished' exhibits both the sense of irremediable individual death and of technical material decay which operate within different linguistic registers ('We perish each alone', we recollect, but rubber perishes.)

The old imperialist Bart and the Christian lady Mrs Swithin, by virtue of old age, live in a shifting time in which prehistory, the Victorian age, and the present are all in synchrony, but as 'orts, scraps, and fragments'. Woolf places all her people this time in a possible final moment (as she wrote the book the bombers moved overhead and the boats set out for their rescue mission to Dunkirk just across the water). Budge's gesture towards Pointz Hall has a double meaning: 'Don't I see the fire (he pointed: one window blazed red) blazing ever higher?'

It is sunset, the war is about to begin. She shows a group who seem to go back uninterrupted to prehistory, but the constant references to the History of Civilization and the dinosaurs remind us, lightly, that civilizations end and the dinosaurs are no more.

She changes the image of 'orts, scraps, and fragments' from its signification in *Troilus and Cressida* as the greasy remains of a meal, into an archaeological image of vestiges, shards. The scraps of the communal and personal past are recuperable only *as* gossip and pastiche, a flotsam of significant fragments. The fragments, significantly, never collapse again into 'synthesis', that Victorian ideal of mind and writing. She jostles Victorian language into new patterns, establishing her separation from them. And that makes it possible for her to acknowledge them as kin.

NOTES

1 For discussion of Woolf's Victorian upbringing, see Noel Annan, *Leslie Stephen: The Godless Victorian* (London: Weidenfeld & Nicolson, 1984), and Phyllis Rose, *Woman of Letters: A Life of Virginia Woolf* (Oxford: Oxford University Press, 1978). Woolf was called Adeline after her mother's sister, Adeline Vaughan, who died the year before Virginia's birth: see Leslie Stephen, *The Mausoleum Book*, ed. A. Bell (Oxford: Clarendon Press, 1977), pp. 59, 66–70. 1832 is the year of Stephen's birth, 1941 of Woolf's death.

2 *Cornhill Magazine*, XLV (1882), pp. 585–93, 481–90; XLVI (1882), pp. 602–12 (quotation from pp. 611–12).

3 *The Diary of Virginia Woolf*, ed. Anne Olivier Bell (London: Hogarth Press, 1980), vol. III, p. 208.

4 Woolf uses Coventry Patmore's title, *The Angel in the House*, for her own oppositional purposes. See *The Death of the Moth* (London: Hogarth Press, 1942), pp. 150–1, where a close relation between her mother and the angel is suggested.

5 Gillian Beer, 'Virginia Woolf and prehistory', reproduced in this volume.

6 Quoted in Annan, op. cit., p. 119.

7 Virginia Woolf, *Collected Essays* (London: Hogarth Press, 1966), vol. I, pp. 212–13.

8 Elizabeth Barrett Browning, *Aurora Leigh* (London, 1857), book I, l. 426.

9 Frederic Harrison, in the *Cornhill Magazine*, XVI (n.s.) (1904) pp. 432–43.

10 *The Diary of Virginia Woolf* (1982), vol. IV, p. 5; *Virginia Woolf's Reading Notebooks*, ed. Brenda Silver (Princeton, NJ: Princeton University Press, 1983) LI, p. 243, and LVIII, pp. 255–73.

11 Virginia Woolf, *Moments of Being: Unpublished Autobiographical Writings*, ed. Jeanne Schulkind (Brighton: Sussex University Press, 1976), p. 161; see also 'Since the war', in *A Haunted House and other Short Stories* (London: Hogarth Press, 1943), p. 44, where she remarks that it was 'shocking and wonderful to discover' that these 'real things, Sunday luncheons, Sunday walks, country houses, and tablecloths, were not entirely real, were indeed half phantoms'.

12 Virginia Woolf, 'A sketch of the past', in *Moments of Being*, p. 132.

13 Virginia Woolf, *Orlando* (London: Hogarth Press, 1928), p. 207. Further page references to this edition are included in the text.

14 *Collected Essays*, vol. I, p. 206.

15 John Ruskin, *Modern Painters* (New York, 1881), vol. III, containing part IV, 'Of many things', pp. 248–9.

16 ibid., vol. III, part IV, p. 161.

17 Perry Meisel, *The Absent Father: Virginia Woolf and Walter Pater* (New Haven, Conn., and London: Yale University Press, 1980); Beer, 'Virginia Woolf and pre-history'.

18 *Collected Essays*, vol. I, p. 214.

19 Virginia Woolf, *Flush: A Biography* (London: Hogarth Press, 1940), p. 19. Further page references are included in the text. Woolf's most rumbustious

representation of chosen Victorians is *Freshwater: A Comedy* (London: Hogarth Press, 1976).

20 *Collected Essays*, vol. IV, p. 39.

21 *Collected Essays*, vol. IV, p. 54.

22 Quoted in Michael Holroyd, *Lytton Strachey: A Biography* (London: Heinemann, 1970), p. 312.

23 Virginia Woolf, 'Women and fiction', in *Granite and Rainbow* (London: Hogarth Press, 1958), p. 83.

24 Federic Harrison, *Cornhill Magazine*.

25 Virginia Woolf, *Mrs Dalloway* (London: Hogarth Press, 1925), p. 88.

26 Thomas Henry Huxley, 'On the physical basis of life', *Lay Sermons, Addresses and Reviews* (London, 1870), pp. 104–27 (quotation from pp. 105–6). Huxley's volume is dedicated to John Tyndall.

27 Virginia Woolf, *The Waves* (London: Hogarth Press, 1931), p. 8.

28 James A. Froude, *Thomas Carlyle: A History of his Life in London, 1834–1881* (London, 1884), vol. I, pp. 289–91.

29 John Tyndall, *On Radiation* (London, 1865), pp. 9–10.

30 John Tyndall, *Six Lectures on Light* (London, 1873), p. 53.

31 See, for example, 'The scientific use of the imagination', in John Tyndall, *Use and Limit of the Imagination in Science* (London, 1870), p. 26, and the responses collected in that volume, for example, *The Times*, 19 September 1870.

32 For a rather general discussion of the possible effects of Woolf's reading in twentieth-century popular physics, see Alan J. Friedman and Carol C. Donley, *Einstein as Myth and Muse* (Cambridge: Cambridge University Press, 1985).

33 Virginia Woolf, *Between the Acts* (London: Hogarth Press, 1941), p. 203. Further page references are included in the text.

9

VIRGINIA WOOLF
AND PREHISTORY

I

The primeval and the prehistoric have powerfully fascinated many twentieth-century writers, notably Conrad and Eliot. The idea of origins and the idea of development are problematically connected in that of prehistory. And in the twentieth century the unconscious has often been presented in the guise of the primeval. These associations have been engendered by the most powerful new metaphor of the past 150 years. The development of the individual organism has always been a rich resource for metaphor; but evolutionary theory and, in particular, Darwin's writing, suggested that species also developed and changed. The analogy between ontogeny (individual development) and phylogeny (species development) has proved to be the most productive, dangerous, and compelling of creative thoughts for our culture, manifesting itself not only in biology, but also in psychology, race theory, humanism, and in the homage of our assumptions about the developmental pattern of history.

What were the particular difficulties raised for Virginia Woolf by the idea of prehistory, and what particular new meanings did she make from it?

The problem of what is truly 'natural and eternal' and what is susceptible to change is one difficulty that expresses itself in Virginia Woolf's work. Social and historical factors claim for themselves 'natural' and 'eternal' authority; social determinism claims to be biological determinism. A wry footnote to *Three Guineas* shows Virginia Woolf tussling with the problem of the imputed permanent characteristics of man and woman and the possibility of change:

The nature of manhood and the nature of womanhood are frequently defined by both Italian and German dictators. Both repeatedly insist that it is the nature of man and indeed the essence of
manhood to fight. . . . Both repeatedly insist that it is the nature of
womanhood to heal the wounds of the fighter. Nevertheless a very
strong movement is on foot towards emancipating man from the
old 'natural and eternal law' that man is essentially a fighter.
. . . Professor Huxley, however, warns us that 'any considerable
alteration of the hereditary constitution is an affair of millennia,
not of decades.' On the other hand, as science also assures us that
our life on earth is 'an affair of millennia, not of decades', some
alteration in the hereditary constitution may be worth attempting.[1]

So the nature/nurture question is one associated issue, here alleviated
by the immense span of time that science promises to humankind in
which to attempt 'alteration in the hereditary constitution'.

But there are other ways, more diffused, expressed more as form,
less as argument, in which the primeval and problems of development
move through her writing. How does she rewrite that major figure in
her own upbringing, her own 'development', Charles Darwin?

Before going further we need to consider her attitudes to 'history'
and to discriminate some meanings of prehistory. Is prehistory and
the primeval in her work simply part of her strong interest in history?
In the last entry recorded in *A Writer's Diary* Virginia Woolf writes:

No: I need no introspection. I mark Henry James' sentence: observe
perpetually. Observe the oncome of age. Observe greed. Observe
my own despondency. . . . Suppose I bought a ticket at the Museum;
biked in daily and read history. Suppose I selected one dominant
figure in every age and wrote round and about. Occupation is
essential.[2]

She didn't do it, of course. Instead she drowned. History here for
Virginia Woolf is a lifeline to pluck her out of the deep waters of
introspection.

'History', almost in a textbook sense, is a recurrent theme in her
work. *Orlando* jubilantly fantasizes the possibility of the self surviving
history, looking different, gendered differently, but not much changed
from century to century. *A Room of One's Own* creates a counter-history
in the image of Shakespeare's sister, and *Night and Day* and *The Years*
follow those long contours of family saga which allow the writer to

160

record changes in how it felt to be alive. History in her writing is a matter of textures (horse-hair or velvet), changing light (flambeaux or gas-light), not of events or 'dominant figures of the age'. In 'A sketch of the past' she writes of the problems of memoir or biography:

> Consider what immense forces society brings to play upon each of us, how that society changes from decade to decade; and also from class to class; well, if we cannot analyse these invisible presences, we know very little of the subject of the memoir; and again how futile life-writing becomes. I see myself as a fish in a stream; deflected; held in place; but cannot describe the stream.[3]

Such analysis, such discriminations, are the business of the historian. But *her* representations of history have something of the picture-book in them, figures held in superb but picturesque moments – a series of tableaux, a pageant. And that, of course, is the image she turns to in her last novel, *Between the Acts*.

> From behind the bushes issued Queen Elizabeth – Eliza Clark, licensed to sell tobacco. Could she be Mrs Clark of the village shop? She was splendidly made up. Her head, pearl-hung, rose from a vast ruff. Shiny satins draped her. Sixpenny brooches glared like cats' eyes and tigers' eyes; pearls looked down; her cape was made in cloth of silver – in fact swabs used to scour saucepans. She looked the age in person. ... *For a moment she stood there, eminent, dominant, on the soap box with the blue and sailing clouds behind her.*[4]

History is stationary, inhabited by replaceable figures whose individuality is less than their community with other lives lived already 'with the blue and sailing clouds behind'. This paradox is at the heart of her representaion of history: with all her acute sense of the shifts in material and intellectual circumstances, she figures human beings as unchanging, standing in for each other across the centuries. This sense of the inertness of the human condition means that history for her is playful, a spume of language. In *Between the Acts* it seems to Isa that the three great words are Love, Hate, Peace. And nothing else matters. The strangeness of the past is all on the surface. At base, it is familiar.

Playfully and with great intensity, such problems create the fabric of thought and association in *Between the Acts*. Mrs Lynn Jones wonders what happened to the home of her youth.

> Change had to come, she said to herself, or there'd have been yards and yards of Papa's beard, of Mama's knitting. ... What she meant

was, change had to come, unless things were perfect; in which case she supposed they resisted Time. Heaven was changeless.

'Were they like that?' Isa asked abruptly. She looked at Mrs Swithin as if she had been a dinosaur or a very diminutive mammoth. Extinct she must be, since she had lived in the reign of Queen Victoria. . . .

'The Victorians,' Mrs Swithin mused. 'I don't believe' . . . 'that there ever were such people. Only you and me and William dressed differently.'

'You don't believe in history,' said William.

The stage remained empty. The cows moved in the field. The shadows were deeper under the trees.[5]

Virginia Woolf's first and last novels, *The Voyage Out* (1915) and *Between the Acts* (1941), are the two works which engage most directly with ideas of the primeval. In *The Voyage Out* it is necessary to travel to remote countries to discover it. The primitive is still figured as outside self. But in *The Waves*, and even more in *Between the Acts*, the prehistoric is seen not simply as part of a remote past, but as contiguous, continuous, a part of ordinary present-day life.

In recent years 'prehistory' has become a useful technical term for describing those conditions of production and of reception which determine the relationship between text and reader. (What do we know about the conditions of production and how does this knowledge define our reading?) The term 'prehistory' is also sometimes used to describe the means by which a work of fiction creates its own past, suggesting a continuity between an unrecorded previous existence for the characters and the language of the text that makes them be. That is, it can be used as a way of claiming a non-linguistic, prior presence for people whom we simultaneously know to be purely the verbal products of a particular act of writing. But there is a further sense of the term which seems particularly apt to Virginia Woolf's work: prehistory implies a pre-narrative domain which will not buckle to plot. Just as Freud said that the unconscious knows no narrative, so prehistory tells no story. It is time without narrative, its only story a conclusion. That story is extinction. Once there were primeval forests, massive land creatures, sea-beasts crawling in the swamp. Now they are gone.

In their place is mankind and its recorded history of war, politics, empire, its unrecorded history of generations obscured by profound oblivion. Virginia Woolf was always distrustful of narrative, finding herself unable to make up plot or accept its resolutions.[6] She was fascinated by recurrence, perpetuity, and both by the difficulty of forgetting and by the fragmentary vestiges which are remembered.

In an early draft of *The Waves* she writes:

I am not concerned with the single life but with lives together. I am trying to find in the folds of the past such fragments as time preserves ... there was a napkin, a flowerpot and a book. I am telling the story of the world from the beginning, and in a small room, whose windows are open.[7]

The single self in the small room with windows open to the outer world attempts to make again from fragments the continuity of time. She seeks to 'explicate', that is, to 'unfold', the folds of time, to renew the lapsed materiality of the past.

'The story of the world from the beginning' has been, in the past hundred years or so, seen predominantly as a story of development and succession. In *Civilization and its Discontents* Freud accepts an evolutionist basis for psychoanalysis but distinguishes between organic and mental evolution:

As a rule the intermediate links [in organic evolution] have died out and are known to us only through reconstruction. In the realm of the mind, on the other hand, what is primitive is so commonly preserved alongside of the transformed version which has arisen from it that it is unnecessary to give instances as evidence.[8]

That is very much the position of Conrad in *Heart of Darkness*. Virginia Woolf, however, emphasizes the extent to which the 'primitive is ... preserved alongside of the transformed version' in the material as well as the mental world. She tempers the triumphalist narrative of development and meditates instead upon ways in which the prehistoric permeates the present day. Sometimes this becomes an opposing comedy to the Tennysonian insistence that we let 'the ape and tiger die' and move beyond the animal:

There is the old brute, too, the savage, the hairy man who dabbles his fingers in ropes of entrails; and gobbles and belches; whose speech is guttural, visceral – well, he is here. He squats in me. Tonight he has been feasted on quails, salad, and sweetbread. He now holds a glass of fine old brandy in his paw. He brindles, purrs and shoots warm thrills all down my spine as I sip. It is true, he washes his hands before dinner, but they are still hairy. He buttons on trousers and waistcoats, but they contain the same organs. ... That man, the hairy, the ape-like, has contributed his part to my life.

That passage from Bernard's final soliloquy in *The Waves* is succeeded by the morphological ecstasy of

I could worship my hand even, with its fan of bones laced by blue mysterious veins and its astonishing look of aptness, suppleness and ability to curl softly or suddenly crush – its infinite sensibility.[9]

The example of the hand was one that Darwin used in *The Origin of Species* to track the identity of structures across species and to establish continuity with our uncouth progenitors, hard to acknowledge as kin.

The ready, inter-metaphorical movement to and fro between the development of the individual and the development of the species makes for new relations and anxieties. It informs the thinking of the past hundred years. Though we take it for granted, Virginia Woolf, like Freud, belonged to a generation in which its novelty of meaning was still perceptible. It is the idea which allows Freud, in 'The Wolf-Man', for example, to speak of 'the pre-historic period of childhood', and which earlier had led T.H. Huxley to explain the lack of experimental evidence for the evolutionary process thus: 'the human race can no more be expected to testify to its own origins than a child can be tendered as witness to its own birth'.[10] Both quotations emphasize oblivion, the impossibility of recording. Darwinian theory required that we accept forgetfulness and the vanishing of matter, and yet insisted at the same time on descent from a remote and changed precursor. Origins can never be fully regained or rediscovered. Origins are always antecedent to language and consciousness. That same emphasis upon lost and unreclaimable origins, upon antecedent oblivion, is found in Freud's working of Darwinian theory. But there is also, in Freud and in Woolf, a counter-insistence on perpetuity and on the survival of what precedes consciousness, precedes history.

In *Moses and Monotheism* (which Virginia Woolf was reading as she worked on *Pointz Hall*, the first title for *Between the Acts*) Freud writes:

assume that in the history of the human species something happened similar to the events in the life of the individual. That is to say mankind as a whole also passed through conflicts of a sexual-aggressive nature, which left permanent traces but which were for the most part warded off and forgotten; later, after a long period of latency, they came to life again.... Since it can no longer be doubted after the discovery of evolution that mankind had a pre-history and since this history is unknown (that is to say, forgotten), such a conclusion has almost the significance of an axiom ... the effective and forgotten traumata relate, here as well as there, to life in the human family.[11]

The gossips in *Between the Acts* muse crudely on these connections:

No, I thought it much too scrappy. Take the idiot. Did she mean, so to speak, something hidden, the unconscious as they call it? But why always drag in sex. ... It's true, there's a sense in which we all, I admit, are savages still. Those women with red nails.[12]

The coinage of evolutionary ideas and of Freudianism is here brought to the surface and daringly trivialized. I say 'daringly' because she thus draws attention to and simultaneously deflects us from the depth of these issues in her own creativity.

Oddly little attention has been given to the possible reading relationships between Woolf and Freud, as opposed to Freudian plumbings of Woolf's neuroses. The Hogarth Press published trans-lations of Freud from 1921 on. Virginia Woolf was reading him in the 1930s. Once, in Freud's old age, they met, and he handed her a narcissus. Frank Sulloway, in *Freud: Biologist of the Mind*, makes the point that what distinguished Freud from earlier psychologists was his adoption of an evolutionist as opposed to a psychologistic descrip-tion of the mind. Prehistory is anterior to knowledge. It lies beneath the polarizations and emplotments of knowledge. It lies, as it were, *beneath* history in that same spatial-geological metaphor that Freud used to describe the relationship of consciousness and the unconscious which lies beneath. The unconscious is both prior in time and beneath in space. It is not known, but equally not gone, nor voided. It escapes registration.

One of the features of Virginia Woolf's style is her fascination with taking language out towards obliterativeness, towards things she feels cannot be described, like the clouds near the beginning of *Between the Acts* and the sky whose blue cannot be symbolized:

Was it their own law, or no law, they obeyed? Some were wisps of white hair merely. One, high up, very distant, had hardened to golden alabaster; was made of immortal marble. Beyond that was blue, pure blue, black blue; blue that had never filtered down; that had escaped registration. It never fell as sun, shadow, or rain upon the world, but disregarded the little coloured ball of earth entirely. No flower felt it; no field; no garden.[13]

The blue 'had escaped registration'. The escape from registration was an ideal, a necessarily unachievable ideal, of her writing. Virginia Woolf is fascinated by the persistence of prehistory as well as its impenetrable distance. The sky, the clouds, changing, unchangeful, are outside history, there from the beginning of time.

These objects of meditation (absence of origins, survival of the primeval, the impacting of race in individuals) haunt Woolf and help to explain certain of the shapes her narratives take, and certain of the exemplary renunciations she makes. Her scepticism about developmental narratives and about irreversible transformations are part of her debate with her Victorian progenitors, her Victorian *self*. Leslie Stephen attributed his loss of faith quite directly to reading *The Origin of Species*. Virginia Woolf, in her career as a writer, assays the forms for experience offered by evolutionary theory. One insistence of evolutionary theory was on changed forms which could not be reversed. Perhaps, in the light of the dominant forms for understanding experience developed by her father's generation, her resistance to the idea of transformation has particular meaning.

It is certainly striking how little transformation means in her work. Certainly there are *oscillations* to and fro between metaphor and the material world. There are momentary illuminations, mistaken identities. But transformations, in her writing, can always be reversed. Indeed, I wonder whether her much discussed frigidity is a necessary renunciation of climax and of the obliterativeness of climax. It is a way of keeping everything persistingly elated, never completed. In our reading experience of Virginia Woolf, one of the most striking attributes of her style is the sensuous arousal it creates in the reader even while it constantly evades moments of completion. She eschews the authoritarian inevitability of sequence implied in plot. Instead, her writing offers constant shifts between discourses from moment to moment. She has abraded some of the conventional notions of 'development' apparently authenticated by evolutionary story, and in doing so she is responding with great subtlety to the other implications of Darwin's myths.[14]

Let me turn now to *The Voyage Out*, the first of her novels, since this bears traces not only of a struggle with Victorian narrative but of Woolf's own reading of Darwin's writing. *The Voyage Out* still uses the form of the *Bildungsroman*. The particular shape that she uses here is that of the voyage which is to be also a voyage of self-discovery. In *Bildungsroman*, typically, the hero learns by means of his growing-up experiences both to know his self and to accept its limitations, to conform to the demands made on the ego by society. A typical form for romantic narrative is that of the circular voyage – away from home until at the furthest point of distance the meaning of home is understood and the return can be accomplished. That narrative was brought into question by other early twentieth-century writers as well as Virginia Woolf; by Conrad, in *Heart of Darkness*, where the voyage upriver and into the forest takes you back into the primeval, into the primal self whose core of darkness is indescribable and can never be taken into narrative. Certainly, as Conrad expresses it, it can be explicated only through negations: unfathomable, immeasurable. These are the forms through which he measures the density of the forest and the activity of the primitive self. Like Freud, Conrad condenses unconscious and prehistoric.[15] We see another reading of the voyage, later, in *A Passage to India*, where Forster shows the voyage out into empire and beyond it, the discovery that the *extent* of India reaches beyond the power of human language to record or British imperial power to suppress. For Virginia Woolf, the *Voyage Out* had a particular meaning.

The book has a closely realistic surface. Rachel Vinrace goes out on her voyage of pleasure and discovery to South America. The narrative implies self-development and promises an according with society's expectations. But in this we are disappointed. Development is thwarted. Rachel dies. There is no voyage back. The book offers an enquiry typical of women's plot: can the heroine survive her own growth? Initiation into society for women involves initiation into descent. They will become vessels of descent, not borne aloft by the boat that carries them, but themselves bearing and carrying: childbearing. At the moment of entry into sexual life, Virginia Woolf's heroine falls ill and dies. Rachel's voyage to South America is extended into a special voyage of exploration upriver into the primeval forests. It is on this voyage that Rachel and Terence declare their love, and on this voyage also that she contracts the fever from which she dies.

In these passages describing the forest Virginia Woolf draws directly on another book about a voyage: *The Voyage of the Beagle*, Darwin's account of his early travels round the globe which provided him with the experience and evidences from which emerged his theory of evolution by means of natural selection. Some of the passages of description of the South American forests in Darwin seem to provide 'local colour' for Virginia Woolf – though I shall argue that they provide more than that. His incandescent, sometimes eerie, descriptions chime in closely with hers.

> In vain we tried to gain the hill. The forest was so impenetrable that no-one who had not beheld it could imagine so entangled a mass of dying and dead trunks. I am sure that often for more than ten minutes together our feet never touched the ground and we were frequently ten or fifteen feet above it, so that the seamen as a joke called out the soundings. At other times we crept one after another on our hands and knees under the rotten trunks. In the lower part of the mountain noble trees with winter's bark and the laurel-like sassafras with fragrant leaves, and others the names of which I do not know were matted together by a trailing bamboo or cane. Here we were more like fishes struggling in a net than any other creature.[16]

That is Darwin. This is *The Voyage Out*:

> As they moved on the country grew wilder and wilder. The trees and the undergrowth seemed to be strangling each other near the ground in a multitudinous wrestle; while here and there a splendid tree towered high above the swarm, shaking its thin green umbrellas lightly in the upper air. . . .
>
> As they passed into the depths of the forest the light grew dimmer, and the noises of the ordinary world were replaced by those creaking and sighing sounds which suggest to the traveller in a forest that he is walking at the bottom of the sea. The path narrowed and turned; it was hedged in by dense creepers which knotted tree to tree, and burst here and there into star-shaped crimson blossoms. . . . The atmosphere was close and the air came at them in languid puffs of scent.[17]

Darwin similarly emphasized the mingling of life and death in the atmosphere of the forests:

The day was beautiful and the number of trees which were in full flower perfumed the air and yet even this could hardly dissipate the gloomy dampness of the forest. Moreover the many dead trunks that stand like skeletons never fail to give these primeval woods a character of solemnity absent in countries long civilised. Death instead of life seemed the predominant spirit.[18]

The return to primary forms may reveal a squandering of life rather than its renewal. Virginia Woolf's writing seems to be quite alert to its own intertextuality here, to be conjuring another prehistory. Darwin's book records the period in his life when, setting sail as an orthodox Christian, he had, by the time he returned to England, begun to conceive the theories which were to change our ways of perceiving experience. *The Voyage of the Beagle* is the pre-text to *The Origin of Species*, its prehistory.

In *The Voyage Out* the scene immediately after that in the forest is full of Darwinian echoes and Darwinian references. An immense amount of sexual force has been generated which spills about among the other characters. People crudely use some of the more specious extensions of evolutionism. Mrs Flushing laughs at the idea of disinterestedness and love. 'Savin' yourself' is all that matters.

> 'One reads a lot about love – that's why poetry's so dull. But what happens in real life, eh? It ain't love!' she cried.
> ... 'Tell them about the bath, Alice.'
> 'In the stable-yard,' said Mrs Flushing. 'Covered with ice in winter. We had to get in; if we didn't we were whipped. The strong ones lived – the others died. What you call the survival of the fittest – a most excellent plan, I daresay, if you've thirteen children!'[19]

The intellectual Hirst is beset by the silence: 'These trees get on one's nerves – it's all so crazy. God's undoubtedly mad. What sane person could have conceived a wilderness like this, and peopled it with apes and alligators?' In the following chapter Rachel and Terence come upon the remote tribe of 'soft instinctive people' where mother 'drew apart her shawl and uncovered her breast to the lips of her baby', watching them the while; Helen, also watching them, 'standing by herself in the sunny space among the native women, was exposed to presentiments of disaster'.

> The cries of the senseless beasts rang in her ears high and low in the air, as they ran from tree-trunk to tree-top. How small the little

figures looked wandering through the trees! She became acutely
conscious of the little limbs, the thin veins, the delicate flesh of men
and women, which breaks so easily and lets the life escape compared
with these great trees and deep waters.[20]

The sense of unchanging life and of the sheer chanciness of survival
are more important here than descent. And the abrupt cutting off of
her heroine's life is her challenge to developmental narrative.

II

Darwin's early writing elated Virginia Woolf, I think. The young
Darwin, like the young Rachel, is discovering the world and in some
of the same regions. But he, active, independent, completes the circular
journey. She, surrounded by protectors, hemmed in by reserve, has
the journey curtailed by death. Virginia Woolf's resistance to transformation does not deny death, but in this book death is received as
silence and diminution, not transformation. The individual life is
muffled. The flesh easily lets life escape 'compared with these great
trees and deep waters'.

Evolutionary theory had made a new myth of the past. Instead of
the garden, the swamp. Instead of fixed and perfect species, forms in
flux. It also renewed the peculiar power of the sea as the first place of
life. Most myth systems had given the sea a primary place in the
formation of life; now scientific theory historicized this concept. The
sea resists transformation. Yet the sea is never old; it is constantly
renewing itself. That, I think, was important for Virginia Woolf, and
became increasingly so. Her fascination with the sea and with the
primeval and prehistoric may be related to her search for a way out
of sexual difference, or, equally, for a continuity with lost origins. Her
mother died when she was 12. Because of this loss, and her own
gender, the mother in her work is conceived as origin, the father as
intervention. In an early version of *The Waves* she wrote of the waves
as 'sinking and falling, many mothers, and again, many mothers, and
behind them many more, endlessly sinking and falling'.[21] Mothers –
matrices: re-formation, not transformation; the acceptance of oblivion:
these are connections crucial to Virginia Woolf's writing. The search
for lost origins had been powerful throughout the nineteenth century.
Darwin himself may have had an unrecognized personal incentive in
his impulse to work back towards ultimate origins, and to repopulate

the past of the world by means of natural history. His own mother died when he was 8 and he was troubled by the scantiness of his memories of her.

What I want to argue is that the need to discover origins, the vehement backward plumbing of history, the insistence on causality and judgement, was *allayed* for Virginia Woolf by her awareness of the survival of prehistory. The continued presence of sea, clouds, leaves, stones, the animal form of man, the unchanged perceptual intensity of the senses, all sustain her awareness of the simultaneity of the prehistoric in our present moment. This absolves her from the causal forms she associates with nineteenth-century narratives.

She is drawn most to what is perpetually changing: and I give equal force here to both elements, perpetual and changing. A passage strikingly related to her imagination of the waves of the sea is to be found in Ruskin's *Modern Painters*, where he writes:

> Most people think of waves as rising and falling. But if they look at the sea carefully, they will perceive that the waves do not rise and fall. They change. Change both place and form, but they do not fall; one wave goes on, and on, and still on; now lower, now higher, now tossing its mane like a horse, now building itself together like a wall, now shaking, now steady, but still the same wave till at last it seems struck by something, and changes, one knows not how, becomes another wave.[22]

For Ruskin, waves change, but are not transformed. They become other waves. This absence of transformation, the acceptance of sustained obliteration and continuity, becomes of great moment in Woolf's later writing.

Writing for her can less and less claim infinity of recall. By the time she reaches her last work she is content with gaps and contradictions. In *Between the Acts* the characters themselves are vestiges of creation, the language is fraught with citation, pastiche, and allusion. 'Orts, scraps, and fragments are we'. Yet the phrase itself, through its recurrence in the text, is a binding chant, linking unlike together in kinship and difference. Merely to look at the work on the page signals difference when we come to *Between the Acts*. Whereas in the submarine world of *The Waves*, 'that mystical eyeless book', as she calls it, we are 'deflected, held in place' by the way in which the language of the book covers every space, the writing occupies the page, in *Between the Acts* white spaces abound, unprinted, unrestored.

Between the Acts is set in June 1939, just before the coming of the war. In it, she deliberately substitutes 'we' for 'I'. She was writing it from 1938 onwards. She was writing it through the coming of the war. In a contemporaneous work, 'Little Gidding', Eliot wrote that 'History is now and England'. In *Between the Acts* history is the past. The *present* is *prehistory* in a double sense. Whenever the action of the historical pageant falters it is saved by the unwilled resurgence of the primeval: the shower of rain, the idiot, the cows bellowing for their lost calves. At the same time, the book describes a moment which may be the last of this culture. The planes swoop overhead. June 1939 is the prehistory to a coming war which, the book makes clear without hysteria, may mark the end of this society:

> 'It all looks very black.'
> 'No one wants it – save those damned Germans.'
> There was a pause.
> 'I'd cut down those trees....'
> 'How they get their roses to grow!'
> 'They say there's been a garden here for five hundred years....'[23]

In the intense comedy of *Between the Acts*, with its shifty lexical play, its apocalyptic imminence, its easy vacillation between the domestic and the monstrous, we reach her most unsettling meditation on the meanings of prehistory. Since Darwin, humankind could no longer take for granted its own centrality or its own permanence.

It is from the period of composition of this work that Virginia Woolf's one direct reference to Darwin in her diaries occurs. We know from references in *To the Lighthouse* that she used him naturally as an example of the apex of human achievement. ('We can't all be Titians and we can't all be Darwins.') In October 1940 the Woolfs' house in Tavistock Square was bombed. She and Leonard Woolf went up to London to salvage some of their possessions.

> A wind blowing through. I began to hunt out diaries. What could we salvage in this little car? Darwin and the silver, and some glass and china.[24]

The diaries, Darwin, some silver, glass, and china. It is an intriguing list and a revealing one. Later she records: 'I forgot the Voyage of the Beagle'. I have already shown, I hope, that the problems bequeathed by Darwin's narratives troubled Virginia Woolf creatively in ways that led her to subtle appraisals and meditations on his work. There is no need to assert the prevalence of evolutionary ideas during Virginia Woolf's lifetime and we know that Darwin's writings had had direct effects upon her early family circumstances. We all live within post-Darwinian assumptions now, and hence, paradoxically, we are not alert to the extent to which imaginatively we take for granted shapes for experience suggested by his theories and their extensions. We need therefore to measure the level of awareness at which Virginia Woolf was engaging with Darwin and the implications of his work. We need to do this in order to clarify the particular difficulties he posed for her as a writer and to perceive the new forms that her rewriting of these difficulties created. In the diary passage we have external evidence that she valued his books. And in *Between the Acts* we have her fullest exploration of the new relations of experience to prehistory that had been fuelled by Darwin's theories. Those theories were indefatigably extended by the two succeeding generations in terms of development, race theory, the unconscious.

> 'Once there was no sea,' said Mrs Swithin. 'No sea at all between us and the continent. I was reading that in a book this morning. There were rhododendrons in the Strand; and mammoths in Piccadilly.'
> 'When we were savages,' said Isa.
> Then she remembered; her dentist had told her that savages could perform very skilful operations on the brain. Savages had false teeth, he said.[25]

Much of the wit of the book depends upon its turning aside any notion of development as implying improvement. And, because so much of it takes the form of thought, past and present lie level, culled as needed by the individual's associations. The novel is a spatial landscape, not a linear sequence. The pastiches of the pageant set periods of the past alongside each other and beside the present. Most of the people in the book say 'Adsum' for their ancestors. Bart's dog is still a wild dog. Bart himself appears a monster, with his rolled newspaper for snout, to his small grandson. The child is convinced, the grandfather is comically offended. The single disturbingly graphic scene of traditional 'action' brings to the surface of the text the matter of prehistory: children, savages, the coming war, the devouring chain of life are all expressed in the awkward scene where Giles acts, running counter to the indications of book and title, 'Between the Acts':

He kicked – a flinty yellow stone, a sharp stone, edged as if cut by
a savage for an arrow. A barbaric stone; a pre-historic. Stone-
kicking was a child's game. He remembered the rules.[26]

He stamps on toad and snake: 'It was birth the wrong way round –
a monstrous inversion. . . . The mass crushed and slithered. The white
canvas on his tennis shoes was bloodstained and sticky. But it was
action. Actions relieved him.' The four-square allegorization of violence, of the oncoming war and greed, is forcefully set apart from the
method of most of the book in a way which apes its own subject-
matter. It is vividly heraldic. In contrast, there is the narrative's sly
habit of pointing, and thus making enigmatic, simple statements by
the intervention of 'he said' or 'she said'. The word 'origin' is a
favourite for such play:

> Lucy rapping her fingers on the table said: 'What's the origin – the
> origin – of that?'
> 'Superstition,' he said.
>
> 'What's the origin,' said a voice, 'of the expression "with a flea in
> his ear"?'[27]

In this work interruption is as important as association. Spaces on the
page give room to the unrecorded areas between the acts of language.
And characters and narrative discourse alike persistently break in
upon thought as well as speech. In the same mode, the prehistoric
breaks in upon the present as well as surviving within it. At the end
of the book 'the great carp himself, which came to the surface so very
seldom' is momentarily visible as a flash of silver. At the end of the
vicar's speech 'Every sound in nature was painfully audible; the swish
of the trees; the gulp of a cow; even the skim of the swallows over the
grass could be heard.' Characters break in on each other's vivid
reveries. The book is permeated with Lucy Swithin's reading of H.G.
Wells.[28] Virginia Woolf here amalgamates his *The Outline of History*
with his *Short History of the World* and writes her own version rather
than quoting Wells directly. Old Mrs Swithin, so pious, repetitive,
and faithful, has an imaginative life swarming with sensual images of
power and birth. During the book's twenty-four hours, she inhabits
the repeated present of the day of pageant, and the primeval worlds
of her book's description. The two sometimes flow together, are sometimes disjunct, are each other's unacted part. Wakened early by the
birds,

174

she had stretched for her favourite reading – an Outline of History – and had spent the hours between three and five thinking of rhododendron forests in Piccadilly; when the entire continent, not then, she understood, divided by a channel, was all one; populated, she understood, by elephant-bodied, seal-necked, heaving, surging, slowly writhing, and, she supposed, barking monsters; the iguanodon, the mammoth, and the mastodon; from whom presumably, she thought, jerking the window open, we descend.

That last thought is taken into narrative discourse to describe 'the great lady in the bath chair' later: 'so indigenous was she that even her body, crippled by arthritis, resembled an uncouth, nocturnal creature, now nearly extinct.' This passage continues:

It took her five seconds in actual time, in mind time ever so much longer, to separate Grace herself, with blue china on a tray, from the leather-covered grunting monster who was about, as the door opened, to demolish a whole tree in the green steaming undergrowth of the primeval forest.[29]

Two pages later the small boy grubbing in the ground, his perceptions unchanged from primitive man, is terrified by 'a terrible peaked eyeless monster moving on legs, brandishing arms'. It is known by us as his grandfather joking, with a newspaper. Lightly, through comic juxtaposition and pastiche, she concurs with Wells's more sonorous description of 'our ancestors' who are also us. Wells writes:

His ancestors, like the ancestors of all the kindred mammals, must have been creatures so rare, so obscure, and so remote that they have left scarcely a trace amidst the abundant vestiges of the monsters that wallowed rejoicing in the steamy air and lush vegetation of the Mesozoic lagoons, or crawled or hopped or fluttered over the great river plains of that time.[30]

No wonder Cleopatra is Mrs Swithin's marvellously unexpected 'unacted part' – Queen of the Nile – in which all first life seethed and grew. 'You've made me feel I could have played ... Cleopatra!' As Wells wrote:

wallowing amphibia and primitive reptiles were the very highest creatures that life had so far produced. Whatever land lay away from the water or high above the water was still altogether barren and lifeless. But steadfastly, generation by generation, life was creeping away from the shallow sea-water of its beginning.[31]

Wells's romantic language infuses that of Mrs Swithin and invigorates the book with its sensual movement: 'Amidst this luxuriant primitive vegetation crawled and glided and flew the first insects.' Diverse scopes of the past are interlaced: hot images of empire thread the work, particularly in Bart's memories of his youth in India. The word 'savages' keeps recurring, tempered, made sceptical, reinvoked. The untamed dog who either cringes or bites, the fish stirring the pond, the membranes of plants, all suggest the primeval pouring through the present.

The swallows lace Africa and Europe, connecting England's present with its prehistory:

'They come every year,' said Mrs Swithin. ... 'From Africa.' As they had come, she supposed, when the Barn was a swamp.

Before there was a channel, when the earth, upon which the Windsor chair was planted, was a riot of rhododendrons, and humming birds quivered at the mouths of scarlet trumpets, as she had read that morning in her Outline of History, they had come.[32]

That is one aspect of the continuance of prehistory; the elegant survival of swallows reassures and sustains a consonance between different time modes in the work. There are other, less beautiful continuities, presented as cliché, as covert allusion, as gossip. Immediately after the description of the swallows we have Mrs Manresa in 'the little game of the woman following the man', connected through Cobbet's observation: 'He had known human nature in the East. It was the same in the West. Plants remained – the carnation, the zinnia, and the geranium.' William Dodge, in the next paragraphs, masturbates as Giles approaches:

'The idiot?' William answered Mrs Parker for her. 'He's in the tradition.'

'But surely,' said Mrs Parker, and told Giles how creepy the idiot – 'We have one in our village' – had made her feel. 'Surely, Mr Oliver, we're more civilized?'

'We?' said Giles. 'We?' He looked, once, at William. He knew not his name; but what his left hand was doing.[33]

176

Giles has blood on his boots. Isa obsessively recalls the scene of rape she read about in the newspaper. The 'sister swallow' is linked, through myth, with the raped woman, and the rape is trivially re-enacted in Giles's insistence in this same passage on the double standard: 'It made no difference; his infidelity – but hers did'. The sexual drive of individuals, though masked by diverse cultural signs, remains fiercely unchanged: 'Vénus toute entière à sa proie attachée'. Racine's metaphor, almost cannibalistic in its intensity, is part of the immoveable repertoire of Isa's thought – Isa, whose *acts* in this book consist merely of receiving a cup of tea from the hand of the gentleman farmer.

It is as though, compacted yet spacious, the matter of the past is more fully *there* the more remote it is. The captious pastiche of the pageant's language presents snatches of English history as a series of linguistic gestures and tropes. But the remote past of prehistory crowds the everyday present in its untransformed actuality. It is as though she concurs with Freud's obervation that individual and masses 'retain an impression of the past in unconscious memory traces' and 'there probably exists in the mental life of the individual not only what he has experienced himself, but also what he brought with him at birth, fragments of phylogenetic origin, an archaic heritage'.[34]

The parallel between ontogeny and phylogeny in Freud's argument here, which Virginia Woolf read as she worked on the novel, strengthens her own imagery of individual and mass. 'Drawn from our island history. England I am', begins the pageant. Why are prehistory, 'unconscious memory traces', and 'our island history' of such importance in the work?

The allusions to all levels of the past function as 'beot', in *Beowulf*'s term. Repetition, encrustation, recurrence, continuity – all are under threat.[35] Plot in this book is the coming of war, the impending obliteration, which makes the ordinary at last *visible* in all its richness. When Miss La Trobe, at the end of the pageant, holds up the mirrors to the audience, they cannot see anything but shallow images of themselves. But we, as outer audience, replenish the emptiness they experience, even while we share it. 'Orts, scraps, and fragments are we.' The entire life (historically bound, and synchronically present) which has been figured in the work is under threat, and momentarily sacred.

Miss La Trobe imagines the scene for her next play:

It was growing dark. Since there were no clouds to trouble the sky the blue was bluer, the green greener. There was no longer a view –

no Folly, no spire of Bolney Minster. It was land merely, no land in particular. She put down her case and stood looking at the land. Then something rose to the surface.

'I should group them', she murmured, 'here.' It would be midnight; there would be two figures, half concealed by a rock. The curtain would rise.[36]

The landscape of sky and land, from which all particular relics of England have been obliterated, could as well be at the beginning of the world as now. The two figures are anonymous, progenitors perhaps, only perhaps. She is 'singing of what was before Time was'. At the end, the book itself repeats Miss La Trobe's project. It takes us back before the beginning of history but it takes us there through reading endoubled:

'England', she was reading, 'was then a swamp. Thick forests covered the land. On the top of their matted branches birds sang. ...' [Bartholomew] looked leafless, spectral, and his chair monumental. As a dog shudders its skin, his skin shuddered. ... 'Prehistoric man,' she read, 'half-human, half-ape, roused himself from his semi-crouching position and raised great stones.'

The old people retire to bed. Giles and Isa are left alone. 'The Record of the Rocks ... begins in the midst of the game', writes H.G. Wells. 'The curtain rises on a drama in the sea that has already begun, and has been going on for some time.'[37]

Giles and Isa, in the final paragraphs, are linked with other species, and with other texts preoccupied with the force of the primeval.

From that embrace another life might be born. But first they must fight, as the dog fox fights with the vixen, in *the heart of darkness*, in the fields of night. ... It was the night before roads were made, or houses. It was the night that dwellers in caves had watched from some high place among rocks.

Then the curtain rose. They spoke.[38]

With the image of the rising curtain and of the bared landscape of night Virginia Woolf simultaneously enregisters the artfulness of history, the perpetuity of the material world. Language, like fishes, rises to the surface. 'Then something rose to the surface', we are told of Miss La Trobe. 'Ourselves', thinks Mrs Swithin as she looks at the fish. But the Dover sole is eaten for lunch. The deftness of the book is in its refusal ever quite to become elegy or threnody. It hopes for survival and gives space to the disruptions of comedy. Simultaneity and conglomeration are, it seems, comic as well as comforting:

> So one thing led to another; and the conglomeration of things pressed you flat; held you fast, like a fish in water. So he came for the week-end, and changed.
> 'How d'you do?' he said all round; nodded to the unknown guest; took against him; and ate his fillet of sole.[39]

Nothing in this work is renounced. But equally nothing is claimed for ever. Levels of discourse persistingly shift, accept their own inadequacy. Not for nothing is Mrs Swithin, who holds history and prehistory together, nicknamed 'Old Flimsy'.

In an almost exactly contemporaneous work, composed equally under the impact of the coming of war, Eliot was writing:

> The river is within us, the sea is all about us;
> The sea is the land's edge also, the granite
> Into which it reaches, the beaches where it tosses
> Its hints of earlier and other creation:
> The starfish, the horseshoe crab, the whale's backbone;
> The pools when it offers to our curiosity
> The more delicate algae and the sea anemone.

In 'Dry Salvages', of which a draft was finished on 4 January 1941, Eliot repudiates 'superficial notions of evolution / Which becomes, in the popular mind, a means of disowning the past'. He continues, in a passage which chimes in with those I have cited from Freud as well as Woolf, responding as they all are to Darwin's writing:

> the past experience revived in the meaning
> Is not the experience of one life only
> But of many generations, not forgetting
> Something that is probably quite ineffable:
> The backward look behind the assurance
> Of recorded history, the backward half-look
> Over the shoulder, towards the primitive terror.[40]

At first, that passage sounds very close to *Between the Acts*, but what is important is that for her that 'backward half-look over the shoulder' does not result in terror. She looks 'behind the assurance of recorded history' *for* assurance.

Prehistory can be described only in the mirror of history, since language and history are inextricable. Yet, outside language and analysis, origins are all about us. She is no longer thrusting back to the past; she has renounced the search for origins. At one level, that is a political act which disengages her from the racial madness of the time. The medium of her work is largely choric, gossip, emerging from 'mass observation'.

> 'No, I don't go by politicians. I've a friend who's been to Russia. He says. ... And my daughter, just back from Rome, she says the common people, in the cafés, hate Dictators.... Well, different people say different things.'...
>
> 'And what about the Jews? The refugees ... the Jews.... People like ourselves, beginning life again.... But it's always been the same....'[41]

In her earlier work, when attention is called to it, the present moment has been empty, as at the conclusion of *Orlando*. Here the present moment lightly engages all the past. She refuses that metaphor which assumes that prehistory is deeper, grander, more sonorous, than the present moment, and instead disperses it throughout the now of *Between the Acts*. The book holds the knowledge that cultures and histories are obliterated, that things may not endure. The immediate history of England is interrupted and threatened by the insistent murmur of aeroplanes moving overhead in preparation for war. Is man 'essentially a fighter'? Does the primeval validate war?[42] Clouds, sky, swallows, pike, sea, earth, appetites, and perceptions figure the simultaneity of prehistory and the present, and yet also sustain the idea of a future. The engorged appetite of empire, the fallacy of 'development' based on notions of dominion or of race, are given the lie by the text's insistence on the untransformed nature of human experience – lightly dressed in diverse languages – absurdly knit together by rhymes. Here she registers for once the fullness of the present, not as moment only. The urgency of the connection between militarism and masculine education which Virginia Woolf asserted in *Three Guineas* is here articulated as part of a text which goes beyond it to emphasize the alternative insights offered by Darwin into kinship between past and present forms, the long pathways of descent, the lateral ties between humankind and other animals, the constancy of the primeval. For us living in an age where we can foresee the possibility of a post-nuclear world inhabited at most by sea, grass, scorpions, and sky, the salutary comedy of *Between the Acts* realizes its fullest intensity.

NOTES

1 Virginia Woolf, *Three Guineas* (1938; repr. London: Hogarth Press, 1943), pp. 326–7. For Julian Huxley's views, see, for example, his presidential address to the zoology section of the British Association in 1936 on 'Natural selection and evolutionary progress'.

2 Virginia Woolf, *A Writer's Diary*, ed. Leonard Woolf (London: Hogarth Press, 1953), p. 365.

3 Virginia Woolf, 'A sketch of the past', *Moments of Being*, ed. J. Schulkind (Brighton: Sussex University Press, 1976), p. 80.

4 Virginia Woolf, *Between the Acts* (London: Hogarth Press, 1941), pp.101–2.

5 ibid., p. 203.

6 For a related discussion of Virginia Woolf's evasion of plot, see my article 'Beyond determinism: George Eliot and Virginia Woolf', reprinted in this volume as chapter 7.

7 Virginia Woolf, *The Waves: The Two Holograph Drafts*, ed. J. Graham (London: Hogarth Press, 1976), I, p. 42.

8 Sigmund Freud, *Civilization and its Discontents* (London: Hogarth Press, 1930; rev. edn 1963), p. 5.

9 Woolf, *The Waves* (1931; repr. London: Hogarth Press, 1946), pp. 205, 206.

10 T.H. Huxley, 'Lectures on evolution', *Science and Hebrew Tradition* (London: Macmillan, 1893), p. 73.

11 Sigmund Freud, *Moses and Monotheism* (London: Hogarth Press, 1939), pp. 129–30.

12 Woolf, *Between the Acts*, pp. 232–3.

13 ibid., p. 30.

14 For an analysis of Darwin's narrative language and of his myths, see my study, *Darwin's Plots* (London: Routledge & Kegan Paul, 1983).

15 For discussion of Conrad's reading of evolutionary theory, see Ian Watt, *Conrad in the Nineteenth Century* (London: Chatto & Windus, 1979).

16 Charles Darwin, *The Voyage of the Beagle* (London: J.M. Dent, n.d.), p. 308.

17 Virginia Woolf, *The Voyage Out* (1915; repr. London: Hogarth Press, 1929), pp. 327, 331.

18 Darwin, op. cit., p. 321.

19 Woolf, *The Voyage Out*, pp. 335–6.

20 ibid., pp. 349–50.

21 Woolf, *The Waves: Holograph Drafts*, I, p. 64.

22 John Ruskin, *Modern Painters*, vol. III (1856; repr. New York: John Wiley, 1881), part IV, chs 12, 6, 11, p. 161. Compare the discussion of Ruskin's meanings for Woolf in chapter 8 of this volume, and my 'Hume, Stephen, and elegy in *To the Lighthouse*', reproduced in this volume as chapter 10.

23 Woolf, *Between the Acts*, p. 177.
24 Virginia Woolf, diary entry dated 20 October 1940, *The Diary of Virginia Woolf*, ed. Anne Olivier Bell and Andrew McNeillie (London: Hogarth Press, 1982), vol. V. In *Between the Acts* itself, Darwin is named at the end of Isa's reading list, p. 26.
25 Woolf, *Between the Acts*, p. 38
26 ibid., p. 118.
27 ibid., pp. 33, 145.
28 H.G. Wells, *The Outline of History: Being a Plain History of Life and Mankind*, rev. edn (London: Cassell, 1920). The quotations are all from ch. 3, on 'Natural selection'.
29 Woolf, *Between the Acts*, pp. 13–14.
30 Wells, op. cit., p. 24.
31 ibid., p. 14.
32 Woolf, *Between the Acts*, pp. 123, 130.
33 ibid., pp. 132–3.
34 Freud, *Moses and Monotheism*, pp. 151, 157.
35 Roger Poole in *The Unknown Virginia Woolf* (Cambridge: Cambridge University Press, 1978), convincingly establishes connections between *Three Guineas* and *Between the Acts*.
36 Woolf, *Between the Acts*, pp. 245–6.
37 ibid., p. 255; Wells, op. cit., p. 11.
38 Woolf, *Between the Acts*, p. 256; my italics.
39 ibid., p. 59. Compare the quotation from 'A sketch of the past' on p. 3.
40 T.S. Eliot, 'Dry Salvages', *Four Quartets, Collected Poems 1909–1962* (London: Faber & Faber, 1974), pp. 205, 208–9.
41 Woolf, *Between the Acts*, pp. 144–5.
42 Compare Woolf's comments on militarism and evolution quoted at the beginning of this essay.

10

HUME, STEPHEN, AND ELEGY IN *TO THE LIGHTHOUSE*

When my perceptions are remov'd for any time, as by sound sleep; so long am I insensible of *myself*, and may truly be said not to exist. And were all my perceptions remov'd by death, and cou'd I neither think, nor feel, nor see, nor love, nor hate after the dissolution of my body, I shou'd be entirely annihilated, nor do I conceive what is farther requisite to make me a perfect non-entity.

(David Hume, A Treatise on Human Nature)[1]

Father's birthday. He would have been 96, 96, yes, today; and could have been 96, like other people one has known; but mercifully was not. His life would have entirely ended mine. What would have happened? No writing, no books; – inconceivable. I used to think of him and mother daily; but writing The Lighthouse, laid them in my mind. And now he comes back sometimes, but differently.

(Virginia Woolf, *Diary*, 28 November 1928)[2]

Several of Virginia Woolf's books compose themselves about an absence: Jacob's absence from his room, Mrs Ramsay's in the second half of *To the Lighthouse*, and in *The Waves* Percival's in India and in death. Absence gives predominance to memory and to imagination. Absence may blur the distinction between those who are dead and those who are away. In one sense, everything is absent in fiction, since nothing can be physically there. Fiction blurs the distinction between recall and reading. It creates a form of immediate memory for the reader.

Writing about Hume, the eighteenth-century philosopher he most admired, Leslie Stephen glosses his position thus:

The whole history of philosophical thought is but a history of

183

attempts to separate the object and the subject, and each new attempt implies that the previous line of separation was erroneously drawn or partly 'fictitious'. (p. 48)[3]

In *To the Lighthouse* the fictitiousness of the separation between object and subject, the question of where to draw the line, is passionately explored, not only by the painter, Lily Briscoe, but by the entire narrative process. It is through Lily that the philosophical and artistic problem is most directly expressed and the connection between Mr Ramsay and Hume first mooted. Near the beginning of the book, Lily asks Andrew what his father's books are about.

> 'Subject and object and the nature of reality,' Andrew had said. And when she said Heavens, she had no notion what that meant. 'Think of a kitchen table then,' he told her, 'when you're not there.' (p. 40)[4]

In the book's last paragraph, remembering Mrs Ramsay, looking at the empty steps, Lily at last solves the problem of the masses in her picture to her own satisfaction:

> She looked at the steps; they were empty; she looked at her canvas; it was blurred. With a sudden intensity, as if she saw it clear for a second, she drew a line there, in the centre. (p. 320)

The separation of the object and the subject, and the drawing of a line less erroneous, less 'fictitious', than in previous attempts, defines the nature of elegy in this work. Virginia Woolf attempts to honour her obligations to family history and yet freely to dispose that history. In the course of doing so, she brings into question our reliance on symbols to confer value.

Virginia Woolf's other books imply aesthetic theories and draw upon the ideas of contemporary philosophers, particularly Bertrand Russell's warning against assuming that language mirrors the structure of the world: 'Against such errors', he writes in *The Analysis of Mind* (1921), 'the only safeguard is to be able, once in a way, to discard words for a moment and contemplate facts more directly through images.'[5] That is an ideal and a difficulty which moves through Virginia Woolf's practice as a writer. Only in *To the Lighthouse*, however, is the power of philosophical thinking and its limitations openly a theme of the book. That has to do with the work's special nature as elegy. In 1925, when she was beginning *To the Lighthouse* Virginia Woolf wrote in her diary:

> I will invent a new name for my books to supplant 'novel'. A new ————— by Virginia Woolf. But what? Elegy?

In elegy there is a repetition of mourning and an allaying of mourning. Elegy lets go of the past, formally transferring it into language, laying ghosts by confining them to a text and giving them its freedom. Surviving and relinquishing are both crucial to the composition of *To the Lighthouse*. Learning how to let go may be as deep a difficulty in writing and concluding a novel as it is in other experience.

The problem of achieving and of letting go is shared by mothers and artists. Mrs Ramsay lets go through death. After her death the book continues to explore what lasts (how far indeed has she let go or will others let her go?). The novel questions the means by which we try to hold meaning and make it communicable.

> Meanwhile the mystic, the visionary, walked the beach, stirred a puddle, looked at a stone, and asked themselves 'What am I?' 'What is this?' and suddenly an answer was vouchsafed them (what it was they could not say). (pp. 203–4)

All Virginia Woolf's novels brood on death, and death, indeed, is essential to their organization as well as their meaning. Death was her special knowledge: her mother, her sister Stella, and her brother Thoby had all died prematurely. But death was also the special knowledge of her entire generation, through the obliterative experience of the First World War. The long succession of family and generation, so typically the material of the nineteenth-century *roman fleuve*, such as Thackeray's *Pendennis* and *The Virginians*, or Zola's Rougon-Macquart series, becomes the site of disruption. The continuity of the family can with greatest intensity express the problems of invasion and even extinction.

Lawrence originally imagined *The Rainbow* and *Women in Love* as one long novel to be called *The Sisters*. But when the two books eventually appeared the first was a rich genealogical sedimentation, the second was thinned, lateral, preoccupied with a single generation. The parents in *Women in Love* are enfeebled and dying; the major relationships explored in the work are chosen, not inherited. In *To the Lighthouse* Virginia Woolf still tried to hold within a single work what

Lawrence had eventually had to separate: the experience of family life and culture, before and after the First World War. She held them together by separating them. 'Time passes', like Lily's line, both joins and parts. It is one formal expression of the profound question: 'What endures?' 'Will you fade? Will you perish?', 'The very stone one kicks with one's boots will outlast Shakespeare'. 'Distant views seem to outlast by a million years (Lily thought) the gazer and to be communing already with a sky which beholds an earth entirely at rest.'

> 'Ah, but how long do you think it'll last?' said somebody. It was as if she had antennae trembling out of her, which, intercepting certain sentences, forced them upon her attention. This was one of them. She scented danger for her husband. A question like that would lead, almost certainly, to something being said which reminded him of his own failure. How long would he be read – he would think at once. (p. 166)

This passage brings home the other anxiety about survival which haunts the book: how long will writing last? Mr Ramsay's ambition to be remembered as a great philosopher registers some of Woolf's ambitions and longings as an artist too. They are expressed in another mode by Lily, who must complete her picture and complete it truly, but who foresees its fate: 'It would be hung in the attics, she thought; it would be destroyed. But what did that matter? she asked herself, taking up her brush again' (p. 320). So the topics of the British empiricists, Locke, Hume, Berkeley – the survival of the object without a perceiver, the nature of identity and non-entity, the scepticism about substance – lie beneath the activity of the narrative. They bear on the question of how we live in our bodies and how we live in the minds of others. Hume writes of mankind in general that 'they are nothing but a bundle or collection of different perceptions, which succeed each other with an inconceivable rapidity, and are in a perpetual flux and movement' (p. 534). The emphasis on perception and on 'flux and movement' is repeated in Virginia Woolf's writing. But, as I have already suggested, there was a more immediate reason for Hume's insistent and sometimes comic presence in *To the Lighthouse*.

When Hume is named in *To the Lighthouse* he is strongly identified with Mr Ramsay's thoughts. He is first mentioned at the end of Mr Ramsay's long meditation on the need for ordinary men and on their relation to great men (exemplified in the twin figures of Shakespeare and the 'liftman in the Tube'). The section ends with Mr Ramsay's self-defeated questioning of his own powers. Yet, he thinks:

> he was for the most part happy; he had his wife; he had his children; he had promised in six weeks' time to talk 'some nonsense' to the young men of Cardiff about Locke, Hume, Berkeley, and the causes of the French Revolution. (p. 73)

His meditation had begun with the question: 'If Shakespeare had never existed ... would the world have differed much from what it is today?' (p. 70). The apposition of empiricism and revolution ('Locke, Hume, Berkeley, and the causes of the French Revolution') suggests a possible partial answer to that question, but it is self-deprecatingly framed as 'some nonsense'. The issue remains unresolved.

Hume's name next appears interrupting, and yet almost a part of, the current of thought generated by Mrs Ramsay in section 11 as she thinks about 'losing personality', eternity, the lighthouse, and finds herself repeating phrases: 'Children don't forget. . . . It will end. . . . It will come. . . . We are in the hands of the Lord.'

> The insincerity slipping in among the truths roused her, annoyed her. She returned to her knitting again. How could any Lord have made this world? she asked. . . . There was no treachery too base for the world to commit; she knew that. No happiness lasted; she knew that. She knitted with firm composure, slightly pursing her lips and, without being aware of it, so stiffened and composed the lines of her face in a habit of sternness that when her husband passed, though he was chuckling at the thought that Hume, the pilosopher, grown enormously fat, had stuck in a bog, he could not help noting, as he passed, the sternness at the heart of her beauty. (p. 102)

Hume, philosopher of mind, has grown so absurdly substantial that he sinks into the bog. That physical episode becomes meta-memory for Mr Ramsay, who *sees* it, not having been there. The full story is reserved for section 13, when at the end:

> the spell was broken. Mr Ramsay felt free now to laugh out loud at Hume, who had stuck in a bog and an old woman rescued him on condition he said the Lord's Prayer, and chuckling to himself he strolled off to his study. (p. 116)

Hume, the sceptical philosopher, is obliged to repeat the words of faith. We remember Mrs Ramsay's involuntary 'We are in the hands of the Lord'. Communal faith usurps the individual will. At the end of this episode (section 13) Mr Ramsay feels comfortable: Hume has been worsted. The giant towering above his own endeavours as a philosopher proves to be a gross man subsiding. For a moment he can be held to scale, contained in anecdote. But Mr Ramsay is himself measured by his will to worst. The narrative engages with the difficulties that Hume's work raises. And by this means, as we shall see, Virginia Woolf movingly allows to her father, Leslie Stephen, within her own work, a power of survival, recomposition, rediscovery even.

Hume's presence in the work allows her to bring sharply into focus the question of what is 'when you're not there', a topic traditional to elegy but here given greater acuity. In 1927 Bertrand Russell wrote in *The Analysis of Matter*:

> I believe that matter is less material, and mind less mental, than is commonly supposed, and that, when this is realized, the difficulties raised by Berkeley largely disappear. Some of the difficulties raised by Hume, it is true, have not yet been disposed of.[6]

Hume's persistence, the fact that his difficulties cannot be disposed of, makes him a necessary part of the book's exploration of substance and absence, of writing as survival.

We know that Virginia Woolf read Hume, perhaps not for the first time, in September 1920. But his importance in *To the Lighthouse* is connected with his special value for Leslie Stephen. In the process of transformation from Leslie Stephen to Mr Ramsay, Virginia Woolf notably raises the level of creativity and attainment at which the father-figure is working, placing him in the rearward and yet within reach of major philosophers. Whereas Leslie Stephen was a doughty thinker, high popularizer, and man of letters, Mr Ramsay is a possibly major, though self-debilitated, philosopher. This raising and enlarging sustains the scale of the father in relation to the writer and at the same time allows a process of identification between writer and father in their artistic obsessions. Virginia Woolf did not acknowledge having read much of Leslie Stephen's work. But when we turn to Stephen's *History of English Thought in the Eighteenth Century* the congruities between the themes of that work and *To the Lighthouse* are remarkable enough, and Stephen's actual exposition of Hume and the directions in which he seeks to move beyond him are closely related to the concerns of *To the Lighthouse*. The first of these is reputation and survival.

The first sentence of Stephen's book simultaneously places Hume at a pinnacle of achievement and presents the problem of literary reputation.

> Between the years of 1739 and 1752 David Hume published philo-sophical speculations destined, by the admission of friends and foes, to form a turning-point in the history of thought. His first book fell dead-born from the press; few of its successors had a much better fate. (p. 1)

The first section of the Introduction is entitled 'The influence of great thinkers' and it grapples with the question of how far the thinker thinks alone or as an expression of communal concerns. How does thought affect society? Stephen argues:

> The soul of the nation was stirred by impulses of which Hume was but one, though by far the ablest, interpreter; or, to speak in less mystical phrase, we must admit that thousands of inferior thinkers were dealing with the same problems which occupied Hume, and though with far less acuteness or logical consistency, arriving at similar conclusions. (p. 2)

Thinking is not exclusively the province of great thinkers, nor – more strikingly – are their conclusions different from those of others.

In *To the Lighthouse* Mr Bankes suggests:

> We can't all be Titians and we can't all be Darwins, he said; at the same time he doubted whether you could have your Darwin and your Titian if it weren't for humble people like ourselves. (p. 114)

The relationship between 'humble people like ourselves' – or not quite like ourselves – and great art, great ideas, great events, haunts and troubles *To the Lighthouse*. It is part of the work's deepest questioning of what will survive. The question includes the questioning of the concept of 'great men', of indomitable achievement, of a world centred on human will, and extends to human memory and the material world.

> Does the progress of civilization depend upon great men? Is the lot of the average human being better now than in the time of the pharaohs? Is the lot of the average human being, however, he asked himself, the criterion by which we judge the measure of civilization?

189

Possibly not. Possibly the greatest good requires the existence of a slave class. The liftman in the Tube is an eternal necessity. The thought was distasteful to him. (p. 70)

Stephen, pursuing the relationship between 'great men' and the mass of thinking, writes:

Society may thus be radically altered by the influence of opinions which have apparently little bearing upon social questions. It would not be extravagant to say that Mr Darwin's observations upon the breeds of pigeons have had a reaction upon the structure of society. (p. 12)

Abstract thought and social action seem at times in *To the Lighthouse* to be polarized between Mr and Mrs Ramsay, but most of the thinking in the book is sustained by the activity of laying alongside and inter-melding the separate thought processes within individuals in such a way that the reader perceives the connections which the characters themselves cannot. The interpenetration of consciousnesses in language on the page allows us to think through problems of substance and absence unreservedly.

In his analysis of Hume's thought Stephen gives particular emphasis to the idea of fictionality. Stephen writes: 'The belief that anything exists outside our mind when not actually perceived, is a "fiction". ... Association is in the mental what gravitation is in the natural world.' (Lily's floating table is anchored by association, not gravitation, we remember.)

We can only explain mental processes of any kind by resolving them into such cases of association. Thus reality is to be found only in the ever-varying stream of feelings, bound together by custom, regarded by a 'fiction' or set of fictions as implying some permanent set of external or internal relations.... Chance, instead of order, must, it would seem, be the ultimate objective fact, as custom, instead of reason, is the ultimate subjective fact. (p. 44)

There are obvious connections with *To the Lighthouse* in such an emphasis on reality as an 'ever-varying stream of feelings'. 'Life', he writes in his discussion of Hume, 'is not entirely occupied in satisfying our material wants, and co-operating or struggling with our fellows. We dream as well as act. We must provide some channel for the emotions generated by contemplation of the world and of ourselves' (p. 11).

Stephen, with Hume, affirms chance and custom rather than order and reason as the basis of perception. Nevertheless, such affinities with Virginia Woolf's writing appear at a very general level and need not imply any particularly intense recall of Stephen's work or conversation. If such consonances were all, I would feel justified only in calling attention to similarity, rather than implying a process of rereading, re-placing. However, the actual examples that Stephen selects are so crucial in the topography of *To the Lighthouse* as to suggest that Virginia Woolf's writing is meditating on problems raised in the father's text.

In the novel there is an extraordinary sense of the substantiality of people. The children are always pelting here and there; words like 'plummeting', 'darting', 'full tilt', express the *impact* of the body. We are, in the moment, in our bodies, and that makes the moment both the most substantial and the most ephemeral of all experiences. We are never for more than a moment in the same place, the same time, in our bodies. That gap between body and time fascinates her in *To the Lighthouse*; and so does the question of substantiality, and its nature. Hume remarks:

> A substance is entirely different from a perception. We have, therefore no idea of substance. (p. 518)

> That table, which just now appears to me, is only a perception and all its qualities are qualities of a perception. (p. 523)

In *To the Lighthouse* we read:

> 'Think of a kitchen table then', he told her, 'when you're not there'.
> So she always saw, when she thought of Mr Ramsay's work, a scrubbed kitchen table. It lodged now in the fork of a pear tree, for they had reached the orchard. And with a painful effort of concentration, she focused her mind, not upon the silver-bossed bark of the tree, or upon its fish-shaped leaves, but upon a phantom kitchen table, one of those scrubbed board tables, grained and knotted, whose virtue seems to have been laid bare by years of muscular integrity, which stuck there, its four legs in the air. (pp. 40–1)

For the reader, pear-tree and table are poised equally as fictive images. The oddness of their conjunction makes us especially aware of them as images in the mind, though Lily's hefty imaginative work concentrates on the individuality of the table as perceived object (scrubbed, grained, and knotted) even more than on the tree (silver-bossed bark, fish-shaped leaves). By her imaginative effort she lurches the table *beyond* table, into some moralized and comically anthropomorphic form. 'Virtue' is shifted from being a question of essence, or of meaning, to one of moral endurance. Lily sees the table *upside-down* so that it becomes humanoid, its legs in the air, bare and muscular, a table of integrity, naked but not violated.

This inversion of the generalized image expresses through comedy the artist's urge towards the particular and the substantial. And yet the major process of Lily's picture throughout the book is *away* from representationalism towards abstraction, as though only pattern finally can satisfy and survive. At the book's end the line in the centre of her picture is distanced almost as far as it is possible to go from the particularity of the tree with which she began. It is almost entirely free of reference. But it was generated out of the referential. The narrative does not itself show any sustained parallel movement away from the referential towards the purely lexical, but it does move away from the burdened authority of symbolic objects. That movement of creativity seems to bear on the function of Virginia Woolf's parents in the work of art she composes, and on the means by which we all seek to make things last.

Table, house, tree, and stone: those four objects, and particularly the first two, are crucial to the narrative and the play of associations in *To the Lighthouse*. Discussing the problem of the relationship between idea and language Stephen remarks in his essay on Hume:

Looking, in the first place, at the external world, nothing seems simpler than the idea corresponding to the name of an individual object, man, or tree, or stone.

But he adds:

The man and the tree change visibly at every moment; if the stone does not change so rapidly, we discover that its qualities are at every instant dependent upon certain conditions which vary, however slowly. All things, as the old sceptics said, are in ceaseless flux; and yet, to find truth, we must find something permanent. (pp. 26–7)

Man, tree, stone: much of the emotion and thought of *To the Lighthouse* moves through those objects, surrounded by the 'ceaseless flux' of the sea. Mr Ramsay meditates on enduring fame and its vicissitudes;

> The very stone one kicks with one's boots will outlast Shakespeare. His own little light would shine, not very brightly, for a year or two, and would then be merged in some bigger light, and that in a bigger light still. (He looked into the darkness, into the intricacy of the twigs.) (p. 59)

Hume sees the attempt to escape from the self into a wider world to free ourselves of our own perceptual constraints as inevitably doomed, and Stephen quotes a famous lyrical passage from Hume to illustrate this:

> Let us fix our attention out of ourselves as much as possible. Let us chase our imaginations to the heavens, or to the utmost limits of the universe; we never can really advance a step beyond ourselves, nor can conceive any kind of existence but those perceptions which have appeared in that narrow compass. This is the universe of the Imagination, nor have we any idea but what is there produced. (p. 46)

Stephen at this point abruptly turns the argument and opens a new paragraph thus: 'Yet it is a plain fact of consciousness that we think of a table or a house as somehow existing independently of our perception of it' (p. 46).

'A table ... a house' begin to suggest more fully the way in which technical daring and emotional homage combine in *To the Lighthouse*, particularly in 'Time Passes'. The empty house, flooded with darkness, has been relinquished by its human inhabitants: 'there was scarcely anything left of body or mind by which one could say "This is he" or "This is she".' No perceiver is there to see the house. The darkness of forgetfulness, death, absence, enters the house. 'Certain airs' ask of the wallpaper, 'would it hang much longer, when would it fall? ... How long would they endure?' At the end of the third section, 'Mrs Ramsay having died rather suddenly the night before', the airs advance in anthropomorphic order, 'advance guards of great armies', to meet 'only hangings that flapped, wood that creaked, the bare legs of tables' (p. 200).

The material world is here sustained by writing, but it is a kind of writing which deliberately obliterates any suggestion of a single perceiver. Language draws attention to its own anthropomorphism, its habit of remaking objects in the image of human perception, the impossibility in Hume's words of 'conceiving any kind of existence but those perceptions which have appeared in that narrow compass'.

Near the book's conclusion, in the section which comes close to ghost story, Mrs Ramsay appears to Lily as Lily strives to resolve her picture.

> One must keep on looking without for a second relaxing the intensity of emotion, the determination not to be put off, not to be bamboozled. One must hold the scene – so – in a vice and let nothing come in and spoil it. One wanted, she thought, dipping her brush deliberately, to be on a level with ordinary experience, to feel simply that's a chair, that's a table, and yet at the same time, It's a miracle, it's an ecstasy. (pp. 309–10)

The precision and obduracy of artistic feeling rejects any raising, or symbolizing, though it floods the ordinary with ecstasy. Lily's old experience of longing, 'to want and want and not to have', itself at last becomes

> part of ordinary experience, was on a level with the chair, with the table. Mrs Ramsay – it was part of her perfect goodness to Lily – sat there quite simply, in the chair, flicked her needles to and fro, knitted her reddish-brown stocking, cast her shadow on the step. There she sat. (p. 310)

Physical (she casts a shadow as no ghost can do), revenant, actual, unhaloed, and unalloyed by symbol, she 'simply' knits her reddish-brown stocking. Absence and substance momentarily resolve.

Earlier in the work Lily had intensely, though fleetingly, seen Mr and Mrs Ramsay as 'symbolical', 'the symbols of marriage, husband and wife'. The moment of transcendence sinks down again and concludes with the anecdote I earlier quoted:

> Still for one moment, there was a sense of things having been blown apart, of space, of irresponsibility as the ball soared high, and they followed it and lost it and saw the one star and the draped branches. ... Then, darting backwards over the vast space (for it seemed as if solidity had vanished altogether), Prue ran full tilt into them and caught the ball brilliantly high up in her left hand, and her mother

said 'Haven't they come back yet?' whereupon the spell was broken. Mr Ramsay felt free now to laugh out loud at Hume, who had stuck in a bog and an old woman rescued him on condition he said the Lord's Prayer, and chuckling to himself he strolled off to his study. (pp. 115–16)

The repertoire of associations is richly at work here: the tree, so freely moved in the course of the book between substance, metaphor, thought, art, until at last it becomes line without reference. (Is Lily's final line tree or lighthouse? By then it no longer matters.) Here the tree figures as space; looking up they saw 'the one star and the draped branches'. In Hume's phrase, they 'chase their imaginations to the heavens' until solidity has vanished, but immediately Prue runs 'full tilt into them'. There is an extraordinary joyousness in that substantiality; the warmth and prowess of the body is regained, and regained as comedy. Mr Ramsay immediately turns to his enjoyment of Hume stuck in the bog and the moment can dissolve as they all take their separate ways. Living, here, means letting things be, holding them a moment, 'a brilliant catch', then letting them go. The 'symbolical' is valuable only if it is not freighted with permanence.

In this novel Virginia Woolf most acutely polarizes the sexes. Never again in her later novels was the binarism of male/female, husband/wife, father/mother allowed predominance. Instead, in works like *The Waves* and *Between the Acts*, she creates a spectrum of gender, a fan of possibilities. In *To the Lighthouse*, however, the formalization of difference is crucial to the activity of the novel. It is her homage to symbol, to generation, and to parenthood, but it represents also the 'writing out' of the symbolic weight of parenthood. It is tempting, in considering difference, and the polarization of sex roles, to see Lily Briscoe as some sort of Hegelian third term, representing the artistic resolution of sexual fracture and contradiction. But geometric patterning offers a false stability of reading, a judging optimism, which serves to protect the reader against the evanescence studied in the work. That emphasis on evanescence requires a reappraisal of the authority of symbol.

To the Lighthouse, is a post-symbolist novel. By this I mean that symbolism is both used and persistently brought into question. The act of symbolizing is one of the major means by which in language we seek to make things hold, to make them survive. But, above all, it is the means by which we make *things* serve the human. Symbol gives primacy to the human because it places the human at the centre, if not of concern, yet of signifying. Symbol depends for its nature on the signifying act. By its means concepts and objects are loaded with human reference.

Though *To the Lighthouse* is weighted with the fullness of human concerns, there is a constant unrest about the search after a permanence which places humanity at the centre. This search manifests itself in many ways: as continuity, through generation; as achieved art object; as storytelling; as memory; as symbol.

Language can never be anything but anthropocentric. In this book, Virginia Woolf struggles not only with the deaths of her father and her mother but with the death of that confidence in human centrality which was already being abraded in her father's generation by evolutionary theory. When Stephen attempts to move beyond Hume he does it by means of evolutionist arguments, emphasizing the progressive, the developmental in the theory. The 'race' is Stephen's new element (and it is an element that Virginia Woolf turns to, much later, in *Between the Acts*):

> Hume's analysis seems to recognise no difference btween the mind of man and a polyp, between the intellectual and the merely sensitive animal . . . the doctrine that belief in the external world is a 'fiction' is apparently self-destructive. If all reason is fiction, fiction is reason. (p. 49)

> Modern thinkers of Hume's school meet the difficulty by distinguishing between the *a priori* element in the individual mind and in the mind of the race. Each man brings with him certain inherited faculties, if not inherited knowledge; but the faculties have been themselves built up out of the experience of the race. (p. 56)

Stephen moves away from individualism to a confidence in communal development. *To the Lighthouse* brings into question all such attempts to propose a stable accord between inner and outer, past and present, to seal the contradiction of subject and object through symbol.

> Did Nature supplement what man advanced? Did she complete what he began? With equal complacence she saw his misery, condoned his meanness, and acquiesced in his torture. That dream, then, of sharing, completing, finding in solitude on the beach an answer, was but a reflection in a mirror. (pp. 207–8)

The signalled anthropomorphism in passages like this ('she saw ... condoned ... acquiesced') edges into sight our assumption of equivalence between inner and outer. In the passage describing the house left without people to observe it Virginia Woolf uses a neoclassical personification which strikes oddly, and which is intermelded with animal imagery. 'It is a plain fact of consciousness that we think of a table or house as somehow existing independently of our perception of it', writes Stephen. Here, Virginia Woolf faces the problem of how we describe a house when it exists 'independently of our perception of it'. The answer in 'Time Passes' is to see the object through time, and to use a discourse which points to human absence, sometimes with playful comfort, as in the following passage, sometimes in mourning or ironic abruptness, as in those passages cut off within square brackets '[A shell exploded. Twenty or thirty young men were blown up in France, among them Andrew Ramsay, whose death, mercifully was instantaneous.]'

> Loveliness and stillness clasped hands in the bedroom, and among the shrouded jugs and sheeted chairs even the prying of the wind, and the soft nose of the clammy sea airs, rubbing, snuffling, iterating, and reiterating their questions – 'Will you fade? Will you perish?' – scarcely disturbed the peace, the indifference, the air of pure integrity, as if the question they asked scarcely needed that they should answer: we remain.

The transposed, ludic quality of this passage is part of the decaying humanism of the concept 'house' – an object constructed for human use and so now, without function, present only as lexical play. Beyond the ordinary house is the *lighthouse*, the furthest reach and limit of human concerns, an attempt to create a margin of safety before the sea's power becomes supreme.

The sound of the waves is heard throughout the book, sometimes louder, sometimes softer, but always there to remind us of the expanse of the world beyond the human, in the face of which all attempts at signifying and stabilizing are both valiant and absurd. House and table are human objects, made to serve. Can the world of objects be made to sustain our need for signification, continuity, or permanence? These questions, brought to the fore by Hume's scepticism, and struggled with anew in the light of evolutionary theory by Stephen's generation, grind, like the dislimning sea, through *To the Lighthouse*.

The formlessness of the sea and the formed completeness of objects challenge equally the authority of the human subject. 'Subject and Object and the nature of reality' turns out not to be a vapid philosophical trope but the book's grounded enquiry, an enquiry which thrives through her father's concerns.

In generation and in language equally (the making of childen and of text) there is an attempt to ward off evanescence. In the course of her novel Virginia Woolf brings these desires within the surveillance of the reader. The tendency of the human to allow predominance to the human, to concur with our sense of our own centrality, is measured. Loading events and objects with symbolic weight comes to be seen as self-gratulation. So, as the work proceeds, she emphasizes momentariness and lightness. She empties and thins. The fullness of part I is replaced by the plainness of part III. The work is filled with a sense of how ephemeral is human memory: bodies gone and minds with them. All substance is transitory.

In May 1925, as she was beginning *To the Lighthouse*, she wrote in her diary:

> This is going to be fairly short: to have father's character done complete in it; and mother's; and St Ives and childhood; and all the usual things I try to put in – life, death etc. But the centre is father's character, sitting in a boat, reciting We perish, each alone, while he crushes a dying mackerel – However I must refrain.
>
> (III, pp. 18–19)

In the completed work Mrs Ramsay becomes characteristically the centre. The start of part I, 'The window', as opposed to part III, 'The Lighthouse', imitates the self-doubting complexity of Mrs Ramsay's sensibility, a fullness which is resolved later into others' simpler and more ideal memories of her. Certainly much of the emotional and artistic resourcefulness of the work goes into the making again, the repossession, of what the writer too soon had ceased to know: of Vita Sackville-West Virginia Woolf said in December 1925 that she 'lavishes on me the maternal protection which, for some reason, is what I have always most wished from everyone'. But the resourcefulness is also in composing what she could never have known: the meditative consciousness of the mother.

The sexual reserve of the writing is considerable. We never known the first names of Mr or Mrs Ramsay. We do not accompany them to the greenhouses. The distance and decorum do not encourage the same knowingness in the reader as does our pleased recognition that the letter of the alphabet of philosophical knowledge that Mr Ramsay cannot quite reach is that which begins his own name. Yet the Ramsays, the text assertively makes clear, are there when we are not. Their withdrawal emphasizes substantiality and sexuality.

All signification relies on memory. In the language of the middle section of 'Time passes' there is a wilful element, a reclaiming, a making demands, by which the distributor of the language seeks to ward off the immersing sea, the elements, the air, the non-linguistic world of human absence. The assertiveness, stylism, the hyperbole of linguistic desire, have parallels with that haunting figure, Grimm's fisherman's wife, whose story Mrs Ramsay reads to James. And the grossness of the wife's demands has links also with the eagerness of the human to dominate the non-human.

> She read on: 'Ah, wife,' said the man, 'why should we be king? I do not want to be king.' 'Well, said the wife, 'if you won't be king, I will; go to the Flounder, for I will be king.' . . . And when he came to the sea, it was quite dark grey, and the water heaved up from below, and smelt putrid. Then he went and stood by it and said,
>
> > 'Flounder, flounder, in the sea,
> > Come, I pray thee, here to me'.

The last pages of the work void that final claim of the human on the world of process. They pare away symbol. The lighthouse itself when approached proves to be 'a stark tower on a bare rock'. The obsessional symbol-making urge of Mr Ramsay, which is associated with his desire to clutch and hold on to experience, begins to ebb. In the fiction, despite his children's fears, he does *not* say, 'But I beneath a rougher sea' or 'we perished, each alone', though in her diary she projected the scene with him 'sitting in a boat, reciting We perish, each alone, while he crushes a dying mackerel' (*Diary*, III p. 19). Throughout the book Mr Ramsay has raucously, anxiously, raised his voice against oblivion, terrified by death, and by that longer obliteration in which writing also is lost. But when they reach the place on their journey to the lighthouse where the boat sank in the war (and in 'Time passes')

> to their surprise all he said was 'Ah' as if he thought to himself, But why make a fuss about that? Naturally men are drowned in a storm,

but it is a perfectly straightforward affair, and the depths of the sea (he sprinkled the crumbs from his sandwich paper over them) are only water after all. (p. 316)

It is a poignant and comic moment. At the moment when highest mystification is expected we are offered a complete demystification. His small gesture, in parenthesis, which recalls and then lets go of the parallel of dust to dust, ashes to ashes, is simply the sprinkling of crumbs on the sea, for the fishes.

That episode is immediately succeeded by another in which symbolism and the mystifying properties of human language and human gesture are relinquished. Lily, thinking their journey, imagines their arrival; ' "He has landed," she said aloud. "It is finished." ' The last words on the cross are half conjured. Mr Ramsay's journey and agony are momentarily, and uneasily, accorded a scale commensurate with his desires, though one on which, as readers, we are not obliged to dwell. The reference is fleetingly there. But it is immediately succeeded, and submerged, by Lily's finishing of her picture. The last words of the book are:

> With a sudden intensity, as if she saw it clear for a second, she drew a line there, in the centre. It was done; it was finished. Yes, she thought, laying down her brush in extreme fatigue, I have had my vision.

The change of tense, 'It was done; it was finished', obliterates the earlier allusion. The scale of reference becomes immediate, and exact. The step is empty. The picture is finished.

The extraordinary serenity of the book, even while it includes desolation and harassment, depends upon its acceptance of attenuation. Loss, completion, ending, absence, are acknowledged. Evanescence is of the nature of experience, and, although language can for a time make things survive, the work calmly rides out the anxieties of authorship. Though rhyme claims to outlive marble monuments, the pebble survives longer than Shakespeare. But people and language have lived. She renounces the grand, the symbolical, the enduring. The moment is the moment of being alive in body and mind. In her diary in June 1927 she wrote: 'Now one stable moment vanquishes chaos. But this I said in The Lighthouse. We have now sold, I think, 2555 copies' (*Diary*, III, p. 141).

*   *   *

Lacan argues that symbol and the act of symbolization represent the father. In freeing characters and text from the appetite for symbol Virginia Woolf may be seen as moving language and persons beyond subjection to patriarchy. And in doing so she transformed and absolved her own father through the act of writing. He comes back, but differently:

> I used to think of him and mother daily; but writing The Light-house, laid them in my mind. And now he comes back sometimes, but differently. . . . He comes back now more as a contemporary. I must read him some day. I wonder if I can feel again, I hear his voice, I know this by heart? (*Diary*, III, p. 208)

A conundrum remains: Virginia Woolf disclaims having 'read' her father. Yet in this essay I have emphasized consonances between their written works. The answer may be that here she purposes a full reading, that act of intimacy, homage, and appraisal in which we subject ourselves to a writer's complete work. She defers any such task, setting it in that warm never-never-land of reading we hope 'some day' to fulfil. The evasion persists. She must delay reading the father. Her earlier familiarity with his work had taken the form of dipping, scanning, listening, a flighty and intrigued resistance which allows rereading and pillaging and avoids immersion.

The wise act of writing in *To the Lighthouse* disperses parenthood and all its symbolic weight. Want and will give way, the want and the will of the fisherman's wife, of Lily Briscoe, of Mrs Ramsay, Mr Ramsay, of Cam and James. Subject ceases to dominate object. We are left with 'the waves rolling and gambolling and slapping the rocks', 'the frail blue shape which seemed like the vapour of something that had burned itself away', the line in Lily's picture which enters and holds 'all its green and blues, its lines running up and across, its attempt at something'. The line is at last freed from the referential. The picture can be completed.

The end of *To the Lighthouse* performs the experience of ending which has already happened in Mrs Ramsay's reading aloud of Grimm's tale of the fisherman's wife. The end of a story allows annihilation and perpetuity at the same time. Things fall apart and – being written – for a time, endure.

So Mrs Ramsay equably reads the apocalyptic conclusion to James:

201

'Houses and trees toppled over, the mountains trembled, rocks rolled into the sea, the sky was pitch black, and it thundered and lightened, and the sea came in with black waves as high as church towers and mountains, and all with white foam on top.'

She turned the page; there were only a few lines more, so that she would finish the story, though it was past bedtime. It was getting late. . . . It was growing quite dark.

But she did not let her voice change in the least as she finished the story, and added, shutting the book, and speaking the last words as if she made them up herself, looking into James's eyes: 'And there they are living still at this very time'. 'And that's the end', she said.

The elegiac triumph of the novel is to sustain entity. People survive when you are not there, when they are not there, in contradiction of Hume's assertion quoted at the beginning of this essay ('were all my perceptions remov'd by death . . . what is farther requisite to make me a perfect non-entity'). But they survive here in a kind of writing which eschews permanence. The last part of the book escapes from symbolic raising, placing its parental figures 'on a level with ordinary existence', with the substance of a chair, a table, a house, with the depths of the sea which (as Mr Ramsay at last thinks) are 'only water after all'.[7]

NOTES

1 David Hume, *A Treatise on Human Nature* (1736), ed. T.H. Green and T.H. Gross (London, 1874), vol. I, p. 534. All further references are to this edition and appear in parentheses.
2 *The Diary of Virginia Woolf*, ed. Anne Olivier Bell (London, 1980), vol. III, p. 208. Further page references appear in the text in parentheses.
3 Leslie Stephen, *English Thought in the Eighteenth Century*, 2 vols (London, 1876). Page references appear in the text in parentheses.
4 Virginia Woolf, *To the Lighthouse* (London, 1927). All page references are to this first edition and appear in the text in parentheses.
5 For discussion of this topic, see Allen McLaurin, *Virginia Woolf: The Echoes Enslaved* (Cambridge, 1973).
6 Bertrand Russell, *The Analysis of Matter* (London, 1927), p. 7.
7 I have written two further essays on Virginia Woolf: 'The body of the people in Virginia Woolf', in Sue Roe (ed.), *Women Reading Women Writing* (Brighton, 1987); 'The island and the aeroplane: the case of Virginia Woolf', in Homi Bhabha (ed.), *Nation and Narration* (London, 1989).

INDEX

Woolf, Virginia—*contd.*
  Lighthouse 9, 127, 128, 141, 142, 172, 183–202 *passim*; *The Voyage Out* 162, 166, 167, 168–70; *The Waves* 127, 128, 132–3, 134, 135, 140, 141, 146–7, 153, 154, 162, 163, 164, 170, 171, 183, 195; *A Writer's Diary* 160; *The Years* 132, 139, 142, 147, 155, 160
Wordsworth, William 82

Zola, Emile 185